A BIG POLE IN OUR GOAL

JERZY DUDEK

MY AUTOBIOGRAPHY

Jerzy Dudek

A BIG POLE IN OUR GOAL

JERZY DUDEK

MY AUTOBIOGRAPHY

Written with Dariusz Kurowski

Sport Media Ⓢ

I dedicate this book to my parents;
wife Mirella; children Alex, Victoria and
Natalia; my supporters who were always with
me in good and bad times;
my coaches – especially Bogusław
Kaczmarek, Jerzy Engel, Leo Beenhakker,
Gerard Houllier, Rafa Benitez, Bernd Schuster,
Manuel Pellegrini and Jose Mourinho – for
their support and inspiration;
my team-mates from the national team
and all the teams I played in.

Special thanks to
Jan de Zeeuw, Norman Gard,
my brothers Dariusz and Piotr
and Tomasz Rząsa.

Hand In Hand Kameraden.
You'll Never Walk Alone.
¡Hala Madrid!

– Jerzy Dudek

Sport Media

JERZY DUDEK: A BIG POLE IN OUR GOAL

© Jerzy Dudek

Written with Dariusz Kurowski

First English Edition
Published in Great Britain in 2016.

Published and produced by: Trinity Mirror Sport Media,
PO Box 48, Old Hall Street, Liverpool, L69 3EB.

Managing Director: Steve Hanrahan
Commercial Director: Will Beedles
Executive Editor: Paul Dove
Executive Art Editor: Rick Cooke
Marketing & Communications Manager: Claire Brown
Editing & Production: Roy Gilfoyle
Editing & Adapting: Chris McLoughlin
Translation: Radosław Chmiel

Media partners: www.theliverbirdside.com

ISBN: 978-1-910335-29-1

Design: Rick Cooke & Lee Ashun
Penalty save illustrations: Ben Renshaw
Photographic acknowledgements:
Jerzy Dudek personal collection, Dariusz Kurowski, Trinity Mirror, PA Photos.

Printed and bound by CPI Group (UK) Ltd, Croydon, CR0 4YY.

CONTENTS

I

Acknowledgements

It has been a great pleasure and a privilege to write this book with Jerzy Dudek, a Liverpool FC Istanbul hero, especially as I was among those lucky people who watched the 2005 Champions League final live. Many thanks my friend.

It would not have been possible to write this book without the great help of a large number of people. So, I would like to thank the following people in alphabetical order: Ewa Biskup, Konrad Cichosz, Aleksandra Górska, Leszek Jasionowski, Elżbieta Kurowska, Magdalena Obtułowicz, Małgorzata Sawicka, Marcin Sikora, Mirosław Tański, Roman Tobjasz and Żaneta Urbańczyk.

Special thanks also to Wojciech Szaniawski from Arskom Group.

I would like to mention two Spaniards who helped me gather information about Real Madrid and Spanish football: Rubén

Rueda Fernández, the manager of the Bernabéu museum and stadium tour, and David Ruiz de la Torre, a journalist for El Confidencial website.

I am also grateful to everyone at Trinity Mirror Sport Media for publishing this book, but especially Paul Dove, Steve Hanrahan, Roy Gilfoyle and Chris McLoughlin. Thank you for all your help and cooperation.

Dariusz Kurowski, author

I would firstly like to thank my parents Anna and Zbigniew for giving me the skills to be able to contribute to this book – my mum signed me up for English lessons when I was seven and my dad taught me the rules of football and was my first coach.

A massive thank you goes to Jerzy Dudek for giving me the chance to work on this magnificent project and for keeping his faith in me; Dariusz Kurowski for all of his advice; James Pearce from the Liverpool ECHO for being a great and supportive friend; Paul Dove and Steve Hanrahan for the opportunity to work with Trinity Mirror; and to Chris McLoughlin and Roy Gilfoyle for all their hard work during the editing and production process.

Special thanks go to Jovi Veith for her patience with me and being supportive in the tough times – your help was huge and priceless.

I also want to thank Paul Wright for his understanding of my passion and his help, and I cannot forget about my friends who always stand right behind me: Michał Czyż, Ula Kowalczyk and Wojtek Pawłowski. Thanks to you I know I'll never walk alone.

Radosław Chmiel, translator

||

Foreword

BY JERZY DUDEK

Wherever I go in the world, two words are mentioned to me more than any others. The first is Liverpool. The second is Istanbul. Every footballer has a career-defining moment, whether good or bad, and for me it happened in Turkey's Ataturk Stadium on Wednesday 25th May, 2005.

I hadn't really thought about whether I'd celebrate the 10th anniversary of Liverpool's historic 2005 Champions League final victory when I received a message asking if I would fancy coming back to the city on that day to attend the Istanbul Reunion Show, being held at the Liverpool ECHO Arena on May 25th, 2015, a bank holiday in England. The plan was to show the match again in full for the supporters to watch and have all the boys on stage talking about their role in what is the most famous Champions League final of all time. It was an opportunity to celebrate what we achieved that night against AC Milan in a city that is special to me, and for all the lads to catch up with each other. It didn't take me too long to say yes.

It was a great, great night, but my choice of clothing earned me plenty of stick. I packed two blazer-style jackets to wear for the event, a blue one and a pink one. The blue one was nice – bang on trend I think they say! – but when I was about to get changed I thought 'hang on Jerzy, you cannot wear blue on a stage in front of thousands of Liverpool fans. That's the kind of crazy thing only John Arne Riise would do!' So, to go with my t-shirt, jeans and trainers, I slipped on my pink jacket and headed off to the Istanbul Reunion Show.

The arena was absolutely packed – there must have been about 10,000 people there – and when I walked onto the stage the sight of me in a pink jacket prompted them all to start wolf-whistling! In fact, every time I spoke they whistled and made high-pitched noises. It was so funny and reminded me of the brilliant sense of humour that people have in Liverpool. In fact, the pink jacket was so popular that when I came back to Liverpool to do some photos for this book I almost brought it with me for the cover shot! Maybe I will give it away to charity, but it is now my favourite jacket. John Arne Riise, of course, turned up in a blue suit!

Because many of us now play for the Liverpool Legends team it wasn't the first time I had seen the lads for a while. Most of them are a bit bigger now! But it is always great to meet up again because one thing you miss when you retire from football is the dressing room camaraderie. You take it for granted as a player because you are in the dressing room with the lads every day, but when you stop playing you realise what a great part of being a footballer it is. You also miss the support that you get from the fans and that is a big reason why I have written this book.

FOREWORD

I wanted to say thanks to everyone who has helped and supported me during my career by sharing my memories so initially I wrote a book in 2015, with help from my friend and author Darek Kurowski, in Poland. When I came back to Liverpool for the Istanbul Reunion Show I was thinking to myself it would be nice to share my story with all the Reds supporters who used to watch me at Anfield, but how could I go about doing this? It came up in conversation with my Liverpool-based friend Rado Chmiel when we were travelling from the airport and he offered to translate my book and put me in touch with publishers Trinity Mirror Sport Media. As you have probably guessed discussions with Sport Media's Steve Hanrahan and Paul Dove went well and now, after my story was adapted and updated by Chris McLoughlin and edited by Roy Gilfoyle, I am proud that you are able to read my autobiography in English.

There is only one place I can start my story. With Liverpool. In Istanbul...

May 25, 2005

FACE TO FACE WITH SHEVCHENKO

For the very first time in my life I was proud of myself. It was a moment I will never forget. Something people remember me for. They called the 2005 Champions League final the 'Miracle of Istanbul'. Well, this was my miracle. The save of my career. Of my life.

But I wasn't thinking that at the time. It was all something of a blur. Before I realised it, one of the AC Milan players – Serginho – had the ball close to the touchline on our right side. He had plenty of space. I was sure that he would cross it perfectly into my penalty area. There are just fractions of seconds to grasp what is happening in those situations, to be aware of who is around you. I barely saw where my defenders were. Jamie Carragher was towards the near post, Djimi Traore at the far post and Sami Hyypia in the middle. Then an AC Milan player flashed between them. This is all a keeper sees in those kind of situations.

The ball was in the air. Sami was closest to me and I knew it would pass him so I realised that someone from Milan would have a great opportunity for a header. I was focused and prepared for the effort on goal. I didn't know that the AC Milan player who the ball was heading towards was none other than Andriy Shevchenko. He was just a flash of white in my eye line, but when the ball flew over Sami he had a free header on goal.

He met it well. His header was pretty powerful. He directed it downwards, slightly to my right. I dived to block it and the ball bounced off me, just two yards in front of goal. Now I was hoping that my team-mates would help me as I wasn't able to get up quickly to dive on the ball or clear it away. All I could do was at least try to get up and be in front of the goal; to give the AC Milan player the ball had bounced towards a slightly smaller target to aim for.

I was on my knees. I think one of my legs was even a little behind the line. The odds were stacked against me. In that split second, with the AC Milan player almost on top of me, I instinctively raised my hands up. It was a pure impulse. I almost screamed: "Here I am! Aim at me!"

I saw that it was Shevchenko who was running for the ball. It landed perfectly for him. He hit it as hard as he possibly could, like he was channelling all his anger.

His shot struck my hand – the 'hand of God' I jokingly called it after the game as I recalled the famous moment when Diego Maradona scored a goal with his hand during the 1986 World Cup against England. The ball could easily have broken my fingers and flown into the net. But it didn't. It flew upwards instead. It was almost like I'd swatted away a giant insect to protect myself. I quickly sprang to my feet to be ready for the ball coming back down from the Istanbul sky, but it landed behind the net.

John Arne Riise – or 'Ginge' as he was known to the lads –

raised his hands in the air like I'd just scored a goal. It felt like I had.

I now saw that Jon Dahl Tomasson was in front of me. I thought that it must have been his header that I'd saved initially before Shevchenko pounced on the rebound. It seemed impossible to me at the time that both chances had fallen to Shevchenko and he hadn't scored. Later on I saw the TV replays and realised how dynamic his jump had been. He put so much into that header that he had naturally taken a few steps forward when he landed to put himself in front of me and ahead of our defenders.

I looked towards the scoreboard and noticed the time. The 117th minute – the 27th minute of extra-time. Had the ball hit the net then our dream would have been all over. 'This is what you wanted' I thought to myself – 'to make such a great contribution in the final few minutes'.

I knew then that we would go to penalties. I knew that it would be a draw, that I'd saved a winning goal, but I couldn't believe what had just happened. I've seen the replays many times since and the expression on my face as the reality of what had just occurred hit me says a thousand words: 'That was impossible'.

But then most people thought Liverpool winning a fifth European Cup was impossible when the half-time whistle blew.

GIFTED BUT LAZY

My grandfather came from Wałbrzych. He moved to Silesia with my grandma and my dad. They lived in Wilcza near Rybnik. My dad met my mum in Ochojec, a village located close to Wilcza, and I arrived in the world on March 23, 1973.

I was born in the hospital in Rybnik. I lived in Ochojec for the first two months of my life. My grandad worked as a bus driver. He was so proud of me. He walked with a pram and boasted about me. Unfortunately I know my grandad only from the family stories about him. He died of a heart attack when I was three months old, just a few weeks after we moved to Szczygłowice – a district of Knurów in southern Poland.

Szczygłowice was built close to the local mine so the miners had a place to live. It was a typical housing estate in the Polish People's Republic (the official name of Poland until 1989) with five skyscrapers, as we called them, towering above the district. There was not even one single family house nearby.

There was one pub in Szczygłowice, called Banderoza. There were a couple of shops and six or seven hotels for mine employees. And that was about it. There was also a lot of tension in the area. Every Sunday after work the employees would leave the hotels, go for a drink and the night would finish with a huge fight between them and the locals. That's why people from Szczygłowice had a bad reputation. There was a lot of fighting.

When someone from Szczygłowice travelled to Knurów for a party, he always looked for a way to show his masculinity. Typical conversations between the lads from Knurów and Szczygłowice in a local nightclub would go as follows:

"Are you from Szczygłowice?"

"Yeah, why?"

"Let's go outside. There are a few things to be discussed."

There were other lads outside and inevitably a big fight would follow. Such things don't do the reputation of a place much good, but it's how it was. Fortunately I know it only from stories. I was too young to be involved.

One of my brothers [I also have another brother named Piotr] is called Dariusz, although everybody calls him Darek. He's two years younger than me. I was raised with him and our cousin. As a family, we were on the top ladder of the local hierarchy. We were afraid of no-one.

I grew up on that estate and it shaped my character. I lived in Szczygłowice for 22 years, until I moved to the Netherlands, but before I got to know Szczygłowice better, something bad happened. I couldn't deal with it for many years. It had a huge influence on my life, although I don't remember the actual incident. Because of one accident, I almost wasn't in this world and wouldn't be telling my story now.

"*Not long after Darek was born, I invited his aunties for a coffee after my return from hospital. It was a time when the water was switched off in our blocks of flats, something that happened from time to time, so Jurek's dad went to buy some mineral water. He returned from the shop and put the groceries on the worktop next to some freshly-made cups of coffee that were sat on saucers. Jurek wanted to see what was in the bags. You can only imagine what happened next.*

Jurek unwittingly nudged the saucer and the hot coffee spilled onto his chest. It was boiling water! We didn't have time to react. It all happened so quickly. Jurek couldn't stop crying. My husband tore off his shirt and took him immediately to the hospital in Rybnik. The doctor looked at Jurek and said: 'Have you brought me a dead child?!'

Jurek stayed in the hospital for a long time. They connected him to a drip. He had looked so adorable with his curly hair before, but they shaved it all off. Things were so bad that they only let us visit him after a month! When we saw him he was covered in bandages that looked like a suit of armour. I broke down when I saw him: 'Mother of Christ, this is wrong! We need to take him home!'

The doctor agreed and said to come back the following week to change the bandages, but fortunately the nurse lived opposite our block of flats. We asked her for help. She brought plenty of ointments and we took the bandages off Jurek. She told us only to use the ointments without any bandages. Jurek cried a lot. It must have hurt him a lot, but the wounds shrank and cracked.

The doctor was really surprised when we returned to the hospital after a week: 'What did you do to him? How have the wounds healed so well?'

All I said to him was that we should have taken him home earlier. The doctor was corrupt. Only when we offered him a bribe did he agree to let Jurek come home, but the important thing was that Jurek was cured and recovered from it. And since that time, all those years ago, I haven't had a single saucer in my home."

Renata Dudek, mother

"Jurek's problems weren't over yet. Because his wound had been covered with bandages for so long his tendons shrank. He also had skin folds under his arm. We spent a long time in the rehabilitation centre. Jurek did different exercises – rungs, tensioning, flips – everything to make sure his tendons would develop normally. I was really afraid about it. When he started to exercise the skin folds became more delicate and started to crack."

Andrzej Dudek, father

I had suffered third-degree burns. The doctor said that I came back from a dark place. In truth I was lucky to survive and then to recover with just scars to show for it.

Until now, this story has only been known by my closest family. It's not something I talked about during my playing career. And although I was, thankfully, too young to remember it happening or recall the pain, I have since made my own scenario from all of the stories I heard from my family. It's like a movie in my head.

Paradoxically, I use a completely different accident, which happened three years later, to create that scenario in my mind.

It was a similar incident, although this time it was Darek who was injured. It was a full house again. My parents' friends were in the kitchen drinking coffee with them and I was playing with Darek. I pushed him and he fell, cutting his head badly after hitting it on the edge of the table. He had to be taken to hospital to be treated and this dramatic situation remains in my head today despite how young I was at the time.

The burns left me scarred and as a result I always felt self-conscious when I had to play football in the 'skins' team – without a shirt – at primary school. I tried to subconsciously cover the scars, telling myself they weren't there, but it was difficult.

I played football and several other sports at school and thankfully the scarring didn't limit my movement. I was still supple enough to be able to play and for that I am thankful.

I have lived with both the physical and the mental scars from that incident for so many years now. That accident will remain in my memory forever. Once my friends asked me why I haven't had plastic surgery to remove the scars. It's for two reasons.

Firstly, I am not convinced by cosmetic surgery. It's not something I am comfortable with.

Secondly, and it might sound a bit strange, but my scars remind me of where I come from and who I am. When I take my shirt off I see an ordinary man. A guy who had to overcome a bad time as a kid to achieve what I did in my career. Those scars remind me to stay humble and help to keep me grounded. But for the grace of God...

Physics attraction

I mainly remember my time at kindergarten for enjoying fancy dress parties. On one occasion I was dressed as an Indian chief.

I attended No 4 Primary School after I graduated from kinder-garten. Ms Okoń was my teacher. She was also the teacher for my father 20 years earlier. One day she stopped when she read my name from the list of pupils:

"Tell me, Jureczek," – she always used pet names – "what was your dad's name? Was it Andrzejek?"

"Yes," I replied.

"Can you bring your dad in to see me then please, Jureczek."

"Did I do something wrong?"

"No, but I think I was your dad's teacher as well!"

I ran home that day and asked my dad if he knew Ms Okoń. Dad confirmed she was his teacher in the past. I asked him to come to school and meet with her. I thought I could benefit from it and I was right! Dad went to school and met with Ms Okoń. They hugged like a family. Since then Ms Okoń always cared more, she treated me almost like her son. She was also the first person who described me as "a gifted but lazy kid!"

It was like this until the final year of primary school. When my mum went to the parent-teacher meetings, she always heard: "If Jureczek wants to do things he can, but usually he's lazy." It was a fair assessment of what I was like at school.

I learned everything in a week when I needed to in order to improve my grades. All I wanted was for lessons to end so I could get out of school and run onto a football pitch to do what I liked to do the most. I passed through my school years with average grades, nothing special, because something different than studying made me happy – football! Apart from football and PE, my favourite subject was geography, but I also enjoyed physics lessons. However, it had nothing to do with physics and everything to do with the physical appearance of our teacher!

It wasn't just me, but I had a crush on my physics teacher, Miss Nowacka. She probably doesn't know it – although she will now – but she always gives me a great welcome when I visit my old school. Maybe she thought I enjoyed the subject, but I don't remember anything about physics lessons apart from the teacher!

The first and last beating

I got into trouble during my sixth year of primary school. It all started when I pushed one of my friends on the playground, fooling about. As she fell she knocked into one of the other boys and all of a sudden other kids started to fall down like dominos until a girl fell from the playground swing and cut her lip. I knew I was going to be in trouble.

I ran home that night feeling scared, but one of my school-mates knew where I lived so she did her 'civic duty' – I think in Liverpool they call it 'grassed me up' – and she, and the mum of the girl who I had pushed, turned up at our flat.

"What are you thinking about?" the woman said to my mum. "Your son pushed my daughter!"

"Yes," said my school friend. "Jurek pushed me, I fell onto another boy and he bumped into the girl who fell off the swing!"

I had come back home from school with a bashed head or cuts and bruises plenty of times so my mum wasn't surprised at all. She looked on kids with compassion and calmly replied to the lady: "If I had to run to all the children's parents when Jurek has had his head smashed, I'd have no time for anything."

My school-mate still moaned: "He has to be punished!"

"Really?" my mum repeated firmly. "Drop it. Goodbye."

I admired my mum for that. I thought 'I ran away from this

situation but she defended me so much'. I was feeling glad far too early though! Mum shut the door, called dad and told him what had happened. He wasn't happy.

"Why are you bringing shame on us?" Whack, whack, whack!

It was the first and the last beating I ever got from my dad and it taught me a lesson. My parents always told me 'don't hurt anyone, but don't let anyone hurt you either'. Even if I got my head smashed, I didn't make a fuss. Once I moaned that someone hit me with a rock and mum replied: "He wouldn't hit you without a reason. What did you do first? Tell me!"

"I was playing in the sandpit when suddenly a little boy hit me with a concrete tile from behind! I touched my head and I felt blood. So I ran home and told you what happened."

"You were in the sandpit and this little kid, who barely walks, came from behind and hit you unprovoked? Do you really think that I believe this story?"

After that day I didn't tell them anything about similar situations. When someone hit me, I kept it to myself. It was another lesson in the tough life of growing up in Szczygłowice.

The wallet on the fishing line

I was a menace when I was a child. I could easily write *The Guide of the Menace: How to Disrupt an Adult's Life*. I can guarantee you it would be a best-seller! My brother and I had many adventures. We played many pranks. Some of them were innocent; some of them a bit naughty! One of the most memorable was 'the wallet on the fishing line'.

We put a wallet, which was attached to the hook of a fishing line, onto the pavement. We then hid in the bushes by the side of the road. When someone went to pick up the wallet, we pulled the fishing line. This gave us a good laugh! Once, two cars stopped in front of the wallet. One of the drivers jumped out to pick it up, but we pulled the line as he got there. He started to chase after us, but we were too quick and he didn't catch us. We liked this prank even more!

It worked even better when we were in the forest. A couple drove past the wallet on a motorbike and the woman who was on the bike spotted it. She told the guy driving to stop, but as this was happening we reeled the wallet in. They got off the bike to pick it up, but it wasn't there! She was trying to convince him that she had really seen a wallet on the ground, but he was angry at her for making him stop the bike unnecessarily. He didn't believe her that it was ever there. Meanwhile, in the bushes, we were crying laughing!

My brother and I were a proper nightmare for our neighbours. We would fill up bags of water and put them above their flat doors. Whoever opened the door ended up with a wet head! Another prank involved the doorbells. Each stairwell in a block of flats has emergency fuses where you can interrupt the supply of electricity when needed. We removed the fuses to turn the electricity off, ran around to each flat, jammed the doorbell switches with matches and then plugged the fuses back in. As soon as this happened every doorbell started to ring continuously prompting the residents to come out into the stairwell wondering what the hell the commotion was!

We didn't just play pranks. When I was bored I used to go to the mining ponds to catch some fish. I became a crayfish specialist. I really like them. You need a mussel for bait to catch a crayfish. I put the mussels into the pond and waited patiently. All I had to do was wait until the crayfish was eating, catch it and pull it out of the water. It was fun, but dangerous. There was a narrow path at the edge of the pond. Once I slipped over and fell into the water. I was in difficulties, I could have died if my friends hadn't helped me, but they pulled me out of the water. It tightly cemented our friendship.

This accident happened on a Sunday morning. People were walking to the church for Sunday Mass and I looked like the youngest Polish miner, dirty and wet from the mining pond. I could have been mistaken for a miner who had just finished his shift and had forgotten to take a shower. How could I walk back home without being noticed? I did it somehow and no-one spotted me, but I couldn't avoid my mum. She realised I had been in the water and punished me. After that I was far more careful when I went to the mining pond.

When I got older I was tempted with more dangerous activities. There was a nice crop of tomatoes growing in the nearby State Agricultural Farm (SAF). Everyone from Szczygłowice went there to grab some tomatoes. My brother Darek and I did the same. I took a miner's bag with me and we went through the fence. Some of the people there broke the windows to get at the tomatoes, but we were more cute. I had a little knife and I used this to chip out the cement from a window frame. I placed the glass on the grass and, with Darek on lookout, I was able to pluck the tomatoes and start to fill the bag. As I was doing so I was asking him from time to time how the situation was. Darek was getting a bit nervous and kept telling me that we've got enough and should go, but I calmly filled the bag. Suddenly we heard a noise and panicked. We ran off, but our bag full of tomatoes was left behind on a barbed-wire fence.

"If Mum finds out she will kill us!" I said.

"Don't worry, she won't," said Darek. "How would she find out?"

"Our address is in the miner's bag!"

Then Darek got scared as well. We were so worried that we stayed outside until the late evening hours as we were frightened to go back home. We imagined that the police would be waiting for us when we got there and that our parents would hit the roof. When we did finally go home the police weren't there, but we were still worried for about a week or two. Luckily, the SAF security didn't inquire about the bag. Nobody was looking for us so we got away with that one, even if we didn't get away with any tomatoes!

Train truancy

One day my friend and I decided not to go to school. We bunked off and went travelling by train for fun. We were in high spirits and before the train stopped my friend opened the door and jumped on the platform. Unfortunately, he didn't time his jump very well and landed in a heap on the platform. I stepped from the train like a normal person and I started to laugh at him. I was helping him to get up, saying: "You loser, you can't even get off a train properly!"

Suddenly someone grabbed him and started to shout: "What are you doing you stripling [young man]?" It was the ticket inspector dressed like a civilian. My friend had been caught and now he was in big trouble.

The inspector took him to the transport police offices. They hadn't collared me so I walked behind them wondering what would happen next. He was taken into an office and I stood behind the doors and listened to how he would explain himself:

"I really didn't do anything wrong. The train already stopped when I was getting off."

The officers weren't having it. "Tell me your name and address," one demanded. "Your parents will pay the penalty for letting you travel without care. Do you have your student ID?"

What they didn't know is that we were prepared for this. We had agreed that in case of emergency situations like this we would always provide fake details. We learned our fake IDs perfectly and could recite them without hesitation. These were our tactics to ensure our parents never found out about any scrapes we got into. My mate didn't have any ID for obvious reasons and gave them the fake details.

"You are not lying are you?" said the officer. "Give me those details one more time quickly!"

He repeated the fake details again without a problem, but the officer started to threaten him: "We're going to put you in the cell and start to heat it up. You'll tell us the truth then."

This made me laugh. I laughed so loudly that the officers heard me and opened the door. Then they asked me if I knew him and demanded to know where he lived. I quickly repeated the fake details. The officers looked at each other and realised they weren't going to catch us out, so they let us go. They said that they would send some kind of official letter to our parents. That got us laughing again because they could send whatever they wanted to the fake address we had given!

Another time we got the train to Katowice and went to the staff room in the electric carriage. There was a box with a switch on the wall. We were a bit bored so my mate pressed the switch and it jumped from one side to the other. We weren't sure what it did, so he pressed it again. Not so long before we arrived in Katowice, four transport police officers came to the staff room and started to press the switch like we did before. One of the officers looked out of the window and said: "It had to be in here."

The officers started to question everyone on the train. Finally they looked at us.

"Where did you get on?"

"Zabrze."

"What were you doing in here? Why did you press the switch?"

My friend admitted what he had done. "Sir, I really didn't know what it was."

The officer got angry. He started to scream at him: "Didn't you know, you little brat? I'll show you!"

He took us from the staff room and told us to stand by the train doors. Then he pressed the switch. It turned out that the switch opened the doors on the whole train! We went pale when we realised this because it dawned on us that we could have caused a real tragedy.

Fortunately, when we were doing this while the train was moving, no-one was close to the doors. The officers took us off the train, wrote down our fake details and let us go without any consequences. But I learned a huge lesson that day and it wasn't the last one in my life.

Train carriage craziness

It was December 1993 when I travelled with my friends to a New Year's Eve party. We were on our way to the Baltic coast. On the same train there were many soldiers returning to their military units from Christmas leave. My friends and I – four couples in total – were sitting in the dining carriage when sud-

31

denly two soldiers started to fight. I was about two metres from them and I really didn't want to get involved, but then one of the soldiers took a little knife from the bar and started to brandish it. I was 20 at the time and I didn't think too much. I grabbed his hand, pushed him onto the bar so he couldn't move and told the barman to get the knife. Then I released my grip on the soldier: "Chill out lad, you drank too much. Get some sleep."

My friends and I left the dining carriage and we were walking towards our seats when I saw another soldier. He was trying to get into one of the train compartments, but one of the girls inside it had blocked the doors from opening with her feet. I tried to help him, but I couldn't open the doors either. I was really surprised, so I tried to find an extreme way to resolve the situation. I headbutted the glass. It shattered and I turned to the soldier. "There you go mate. The doors are open."

Why did I smash a glass window with my head? I still cannot find the answer to that question. I can't explain it in a rational way. I think I'd had a few too many beers! When I was on the way to my compartment I was stopped by another soldier: "Do you know you're covered in blood mate?"

I took a towel out from my bag and put it against my forehead. I'd done myself a bit of damage. Minutes later my friend came over: "Something's going on Jurek. The ticket inspector wants the girls to pay for the broken glass but they said they won't do it as they didn't break it. So now they are probably looking for you."

We arrived in Tczew and I saw plenty of police and military police on the platform waiting to get on the train. I thought 'it's all over for me here' so I hid under the seats and covered the gap up with bags. The ticket inspector came into the compartment asking if anyone had seen me. There was only one woman in the compartment and she said that she hadn't seen anyone. The inspector left and the train pulled out of the station. I was told that all the soldiers had been taken off the train by the military police. I felt safe hearing that so I clambered out from under the seat and sat back down like an ordinary passenger, albeit one with a gashed forehead!

The girls who had been in the compartment with the broken window were still looking for me though and suddenly they appeared and pointed at me. I started to realise that I wasn't going to escape this situation and sure enough there were police waiting for me at the Gdańsk-Wrzeszcz station. I left the train with my friend. The rest of our gang continued to travel to our final destination in Łeba and I promised them that we'd be there soon. I was taken to the police station and locked in a cell overnight. The following morning I was questioned and started to write down my version of events. As I was doing this my mate said: "Why do you want to punish him? He saved the life of one of the soldiers on the train, let him go!"

He shouldn't have said that. The police officers started to ask for the details. They called the military unit in Bydgoszcz. They found out everything about the incident regarding the soldier with the knife on the train and told me we had to travel there. We were taken there on a train and as I looked at the glass in the doors of the compartment I was sitting in it made me think about the one I had smashed with my head the night before. "Is it a nightmare?" I asked myself. "Why on earth did I do that?"

Maybe the 20-year-old lad without any social status wanted to show off? Maybe I had wanted to impress to get recognised?

Maybe I thought I would gain respect by doing something completely irrational? Maybe that was the explanation of my immature behaviour. To this day I still do not know.

We reached the military unit in Bydgoszcz. I was standing in front of a delegation of differently-ranked soldiers and was questioned by one of them. I told him everything in detail. There was no other option. They also asked me if I had served in the army and if I had ever been convicted of any other offences? I explained that I hadn't. The officer said that if my testimony was proven to be true there would be no charges against me. I signed the statement I had given and I was free to leave.

There was still time to get to Łeba for our New Year's Eve party so we continued with our journey. I looked awful, as you would look after head-butting a glass door and spending a night in the cells! My friends took care of me when we arrived and we ended up having a nice evening.

One of the songs that was played was *Dzieci* [*Children*] by Elektryczne Gitary. I knew the lyrics to that song word by word and we all sang along to it loudly. It includes the line 'we all are out of our minds that we're still living'. I definitely sang that bit the loudest as the lyrics matched the situation I had just been through perfectly. That night I also stood in front of the mirror and looked at the wound on my head. I promised myself that I wouldn't do anything so stupid ever again.

I was playing for Concordia Knurów at the time and returned to training with them in the new year. A few weeks later my coach called me in for a chat: "What the hell did you do?" he said. "You have been summoned to go to court in Bydgoszcz. What's going on?"

So I had to tell him the whole story and that I had witnessed an incident involving some soldiers, but when I saw the court summons it wasn't relating to that. They were prosecuting me for what happened with the broken glass on the train – a destruction of state property.

I went to the court in Bydgoszcz, but I didn't have to. They started the case automatically and I got the sentence two weeks after. I had to pay about £300 for the damage I had caused to the train. I had managed to save roughly that amount, but that fine wiped it out. They made me pay for my stupidity and it gave me a reality check. I was turning 21 that year and I decided that it was time to stop playing pranks and behaving stupidly. I had learned a serious lesson in life and realised that if I didn't learn from a mistake like this then I never would. I'm pleased to say that I've never been involved in anything like that since. I grew up!

Perhaps some people have heard about this incident before. I mentioned it in an interview I gave once and one of the tabloids made a big deal about it. They painted me as a criminal and an alcoholic who – fortunately – found an escape in football. They said that if I wasn't a footballer I would probably be in jail now! I dispute that. Yes, I was a menace, a foolish kid who got into avoidable situations, but I was not a criminal and I didn't have an alcohol problem. Football wasn't an escape for me either. It was always a love of my life!

ESCAPE FROM THE MINE

The first football pitch I played on was located between a block of flats and the workers' hotel. There were three trees on it and one was in the middle of our pitch! The other trees were used by us as goalposts. We used the block of flats as one of the touchlines, the other one was the kerb of the road. We didn't want to walk a couple of hundred yards to play on the school pitch. This was our home ground!

Every so often we would end up breaking a window... with the ball, not my head! Luckily, they were double-glazed. When a ball hit one, it broke it, but the ball didn't disappear into the flat. We had time to grab the ball and run away.

The first big football competition I remember was the 1982 World Cup in Spain. I was nine years old at the time. Poland drew their first two group games 0-0 against Italy and Cameroon so we didn't want to watch the third one against Peru. Instead we decided to go outside and play on the pitch. Everyone else was watching the game but at that age we were playing football all the time.

We were exhausted, sitting on a bench for a rest, when we heard shouting and cheers from the workers' hotel. GOAL! Moments later they were jubilantly cheering again. We counted five cheers and we couldn't believe it. Poland scored four goals in 14 minutes in La Coruna and went on to beat Peru 5-1. What a change after two 0-0 draws! We remembered that game and from then on, when we scored lots of goals on the pitch outside, we said we were playing like Poland v Peru.

I remember all the players from that game: Młynarczyk, Żmuda, Boniek, Majewski, Kupcewicz, Matysik, Buncol, Lato, Jałocha, Smolarek, Janas, Dziuba, Ciołek. They were my first football idols. These are the players I grew up wanting to emulate. After that 5-1 win, when that Poland team were playing, the streets were empty. Poland reached the semi-final of that World Cup having finished top of their group in the second round. This was at a time when the World Cup featured two group stages and after Zbigniew Boniek scored a hat-trick in a 3-0 victory against Belgium, a 0-0 draw with the Soviet Union was enough to put Poland into the semi-final for only the second time, where we would face Italy. The country was going crazy! But unfortunately Boniek was suspended and Italy won the game 2-0. Poland finished third after beating France 3-2.

Boxer, gymnast, tennis player

I seriously started to play football in year two at my primary school. We went out for break-time and looked for a place to play out of the way of the older pupils. I started to grow up and became a leader in my class with two other lads. We were playing football somewhere all the time. It was the only enter-tainment we had and the biggest attraction. We played games block versus block.

Anyone who owned a leather ball had the most respect in the area. The lads usually got hold of a leather football if they had family who travelled abroad, mainly to Czechoslovakia or Hungary. A real ball was a rarity at the time. You couldn't even buy one normally. You needed special vouchers from the waste paper collection centre to get one. But, to be honest, you would need to deliver two lorries full of paper to collect enough vouchers to get one ball. That's why we were happy even with a rubber one.

We usually played to one goal and would start with a game where you could only take one touch to have a shot. The first person who broke the rules, or didn't hit the target with his shot, was the goalkeeper. Nobody wants to play in goal as a kid! We could only shoot from in the air – I think it's known as 'headers and volleys' in Liverpool – and when the goalie conceded five goals he was ruled out of the game. It was knock-out-style football. We eliminated the weakest and played until we had a winner.

That was a kids' life in Poland – study, football, study, break some windows! There were no computers or smartphones like today. We would also play table tennis or chess in a school common-room. I tried every sport at school. I competed in the Knurów Championships in volleyball and basketball. I also did some running, although quickly realised I wasn't cut out to be a distance runner.

I was also selected to be on the school gymnastics team and attended boxing training alongside football. I trained with the volleyball team to work on my jumping skills and I played table tennis with the professional lads every day. They helped me to learn perfect backhands, forehands and smashes and I was so good that the coach of AZS Gliwice (they played Premier League table tennis!) tried to convince me to play in their junior teams. It was something for me to consider, but I didn't want to miss football training so I refused. When I think about it now, though, playing a variety of sports where multi-skills are required as part of my normal routine paid off for me later.

A brick in the head

Once we stayed after school to do some penalty shoot-outs with a tennis ball. We used two bricks as posts. One of my mates was the goalie. It was my turn to shoot, but another lad started to push the goalie, screaming that it was his turn to be the keeper.

"Get lost," I said to him firmly and threw the tennis ball straight at the lad's head. Everyone started to laugh except him, obviously. Suddenly I saw the smiles on their faces turn to anxious expressions. I turned around to see the lad who I had hit had returned the throw. He hit me straight on the head, just as I had done to him, but he used a brick.

I was covered in blood. Someone ran for my dad. They took me to the health centre, which was not too far away from school, and the doctor who treated me was a great psychologist too: "I can see that you're a big man, young boy. There's no need to be afraid, nothing terrible happened. It will hurt you a bit when we put some stitches behind your ear, but I wonder if you'll be as brave as your father is." I was proud of myself when the doctor added: "Such a brave young man! You didn't even cry, well done!"

I still have that same motivation today. When someone praises me I work harder to justify the praise. And I also have a scar from the six stitches behind my ear. When the doctor had finished I looked like a war child with the bandage on my head, like Franek Dolas from my favourite movie *How I Unleashed World War II*.

I must stress that the brick I was hit with was our goal post. I think that was the first moment when I met my destiny – to be a goalkeeper. My mum has a different view on it. She says it was earlier when I was a toddler on a day when she took me to see my auntie (her sister) who lived in a typical Polish village. Her son, my cousin, wanted to take the pram and had a walk, pushing me. It was perfectly fine until the moment when he was chased by geese. He got scared, ran off and left the pram moving with me sitting in it. I fell out of the pram and was unhurt, but Mum always laughs like a drain when she recalls this situation. She says that it was my first proper goalkeeper dive!

Captain of the class

I was in year four at school and we had a football competition every year. We played eight-a-side and we were released from other subjects to play football. I was the captain of my class and I was so proud of it. My class didn't have too many good players, maybe four or five of them were good, but the others only thought about studying. I asked them to stay after school to train a bit, but I felt frustrated because we could never win the competition.

When I played in goal, I worried because there was no-one to score goals up front. When I played as a striker, we didn't have a proper keeper to replace me so we let goals in. At least we did until I found Piotr Jurski. He had a nickname – 'Big Hand' – and it was true. Piotr used this to good effect and went in goal so I could play up front, dribble a bit and score some goals. I cared a lot about trying to win because football was my life.

Every two years the school organised a typical sports day. I was unlucky because I started the school during the year they didn't do it! It made me jealous of my older friends. They decided to form a junior team and they played in real competitions as Górnik II Knurów.

I had an idea to play a friendly against them. I spoke to the captains from the whole of year four and we decided to form a team. Our PE teacher, Jan Korepta, watched us carefully and asked: "Where do you want to play?" He looked at me again and said: "You've got long legs, so you can play up front as you should be quick."

"I always tried to extend the lessons into the long break time. The whole school went outside and I always steered them to have a penalty shoot-out and a real competition. Nobody wanted to be in goal so they called Jurek. He stood in goal in casual clothes. He was younger than the others, but they insisted on giving him a try."

Jan Korepta, PE teacher and first coach

Nobody wanted to be in goal. I played in goal for my class, so I said I would play there. The teacher looked at me carefully and called the goalkeeper from the sport class. We stood back to back. He was maybe two centimetres taller than me: "This is your rival," said Mr Korepta. "I'm not sure if you can beat your rival. We'll see how it goes."

This was the first time I tasted rivalry in goal. Mr Korepta asked me about my parents. I told him that both are tall. He liked this news.

"That's fine, you might be a keeper then. You need to be tall to play in that position."

We lost the game 2-1, but everybody who watched the match was hugely impressed with our performance. We really fought bravely. It was nice, but our team had to disband because the sports class was one year higher. That's why we decided to train on our own. Maybe 'train' is the wrong word to describe it. We just played eight-a-side games until we were exhausted.

Football was such a passion for me that after training I went back home and trained there. We had a sofa in our flat so I threw the ball at the wall and dived onto the sofa trying to catch it. I also tried to improve my physical fitness. My dad's friend brought me 12kg dumbbells. I raised them maybe three times. My cousin, who was a speedway racer, had a dumbbell connected to a line and he always worked on strengthening his arms. I realised that strong arms are important for a goalkeeper so I worked with dumbbells too. I also did push-ups. I worked on my jumping skills at home too. I put a bar at hip height and I tried to jump over it. I loved that exercise. I'd still enjoy doing them now. Those 'training' sessions were never a chore. They were a pleasure for me.

A magical bus

Mr Korepta and Krzysztof Mikołajczyk – who was my main teacher from year five to year eight – organised all the sports competitions at school. When I was in year six, they decided to create a new team for us. The teachers knew that there were plenty of talented boys in Szczygłowice, but we were treated differently because of where we were from. We could feel those social differences. Our teachers worked hard to create the team and finally we also started to play as Górnik II Knurów in junior competitions. We travelled to play in neighbouring towns Rybnik, Jastrzębie, Żory... it was such a great experience for us.

The coach started to take the most talented players from our team to play for the team that was one year older. The age difference is an important thing and when I was in year seven, they decided to merge the teams of lads born in 1972 and 1973. It was a tough competition against the older keeper, so I decided to play as left-back instead and I really liked it.

The following year was very difficult for us. The new goalkeeper from the year below me was agile, but he lacked height. He conceded lots of goals and the coach decided that he needed me in goal instead. I really didn't want to play there as I was really enjoying playing at left-back. I felt as good as Roberto Carlos in the late '90s playing there! This upset Mr Korepta, who talked with Mr Mikołajczyk, who in turn tried to persuade me to change my mind saying: "Listen, you'd be good back in goal, but you can also play on the left if you like. You never know when you can be useful."

I thought that if they cared so much about my place in the team I would have to make a proper decision. I said yes, but only if I'd be back in goal permanently. "I'll go in goal but don't ask me to play as a left-back any more. I will stay in goal and I am responsible for this position."

They agreed and so the goalkeeper position was finally mine for keeps. We had Saturday training sessions at school and it was the first time that the coach gave me instructions on how to hold my arms, how to position myself and when I should be ready to intervene. I felt like a real goalkeeper!

I've liked rivalry since I was a kid. I've always had to fight for something. We played against the No 1 sports school in the Knurów Championships. The most gifted boys attended that school. They had everything – beautiful shirts, bags, real football boots and tracksuits with 'Górnik Knurów' on them. We were jealous. Not to mention that we didn't like them in Szczygłowice. They didn't like us either. It was a genuine rivalry. We always met them in the final of the City Championships. We beat them in the futsal tournament and after that someone finally thought it was worth investing in us. Because we won the final they gave us new boots, tracksuits and a couple of new balls. We had to fight for something that others had for free, but at least we had character.

The biggest prize was travelling for away games on the original team bus used by the first-team. There were tables between the seats and it had a huge banner 'MINERS FOOTBALL CLUB – GÓRNIK' on the side. The driver was Mr Pierończyk. We couldn't believe they let us travel by bus. It was something magical, like a fairytale. We travelled on that bus maybe three times during the season. The driver came on and said: "Do not touch anything. Don't put bags on the tables. And if you lose today, you never travel with me again!"

More motivation. We fought on the pitch for that bus. We had to fight for something all the time. First for the kits, then for that bus.

It meant that our attitude and focus was very good, but it was also when I first experienced football scams. One involved altering the paper student IDs, let's say changing the number three to number five in a birth date so a lad was eligible to play in a game. I remember a lad older than me, who should have been too old to play, who scored a couple of goals. The referee was suspicious and checked his ID, but everything was 'correct' so he couldn't do anything about it.

We played a game against Naprzód Rydułtowy. We lost 4-0. One of their players scored three goals. He looked like an older player. After the game, when we were leaving the stadium, there was a match being played between the older age group. We stopped for a moment. Our coach went to check if that lad who had scored three goals against us was playing there. It was no surprise when the coach discovered he was. Those kind of situations happened on a regular basis.

Vocational school

I finished my primary school and I had to choose where I'd like to continue my education. Our teacher asked us about our plans. The grades from our final exams were very important in making this decision. When someone wanted to go to the city technology college teachers usually gave them the chance to improve their grades.

"Dudek, where do you want to go?" the teacher asked me one day. I said that I wanted to go to Miners CTC. She was surprised, but I had a reason. Górnik Knurów cooperated with Miners CTC in Zabrze. If I passed the entry tests, I could play football and attend the sports class at CTC. Górnik had lots of problems with the lads in the past. They didn't care about studying. They knew they would pass the year. Football was the most important thing and when a teacher asked one pupil if he wanted to improve his grades he said: "I came to your CTC to play football, not to study. I'll pass the year anyway."

The principal went mad and he said to the chairman of Górnik that this situation cannot be tolerated because teachers were not able to keep discipline in school.

The maths teacher took my plan on board but told me honestly: "Dudek, I think you have no chance of passing the tests for CTC, but you can try." So I tried. I took the exam but I didn't know how to answer some of the questions. I failed, and the teacher said: "Now maybe you'll think twice about your school choice?"

I had nothing to think about. I didn't care too much about CTC Zabrze anyway. I wanted to play football. Fortunately, Szczygłowice Mine decided to create the Elementary Miners' Vocational School at that time to prepare students for working down the mine. Instead of travelling to Zabrze every day, I attended classes on my estate. I started to learn the skills to become a mechanic specialising in mining equipment. It was the best choice for me as I passed the years easily and had plenty of time to play football.

Like a bag of potatoes

Roman Kensy – Górnik Knurów's coach – came to Szczygłowice just before I finished year eight at school. Kensy was responsible for coaching young players. He took me and the lads from our team to the first youth team as he wanted to make a natural selection, to choose the best players. I started to train in Knurów and I was delighted. I got changed in the real dressing room. I had real football stuff – tracksuits, boots – and most importantly I had a proper training session every time.

However, it wasn't easy in the dressing room. We came from Szczygłowice. The lads from Knurów had a laugh at our expense. We were fighting for a place in the team before the training session had even started. There's a Polish saying that 'difficulties create the character'. My character started to be created quite early. A couple of lads missed the training sessions. They didn't want to travel to play with 'those Knurów lads' and they were turfed out, stopped from coming to any training sessions. I tried to ignore the stick that came my way. I knew what my goals were.

I met coach Witold Słabkowski in Górnik. I cannot describe how much I owe him. He would help everybody. I finished school around 1pm and I couldn't wait for training to start at 4pm. I was so professional that when the coach said that we needed to prepare for training by not eating anything for a couple of hours, I ate nothing. I was at the club two hours before training. I played football-tennis or I did some stretching. Or both. I liked it and nobody had to tell me what to do.

"At the beginning Jurek hadn't got a clue what goalkeeping was. Once I said to him: "You dive like a bag of potatoes." He was physically underdeveloped. I started to work with him on the basics. He strived to be the best. We had classes in the big and small gyms. The team was in the bigger one, meanwhile I went with Jurek to the small one and we had an individual training session. We worked hard on jumping, manoeuvrability and agility. He had a great appetite and it helped."

Witold Słabkowski, Górnik Knurów junior coach

I really worked hard with coach Słabkowski. I made huge progress and I was ready to work more. I went to a training camp with the older lads during the winter. I played with them over the spring. Then Roman Kensy called me. He asked me to sit on his team bench. I thought he was joking. I had a seat on the bench with almost grown up, 18-year-old men. And we used the kits the senior team played in. I was totally made up!

I was on the bench in the first game. I debuted in the next one, against GKS Tychy, when I was 16 years old. I played once more and the season was over. The playing standard was high. In other teams there were lads who played in the national team like the Stanek brothers in Odra Wodzisław.

The kidnapping of Waldi

I was in Kensy's team the following season. We were second for most of the season but our best striker, Wojciech Kluska, got a serious injury. He couldn't play for four months and we struggled to score. Górnik finished the league in mid-table.

I was an experienced player in the youth team the following season. I played with lads of the same age, but I still stayed later after training as I was focused on trying to improve.

Górnik youth teams played their matches ahead of reserve team games. The matches were usually played in midweek and we had our own name for them. We said that we were going to 'play like the English', but I had no idea why. The team consisted of players who didn't get a match for their junior teams at the weekend. It was a mixed bunch and nobody wanted to play, but I was quite the opposite. Nobody had to ask me to play – I wanted to do it.

We were struggling to get a team together and before one

game there were about nine players at the most who turned up at the pre-match assembly. The coach had a radical plan. He asked the bus driver to drive through the city centre and he jumped off and grabbed some boys walking through town. He chose lads who were similar to the players on the pictures of health cards he had for each player. The coach asked our new team members to learn 'their' data – such as their new names! – quickly. Fortunately, the boys wanted to play and had no problems with their new identities!

As we were driving past a bus stop we spotted Waldek Pindur. He was a Górnik player and was three years older than me. Waldi – that's what we called him – was on his way to see his girlfriend and the coach offered to give him a lift on the bus. Waldi was happy until he realised that his date was going to be cancelled as he had been 'kidnapped' and was going to play with us due to a lack of players! This pissed Waldi off and he threatened to jump off the bus, but the driver drove quickly so he couldn't. It meant that we had one more player for the game. Oh, and in case you are wondering how they played without having any kit, our coach took out a bag full of football boots and told them to find their size! As you can see, it wasn't the most conventional way of putting a football team together!

The hospital escape

By now I was in year three of my mining vocational course at college. I didn't care too much about studying, but I was one of the best students in school. To be honest I didn't have any problems with the lessons, but the football training was the most important thing to me.

It was now reaching a stage where the vocation I had chosen

was about to become very real. I was 17 years old when I started to go to the mine. We went underground to do our work experience. I felt like an adult, like a real miner. I had to be at the mine for 6.45am, we went down at 7.30am. Four hours of practice followed and I was free around 1.15pm. I came back home, dropped my bag and I went to the stadium for my training having eaten almost nothing. The days flew by.

Around that time the school asked us to do regular medical tests. If you didn't pass your medical you were unable to pass the work experience. It emerged that I was one of two lads who had to be rechecked. My haemoglobin level was very low. The diagnosis was anaemia. Ironically, I felt great. I was tall, but thin, not least because I wasn't eating properly. The doctors didn't want to let me go home with those test results so within one hour they gave me a blood transfusion. I received about one litre of blood and had to stay in the hospital for a week.

Adam Tąpała, who was my coach, visited me. He spoke to the doctor, Tomasz Reginek.

"What's wrong with the lad?" he asked. "Do we need to give him some vitamins to make him stronger?"

The doctor answered: "He needs to eat lunch every day and everything will be fine. That's all he needs."

Coach Tąpała told me to do some stretching in the hospital to keep myself fit as we were due to play a very important game on the Sunday against Carbo Gliwice and he was hoping I would be able to play. However, the doctors refused to let me go home on the Friday so I whispered a solution to the coach. I told him that I would go for a walk in front of the hospital on the Sunday morning and he should be waiting for me there in the car with my bag, tracksuit, boots and gloves. I'd play the game and return to the hospital. Hopefully they wouldn't notice I was missing for a few hours!

The next tests they carried out on me went well, so I had nothing to fear health-wise that Sunday morning. Time to execute the plan! I went for a walk outside dressed in pyjamas and the coach was there with my kit. He was with Tadeusz Wiercioch, the team executive who deserves to have a monument in Knurów as he was so helpful to everyone. I jumped in the car and we travelled to Gliwice. I had missed training for a week, so I was a bit stiff. We won the game 2-1 and I was one of the best players. In the dressing room after the game, the coach pointed at me and said: "Do you see him, lads? He was out of football for a week, lying in hospital! And you? How many times did he save your asses today? Get off your backsides!"

I felt good and although I had to go back to the hospital as I hadn't been discharged, I told the coach that I'd be back in training on Tuesday. First of all I had to get back into the hospital but there were no problems, mainly because I made friends with the nurses. I told them I had been on a long walk. The doctor came over on the Monday and spoke to me: "How are you feeling young man? You're alright? I will let you go home then, but no exercises for at least a week. And drink lots of orange juice. I'll see you next month for a check-up."

I went to training the following day. I didn't listen to the doctor, I preferred to think about what my coach Słabkowski always repeated to us: "You have to have strong bones. That's why you have to drink lots of milk." I tried to drink as much as I could simply to avoid going back to the hospital again. I didn't get overweight, but I had strong bones and throughout my career I wasn't an injury-prone player. I owe that to coach Słabkowski.

A Velen fiddle

Coach Tąpała got us together and passed us some sensational news – we were going to Germany for a football tournament! The only issue was that we were going there unofficially. The invitation came for LZS Gierałtowice, a village near Knurów. They had been invited to send a team to play in Germany, but they didn't have a youth team. Not wishing to turn the invitation down they asked us to go to Germany and play on their behalf. It was a bit of a fiddle, pretending to be a team that we weren't, but thanks to them we saw a completely different world.

We played in Velen, near Gelsenkirchen. We won the tournament and I didn't concede a single goal. I was the winner of a cup for the club that I didn't play for officially!

Everyone bought some gifts for their families. It might sound unbelievable today, but at the time a can of beer or Coca-Cola was a rarity where we lived. We bought goods which were unavailable in Poland. I bought a multi-pack of cans for the family.

We came back to Poland with the cup that we had won but that created a problem. Where should it be kept? Gierałtowice was the club that had officially won the tournament, but the team that won it was Knurów. I don't know how the decision was made, but finally the cup went to Gierałtowice to go on display. My picture is apparently still in Velen's gallery.

A mining transfer

I finished junior age football and my vocational school at the same time. Because of my very good grades I could choose the mine unit I wanted to work in. I was thinking about the decision when suddenly Mr Wiercioch asked me if I'd like to join the senior team of Górnik Knurów: "Listen, we take six lads from the youth team and we want them to join the first-team. You're finishing school now so we'd like to offer you a full-time position." I was floored. "A full-time position in Knurów Mine?"

I got a job as a miner. I got my badge, my pay slip and my hook, but instead of working down a pit, I was based at the stadium. I was lucky because I was the last one of the players who got that position! It was unreal as I was now the fourth-choice keeper in a professional Polish football team. Wiercioch reiterated to me that he believed in me and I would be the best keeper at the club one day.

On the 15th day of every month I went to get my salary. I felt a little bit embarrassed that I was queuing in line with the real miners as I knew they had to go down the pit and work really hard for the same money I got for working at the stadium. For two years I checked in at 7am on the pitch and I worked until 11am.

I cleaned the stands, cut the grass, did any job that needed doing. I know everything about pitch maintenance to this very day and I still really like to cut the grass at home.

After two years of this the deal finished. The mine couldn't afford to hire the players. Lots of them decided to stay on and work as miners, but I was advised that I could stay at the club. I was single at the time and I got a small payment from the club. Sometimes I helped to unload coal into the boiler room, but in general the only thing I did was train. I did it for the following two years.

I trained with even more passion and desire because Concordia (the club was renamed Concordia Knurów in 1991) had a real goalkeeper coach – Jerzy Ogierman. I experienced my first drills with the professional coach Ogierman and loved it. I stayed an extra 30 minutes after the sessions and asked someone to practise taking free-kicks and penalties at me. I didn't do it for my career. I was simply hungry to play football.

Step by step, I started to knock on the first-team door. My debut was in the third division, a month after my 19th birthday. We were losing 1-0 against Carbo Gliwice when I replaced Tomasz Jarosławski in the second half, but I was on the bench the following game. I played in two more games during the season and I felt more and more confident. Experienced players started to tell me that I would soon be a first-team regular. "Keep working hard lad. Don't worry about anything, just work hard and you'll get there."

And I did it. I was first-choice goalkeeper for Concordia for the following three years. We tried to win promotion to the second division. Unfortunately we failed. We were second going into the 1993/94 season break. After the season resumed we played an away game against Krisbut Myszków, which was billed as 'the battle for promotion' to the second division. We were five points behind Krisbut, which was quite a gap as you got two points for a win, not three like now. We had to win to have a chance to get promoted. Unfortunately, we drew the game 0-0 and we didn't catch Krisbut.

The best period of time for me at Concordia was when they hired Marcin Bochynek. He worked previously for one of Poland's most successful clubs, Górnik Zabrze, and Greek side, Larissa. He sorted a lot of things out at Concordia. He instigated change and ensured we had much better conditions under his management. Bochynek started to talk me up across the region and help me to build a reputation. This inspired me. I wanted to show more and more and I began to play better and better. So did the team. Our coach stated that we wanted to win promotion to the second division and this time we led at the season break, but by the end of the season we had again failed to do so. Varta Namysłów finished ahead of us, which was a huge disappointment.

Legia wind-up

With Bochynek as the manager of Concordia and my form earning recognition, there was interest from other clubs to sign me. Górnik Zabrze were the first to make an approach. Marek Kostrzewa – Zabrze's assistant manager – came to Knurów to ask if I'd like to join them. Arkadiusz Kłak was their goalkeeper and I would have to challenge him for a place on the team. Our press officer, Tadeusz Ratuszyński, told me to refuse the offer: "Jurek, wait a year. You're not the type of person who will be happy being back-up for someone."

I thought that I wouldn't mind being back-up for Kłak – he was one of the stars in the Polish Ekstraklasa [the top division] – but Bochynek nailed the speculation: "There's nothing to talk about. He stays here."

He wanted us to get promoted to the second division and I was a key member of his team, but Górnik wouldn't let it go. Kostrzewa arrived again to try and sign me so Bochynek called me before I even had a chance to speak to him.

"Listen kid, you go there and you f***ing say that you feel sorry to waste his time, but you are signing for Legia Warsaw in the summer because you have to serve in the army there." [Drafting was mandatory in Poland at the time. A footballer could do it by playing with a military football club like Legia Warsaw].

I thought to myself that they won't believe me, but I went along with what he wanted me to do: "Sorry, but I've got a deal with Legia. I'll be serving in the army in Warsaw."

Kostrzewa was an old hand and he instantly knew I was lying: "Kid, what the f*** are you saying to me? Did Bochynek tell you to say that? Do you want to join us or not?" I answered quietly that I don't want to. Kostrzewa wasn't happy, but he didn't insist that I change my mind. He knew that Concordia didn't want to let me go and so no deal was done.

Tug of war

Marek Kłodko was a friend of mine who went from Concordia to Petrochemia Płock. He praised that club a lot. He worked with Hubert Kostka and had some good news for me: "I talked with Kostka about you and he is interested in signing you. He's a former goalkeeper and he can spot a talent. The only issue is the price."

I was waiting for an approach, but months went by and nothing happened. Before the 1995/96 season Bochynek left the club to manage second division Odra Wodzisław and although we would be fighting for promotion again, I didn't believe we could achieve it because of our failures to go up in previous years. I realised that my ambitions could not be fulfilled at Concordia and felt I needed to change clubs. Bochynek was keen to take me to Odra Wodzisław and came to Knurów to see me: "Join me in Wodzisław. I'll help you to sort a move out. We are the leaders now and once you join us, you'll get enough game time to get experience and next season we'll play in Ekstraklasa."

I really liked the idea of working with him again in a higher division, but suddenly Kostrzewa returned to Knurów to meet me: "Listen, kid, Bochynek always talks like that, but I'm coming for you for the third f***ing time. This is the last time I'll do so."

Kostrzewa was now assistant manager to Bogusław 'Bobo' Kaczmarek at Sokół Tychy. He started to talk about the club and their ambitions: "Mr Buller, the club owner, is a good man. Buller has money. It will be good, you'll see. We will stay in the top division. Bobo signs good players and we will fight for cups next season. And two years from now we're going to have a stadium like Schalke 04 do in Gelsenkirchen with a retractable roof. Buller saw it at Schalke and will build it here. We have plans to play in Europe."

Following a merger between Sokół Pniewy and GKS Tychy in 1995, Sokół Tychy had been formed and had taken Sokół Pniewy's place in Ekstraklasa. This was beneficial to GKS Tychy as they had been in the third division. I liked what I had heard from Kostrzewa and thought this would be a good move for me, but I went to see Waldemar Waleszczyk for advice. We played together for Concordia and I respected him a lot. I told him of my options and he advised me to choose Wodzisław: "You'll have time for acclimatisation and within six months you'll play in the top league. They'll definitely get promoted. Tychy is the opposite. You have one bad moment and if they go down they will blame you for the relegation. There are no jokes out there."

I listened to his advice and got in touch with Bochynek. He arrived in Knurów to pick me up and we drove to Wodzisław for a meeting with chairman Serwotka.

"Be quiet," said Bochynek. "I'll sort it out."

We went to Serwotka's office: "I've got this Dudek lad, chairman. The issue is how much he wants to be paid. And if he is ready to come to us."

I stared at him and thought to myself that I didn't have a clue what was going on. Serwotka looked at me and asked how much I'd like to earn?

"I don't know, to be honest," I stuttered. "Definitely more than in Knurów."

The chairman said that he'd think about it, but then Bochynek suddenly said: "Sir, I'm not sure if this is the Dudek we want to sign!"

There was another Dudek at Concordia, a striker, and now I was wondering what the hell Bochynek was doing. Was taking me to Wodzisław some kind of smoke screen? I knew that Odra were interested in signing Miedź Legnica's keeper Paweł Primel, so maybe I was being used to try to get that deal done. Bochynek told me at the end of the meeting that there was nothing to worry about, he was controlling everything, but I felt concerned about his intentions.

The next day I had a call from Kostrzewa: "Kid, we train indoors. Come along if you like. Get yourself to Przyszowice and I'll take you from there." So I went with Kostrzewa to train with Sokół.

It was during the winter between Christmas and New Year's Eve. I loved to play indoors when I had the chance and I played in six-a-sides, but always as a guest keeper. It was December 31 when Sokół were going to play in a tournament, but first there was an indoor tournament in Szczygłowice. The best indoor teams played there, but the winner was my team – Milano. We were sponsored by the owner of the local night club. I was named as the best goalkeeper of the tournament and received a trophy and a radio cassette recorder. I was extremely happy.

I went to Chorzów to play in the other tournament and I saw Bochynek: "So you betrayed us, huh?" I calmly answered that I didn't betray anyone and was playing at Sokół because I felt good there. I must have played pretty well during that six-a-side tournament as they asked me to come to Tychy for their training session on January 5. Sokół started to negotiate with Concordia about my transfer.

Straight after the tournament in Chorzów I went to celebrate New Year's Eve with my friends in Struża, near Myślenice. It was the best party of my life! We had pretty extreme conditions as the heating in the holiday cottages we rented was broken. But we didn't care. We partied until dawn. When you experience extraordinary conditions, you have the best fun. So I started 1996 in a great mood, but I didn't know that this year would be a crucial one both in my life and for my career.

NOT SO SCARY
AFTER ALL

Sokół started negotiations with Concordia about my transfer. There were no agents, so I went to Knurów on my own to talk about my move. I wanted to know how much they wanted for me and if they would let me go. "Jurek, we can't let you go for a bag of crisps. You have an international future," they said to me.

"Okay, let me get some sedatives and we'll talk after I've taken some!" I joked. "You cannot ask 1.8 billion zlotys (around £47,000) for me [in the days before Polish currency was adjusted due to inflation]. If you got that much money you could close the club and dine out on it!"

They were being stubborn so in the meantime I continued to train in Tychy. Two weeks later I visited Concordia and the guys started to ask me about Sokół. They listened to me with incredulity: "There's a proper professionalism. If you need new boots and a new tracksuit it's no problem. You get world class care! And we go to the Netherlands to prepare before the season restarts." It was a different world to how life was at Concordia.

Sokół were still in negotiations with Concordia and their new coach, Józek Dankowski, insisted that I must stay in Knurów. He was promising promotion to the second division, but I didn't want to listen to that: "Józek, I respect you a lot, but stop talking such bullshit to me, please. We are currently third, right? We didn't get promoted in the past and I feel that if I stay another six months here I'll melt into the greyness. I may not have this chance to move clubs again."

I travelled to the Netherlands with Sokół for a winter camp, but they advised me to return to Knurów again to talk them into cutting the transfer fee for me. So I did, and the price they were requesting dropped to 1.4 billion zlotys, but I wasn't aware of all the behind-the-scenes games that were being played when I returned to Tychy. So I had to travel to Knurów again and asked Dankowski for an explanation: "Józek, tell me what on earth is going on."

"There is a guy who came from Sokół and he asks: 'How much do you want for Dudek?' We said we want 1.6 billion zlotys for you. He said that it's fine and he almost signed the papers, but he didn't like one point – the 40 per cent sell-on fee for Concordia from your next transfer if they sell you in the first year, a 20 per cent sell-on fee from a transfer within two years and a 10 per cent sell-on fee from a transfer within three to five years."

It seemed like quite a logical condition to me, so Dankowski asked me to check why Tychy had stalled over it. I went to Tychy and asked them: "Why are you not happy with that sell-on fee clause? Do you want to sell me straight away so are worried about the 40 per cent? Who would want to buy me within a year anyway?"

The sporting director, Edmund Mikołajczak, constantly said he cannot agree with such a clause. There would be no transfer for me under those conditions. Sokół told me to go back to Knurów to force a deal through by threatening never to play for them again if the transfer collapsed. I told them I would serve the rest of my contract out that season and then join Sokół as a free agent in the summer, meaning they would completely miss out on a transfer fee.

It worked. Within a couple of hours the issues had been resolved and I was told that my transfer could now be completed. It was another six months before I discovered why Mikołajczak was so adamant that the sell-on fee clause wasn't acceptable.

Unbeknown to me, Feyenoord Rotterdam were interested in signing me. They had seen me when I was in the Netherlands with Sokół and made an enquiry. The problem was that I wasn't an official Sokół player. The chancers from Sokół suddenly realised they could buy me for a bag of crisps and then transfer me for a big profit so obviously they didn't want 40 per cent of that going to Concordia. Sokół didn't want to share the profit, so it was ironic what happened when I was transferred to Feyenoord just six months later. Nobody saw the money Feyenoord paid because Sokół went bankrupt a few months after my move to Rotterdam. The club actually withdrew from the league halfway through the 1996/97 season because of their financial issues and were demoted.

When I think about my transfer to Sokół it makes me laugh

now. I was travelling between Knurów and Tychy to secure my transfer while Sokół were already thinking about selling me to Feyenoord. At least I have good memories from the six months I spent in Tychy. There was a great atmosphere among the team.

The Polish Tommo

My first real test in Sokół was an indoor tournament in Poznan. We played on astroturf with little 5m x 2m goals – exactly the same as I had on my primary school pitch in Szczygłowice. The arena was full of supporters and on the pitch there were top Polish teams and Aalborg from Denmark. They played in the Champions League at that time.

These were the perfect conditions for me to play in. There was great interest and even more excitement for a player experiencing this for the first time in his life. It was a privilege, but I got stressed. I felt that my muscles were not as flexible as usual. Maybe I was a bit frozen with nerves, but then I got hit very hard in the chest while I was making a save. I think that was a game-changing moment as all the stress oozed away and I played at my usual level.

They offered me 12 million zlotys (about £310) a month in wages, which was three times higher than in Knurów, plus game bonuses, but the money wasn't that important. I could play in Ekstraklasa. Sokół was better organised than Concordia, although the training facilities were a bit worse.

I have to give praise to Marek Kostrzewa. He might have had a specific, direct style of talking to the players, but he was a great assistant – top class in Poland!

During training sessions we had indoor five-a-sides and the losers had to buy beers for the winners! Everyone wanted

Kostrzewa in their team because he was a real fighter. He showed his commitment, desire and determination to win even in those innocent five-a-sides. I think he was the Polish Phil Thompson!

Debut against Legia

My debut was an away game against Legia Warsaw, a team that had played against Panathinaikos in the Champions League quarter-final a week earlier. I wasn't too sure if I was playing when we were on the way to the capital, but I felt pretty confident anyway as I had settled into the squad quickly. Bobo came to me on the bus and said: "Alright, kid. I know it's Legia, but you play tomorrow. Get ready!"

I instantly started to sweat! In fact, I was so nervous I didn't eat anything until the following day. I barely slept the night before the game and I didn't touch my breakfast either. I relaxed a bit during the team walk, but inside my stomach was churning and I was thinking about it all the time. I had a doomsday scenario in my head where everything had gone wrong. 'It's over mate. We thank you for trying but that's it'. 'Well, at least I'll be a free man if it goes that badly wrong', I thought to myself.

We were in the tunnel before the game. Maciej Szczęsny [whose son, Wojciech, played for Arsenal and Roma] was standing face-to-face with me. I had read the interviews with him before the game. He said that the pitch was not in a good condition, that it stank like a barn and was not prepared for a game of football to be played on it. When I saw him on the TV, I thought he was so tall that his head must tower above the crossbar, but when he was standing next to me – eyeballing me in Legia's tunnel – I realised that we were the same height.

Szczęsny looked at me and said: "Look at what kind of shit we have to play on." He was very direct towards me and I relaxed immediately as a result. He was one of the biggest stars in the league yet now I could see he was still an ordinary lad. Before we went onto the pitch, he added: "Is this your debut today? Good luck, kid."

The game kicked off and I was totally stress-free. I got more confidence after making a couple of saves. It was goalless until Tomasz Sokołowski scored a real stunner. We conceded another goal in the dying minutes of the game. I didn't make an error, so even though we lost 2-0 my debut was quite good.

I saw the replays the following day and Legia defender Marek Jóźwiak was the expert in the studio: "Despite conceding two goals, Dudek played well. He couldn't save any of the goals and he prevented Legia from scoring more." I thought that Ekstraklasa was not as scary as I had imagined. Indeed, nobody had any disputes with me until the end of the season.

"Once I was angry with him, but just a little bit. We played in Kraków against Hutnik. Andrzej Jaskot had a shot from about 30 yards. It was nothing dangerous in theory, but Jurek tried to catch the ball with his typical low catching style. He didn't close his elbows properly and the ball went between his arms and legs. I didn't worry too much about it. It was a typical lack of experience. Every goalkeeper has to concede some silly goals."
Bogusław 'Bobo' Kaczmarek, Sokół Tychy coach

Fifty million zlotys for a wedding

I hadn't been at Sokół long when I paid a visit to chairman Buller and spoke to him directly.

"I am getting married soon and I need some money. I got paid in February and I've had one bonus for the win against Lech Poznan. But basically, for the last three-and-a-half months I have been living in debt. Thankfully I spend my money wisely, so it's not catastrophic, but I am really struggling here."

I wanted to earn at least 50 million zlotys, as did Tomasz Kos, who came with me to ask for the same pay rise. Buller agreed to our demands and called his driver and told him to bring the money for us the next day. Now I could afford our wedding!

I asked the coach if I could at least buy a beer for the lads to celebrate my forthcoming marriage with them. I wanted to have a little stag party and a barbecue, but we had training the following day. Kaczmarek said yes but warned me: "Jurek, just one beer each, okay?"

So that's what I did. I supplied one beer for each player. The guys were surprised so made an offer I couldn't refuse: "You have done as you were told mate, you've officially given us one beer. So now we'll have a whip-round and get the rest!"

We met in a local restaurant and my stag party was unforgettable. I was so happy that when I went in for training the following day I said to the lads: "I didn't know you could party like that!"

They laughed. "Jurek, Jurek, we have parties like that every week!"

Every week! I thought they went to sleep at 10pm every night like I did. Young and naïve, I didn't believe them: "Every week? Come on! You can't be, we're fighting for survival in the league!"

"You see, kid, this is why we are so harmonic on and off the pitch. We stick together. The best parties are once a week straight after the game!"

Given my team-mates were drinking and partying all the time maybe it's hard to believe, but we avoided relegation. We played the last game of the season against GKS Katowice and had to win to keep ourselves in the league. They really didn't care about the result as they were safe so it wasn't as difficult a match as it could have been. We controlled the entire game, won 1-0 and we could have scored more. Avoiding the drop was an achievement for us as we were battling against relegation for the whole second half of that season.

The team was full of lads from outside of Silesia. Paradoxically, it helped a lot. We encouraged each other. No-one refused to get stuck in and I have to say that I worked with a bunch of great lads during my six months with Sokół.

Darek Jaskulski was one of them, Robert Wilk – who played in the national team – was another and so was Darek Placzkiewicz. I got on well with the young guns like the three Krzysztofs – Bizacki, Konon and Nowak – and who could ever forget about the famous Janusz Nawrocki? He played at GKS Katowice for years. We called him 'The Pearl Diver'. The real pearl divers have a massive lung volume that means they can survive underwater for a long time. Janusz – or 'Nawrot' as he was also called – was just as strong. His stamina levels were phenomenal. He ran box-to-box at full speed the whole 90 minutes and made it look like he'd only been playing for 45 minutes.

When we played away it would often take hours to drive back home so the lads would shower quickly and then scramble to get a seat on the bus near Janusz.

He would start with his stories about playing in league football. His stories were worth hearing so that's why we only took a very quick shower after away games!

No matter what time we arrived back from an away game (usually late in the night), we had to be ready at 11am for 'regeneration'. Instead of saying "goodnight," coach Kaczmarek warned us: "I hope nobody will be late!"

When we arrived for regeneration the coach started his post-game analysis: "We played quite a good game yesterday, but Jurek... unnecessary kicks. You should play the ball to the defence more. Bizacki – how many opportunities do you need to score? You scored, but you should have got at least 10!"

He had a recognisable tone of voice, like he was sleepy, but suddenly Bobo would open his eyes widely:

"Nawrot, where have you been?"

"Are you talking to me, gaffer?"

"I've been talking to you for five minutes!"

"But..."

"Who did you think I was talking to? You can barely see five feet in front of your nose."

"But we travelled all night gaffer!"

"Open your eyes. WAKE UP!"

The atmosphere immediately lightened up. They had a good rapport.

Kaczmarek always repeated at the end of these talks: "Gentlemen, I beg you... Nawrot, can you hear me? All of you look rough. There is no drinking and smoking at all! I'm a teetotaller and I can smell from a mile who touches this crap. I warn you – you'd better stay home if you're drunk or hungover. It can cost you a lot if you turn up here like that. We have a goal – to avoid relegation – and I do not want that compromised."

I spent only six months with Sokół, but I could write another book just with anecdotes about my time there!

Feyenoord

It was June 15, 1996 and I was getting married to Mirella, but the following day I had to go to South America with Poland Under-23s to play against Argentina and Brazil. The wedding do finished at 5am, but instead of returning to the hotel with my wife, I went back home for a while because I had to travel to Warsaw at 8am. Mirella cried. So did I. That's how my honeymoon started. In tears.

My neighbours must have wondered what was going on when I left home alone. They were probably talking about me as I'd just got married but nobody saw me for a couple of weeks! I checked in at the hotel in Warsaw on the Sunday at 2pm and I asked what time our flight to South America was. "Monday, 6.15am!" So I had to run away from my own wedding party to stay alone in a hotel in Warsaw.

When I came back to Poland from South America I got a call to join up with the senior Poland national team at their training camp. I was in the taxi and I was wondering if coach Piechniczek would give me at least one day off. He did, so on the Sunday I went to see my wife for the first time since we had been married!

On the Monday I had to return to train with the national team and stay in the camp in Wisła, southern Poland, for 10 days. When I was there, I met Tadeusz Fogiel. He was an agent and he was looking for players that he could sell to France. I also had the opportunity to talk to Widzew Łódź, a big Polish club that folded in 2015 but is now an amateur club. Their coach, Franciszek Smuda, and director, Tadeusz Gapiński, asked me if I'd like to play in Łódź. I said yes, but first of all they had to negotiate with Sokół. I knew they needed money because of the emerging financial problems, so I thought it wouldn't be a problem.

But Mr Buller wasn't letting me go anywhere on the cheap! He told them he wanted around £500,000 for me, which was an enormous price at the time.

After the international break I returned to Sokół. I started to wonder why I did so. I felt great with the national team in Wisła and I saw changes in Sokół I did not like. There were a few new players and coaches including the goalkeeper coach. I was devastated.

I really wanted to get out of there as soon as possible and suddenly Buller called me: "Do you want to go to Feyenoord for a trial?"

I smiled. I thought he was kidding: "Excuse me, where? Feyenoord? In Rotterdam? Me?"

As I mentioned earlier, Feyenoord had scouted me since that winter camp in Holland and they wanted to see more. It was crazy. I'd recently got married, I hadn't seen my wife for a month, I didn't even have any non-club clothes or my passport with me, just a bag with my football gear in.

I said to Buller I needed to think about it, but Darek Jaskulski and Marek Rzepka – my two friends from the team – had a word with me. "There's nothing to think about, mate. Five minutes and you're off. Run if you can as Sokół might be bankrupt soon."

We went to Bydgoszcz for a friendly. A big agent arrived to watch the game – Jan de Zeeuw – who would later become my agent and a friend. He took me to his home in Sitno and provided all the details about my flight from Gdańsk to Amsterdam, via Hamburg.

Jan told me that I had to travel alone. I was so stressed. I thought I couldn't do it. I'd never travelled out of the country before on my own. It was a nerve-wracking prospect. Finally, I got onto the plane with two pairs of football boots and my goalkeeper gloves. My next adventure was about to begin...

DUTCH DISNEYLAND

In January 1996 we travelled with Sokół for a camp in the Netherlands. It was a 24-hour trip by bus, but I was delighted. I hadn't travelled on such a luxurious bus in my life. It was real fun.

Bobo Kaczmarek was the only one who could speak any English and he wasn't fluent.

This was only my second trip abroad in my life. I was excited at everything. The hotel was awesome, as was the football pitch. The Netherlands was brilliant, so clean and tidy that I was scared to go out on the streets. It looked too neat!

Sokół gave us beautiful jackets and tracksuits for the trip. We visited Rotterdam during our spare time and also played friendlies with Excelsior and Feyenoord II Rotterdam. We were over the moon just to be there, it was a completely different experience for us all, and this was despite there being terrible snow in Rotterdam at the time. That didn't bother us coming from Poland. We were still happy to train in the park, even though it was the worst snowfall in the Netherlands for 20 years.

We won 3-1 against Excelsior in our first friendly, but because of the weather we had to play our next game against Feyenoord's reserve team on astroturf. Usually the youngest player at Sokół had to pick up the team kits and load them onto the bus. I was the youngest and new to the team, so it was my duty to do it. All of us were excited as there were rumours that we might even play against the Feyenoord first-team.

We arrived at Feyenoord's training ground and started to get off our bus. Someone shouted to grab the bag with kits in it. Then the masseur came over to me and said: "Kid, where are the kits? The bag was in the hotel reception, did you take it?"

My heart sank. I'd forgotten it! Our entire kit was 18 kilometres away in the hotel – too far to go back and get it in time for the match – and it was my fault. I had no option but to admit my mistake so I went to our assistant manager Kostrzewa and shakily said: "Coach... I forgot to bring the kit bag."

Kostrzewa went ballistic. He started to scream and shout: "Are you crazy? How did you forget the kits for the whole team?! Go and explain it to Bobo. Don't you f***ing think that I will go and explain it for you!"

Finally it was Kostrzewa who passed the message to Bobo. I saw how angry he was and, for my own safety, I didn't want to get close to him. "We don't have a kit, this young fella forgot to grab the bag from the hotel," said Kaczmarek to Jan de Zeeuw and pointed at me. De Zeeuw went to Johnny Metgod – Feyenoord's reserve coach – and asked if we could borrow a kit for the game. Metgod said it wouldn't be a problem and winked knowingly: "But you owe me a bottle of vodka!"

Luckily, we had plenty of vodka with us!

Next I had to go into the dressing room to tell the lads what had happened. They thought that I was messing with them, winding them up, but a moment later they realised I wasn't joking when they saw a full set of green Feyenoord kits being brought into the dressing room. "Eighteen full kits we've got," said the team technical director, "Nobody even think about taking a f***ing thing. Understood?"

I felt bad, but the lads were actually grateful to me for forgetting to bring the Sokół strip because it meant they got to wear Feyenoord shirts instead. They started to take pictures of themselves in it, one by one. I was given Ed de Goey's number one shirt to wear and I think I took about 10 pictures in it. Everyone thought it was a once-in-a-lifetime opportunity and we had to make the most of it. To be honest I wasn't sure if I was going to play in that game – I was afraid that the gaffer would punish me for my forgetfulness – but I started and we won 2-1.

After the game I timidly asked Kaczmarek if maybe we could ask Feyenoord to let us keep the kits. Bobo looked at me angrily again. "Dudek, you'd better shut up for today…"

So we got changed out of them and they were counted. Eighteen full sets were still there. Our hearts bled when we had to return them. I didn't imagine at that time that I would one day play for Feyenoord so it felt like we'd never get the opportunity to wear such prestigious shirts again.

We travelled to see Feyenoord's De Kuip stadium. When we got there the first-team players were just about to finish their training session. Everyone was waiting for the legendary Ronald

Koeman to take a picture with him when Bobo suddenly called me over and started to talk to Ed de Goey: "Ed, this is Jerzy Dudek, a young, talented goalkeeper from Poland."

"Nice to meet you," replied de Goey. Myself, de Goey and Kaczmarek had our picture taken together. When I look at it today I can see my awestruck face. It was the highlight of my career at that time to stand next to the famous Ed de Goey, who had also been the Netherlands' first choice goalkeeper at the 1994 World Cup in USA.

We took pictures everywhere inside De Kuip. We couldn't believe that players had the opportunity to play at this beautiful stadium week in, week out. We were like kids at Disneyland. Little did I know that I would get the opportunity to play in De Kuip for myself in the not-too-distant future.

Five-year contract

I returned to the Netherlands six months later for my trial with Feyenoord. Jan put me on the plane in Gdańsk, saying: "Don't worry at all. Włodzimierz Smolarek will be waiting for you." It was the first time I'd travelled on a plane alone, I only knew about 10 words in English and I was scared I would get lost in Amsterdam's Schiphol Airport.

I came out of the arrivals hall and I saw a familiar face – Włodzimierz Smolarek, the former Polish international striker who also played for Feyenoord between 1988 and 1990. He took me to The Savoy Hotel in Rotterdam city centre – new Feyenoord players always stayed in this hotel – and I was told to turn up for a training session the following day. I met Belgian defender Geoffrey Claeys in the hotel. He took care of me and gave me a lift to training, but we didn't speak too much as while he could speak English, German, French, Spanish and Dutch, I could only speak Polish. When we arrived at training for the first time I was speechless when I saw who I had to train with: Henrik Larsson, Ronald Koeman, Gaston Taument, Ed de Goey and Tomasz 'Tomek' Iwan. Me? Train with these superstars? I felt out of my depth and when training started every shot went past me, like all the outfield players were in their best form and I was the opposite. I thought it was a galactic level for me, far too high a standard. What was I doing there?

In truth, it depressed me. I started to wonder why I'd asked for this move. We had a second training session in the afternoon and I made a quick calculation. It was Monday and my return ticket was scheduled for Friday. I could train on Tuesday, then maybe they would let me train on Wednesday. But Thursday? I doubted that they'd still want me by then.

I called Mirella a couple of times per day and my head was all over the place. "I'm coming back home, definitely coming back." Three hours later: "I'm staying. I'll try to fight for a place." Then it was: "Mirella, please come to me!" But after training: "Don't come! I'm coming back!" I was so stressed, on an emotional roller coaster, so I called Jan after my second day and told him: "Take me out of here. I want to come back home. This is not a life for me." But things improved.

Marek Saganowski and Grzegorz Król came to Rotterdam as Feyenoord were also interested in signing them and I started to feel better. We went to Doorwerth, near Arnhem, and I met with Jan and Bobo there. Jan translated the basic words that I needed to shout when playing: 'keeper, away, forward' etc and wrote them phonetically. I had started to learn a new language and a new life. I played in a trial match against the local amateurs the next day and they attacked constantly. I saved about two or three one-on-one situations. It was a usual thing for me, but everyone started to praise me. Henk Fräser, an international player for the Netherlands, came to me after the game and said in English: "Congratulations! Good boy!" It boosted my confidence.

I had a meeting with Jan, Bobo and Hans Hagelstein, the Feyenoord general manager. He passed a piece of paper to Jan: "These are our conditions." They offered me a five-year contract. Jan asked me if the financial details were fine for me. "How do I know?" I said, "I don't understand a single word!"

De Zeeuw started to convince me that – at this stage of my career – it was a good deal for me. I called Mirella: "Listen, they really want to sign me for five years! I'm going to earn 10 times better money than in Poland. What should I do? If I fail, I could go back to Poland. Until then I would earn the money which would give us a good start in life. We're only going to leave a studio flat, which we still need to finish off. We have no money and I haven't earned any for five months..."

Mirella replied that if I signed the deal, she would move to the Netherlands.

"I travelled to the Netherlands by bus with one bag. I had some clothes and a book called 'Mother and a child'. I was going to give birth in a couple of months. I hadn't travelled abroad before then. I was afraid to travel on my own, so I asked my friend if she would come with me. We got out in Rotterdam and we didn't see Jurek! I started to panic! I didn't know what to do, but immediately I saw a car. It was Jurek with Marek Saganowski's uncle. We went to the hotel. Tomek Iwan and his wife Ania visited us.

They were settled already in the Netherlands. They spoke perfect Dutch. I thought we would be fine with them around."

Mirella Dudek, wife

Where's my parachute?

I remember my presentation at Feyenoord very well. It was an open day for the supporters. I was one of five new players in the team. We travelled to the airport to get into a helicopter which was to land on the pitch inside De Kuip, so it was a bit different than holding up a scarf next to the coach like it was with Gerard Houllier at Liverpool!

The organisers said the helicopter would land in five minutes, but we made about 20 circles around the stadium before landing. I'd had enough. If someone had given me a parachute I'd have jumped without a doubt.

Before we got out, the pilot told us not to wave to the supporters but as I didn't speak Dutch fluently I didn't understand. Anyway, with 52,000 supporters having turned out to welcome us how could I not wave? Thankfully I realised why as I jumped out of the helicopter – the blades were still rotating and Feyenoord wouldn't have much use for a goalkeeper with no hands!

Three days later we played a friendly against Gremio and I made my debut in the second half.

The pitch was amazing and the stadium was full, but I made the mistake of trying to pass to Koeman when he had turned away from goal. One of the Brazilians intercepted the pass, but shot wide of the goal.

I heard the groan from the stands when I gave the ball away – the supporters must have wondered what I was doing – but I also made a couple of good saves.

Ronald Koeman

About 60 minutes after I'd arrived by helicopter at De Kuip we heard news that Feyenoord had signed another player. It was Marek Saganowski, who considered the deal for quite a long time before he became another Polish player at Feyenoord alongside myself and Tomek Iwan.

That first season flew by. I played in the reserves and I had to train with the first-team in the morning. I was on the bench during the Eredivisie matches, as second choice to de Goey, took Dutch lessons and I was busy at home after Alexander was born on December 9, 1996. This was my world and I loved it!

When I joined Feyenoord I knew they had two stars: Koeman and de Goey. I looked closely at Koeman during my days there. What did he do on the pitch? What did he do in the gym? How did he move? How did he shoot? I wanted to learn from his behaviour. He'd been part of the great Dutch Euro '88 winning team so although he was now 33 I saw him as a role model. But there was conflict between him and our coach, Arie Haan, who had also been a legendary player for the Netherlands.

We travelled to Kazakhstan to play in a friendly. We won the match easily and afterwards Koeman, Gaston Taument and Henk Vos went into town to experience the Kazakhstan night-life. I have never slept in such a modern and beautiful hotel – a round building, half of which was made of glass allowing you to see everyone who came in and out, which has an importance in this story. Myself and Tomek wanted to go out too, but Haan was sitting downstairs in the hotel with the club director and two other officials. We hoped they would go to bed, but they didn't have any intention of doing so. They knew exactly what they were doing. They ordered drinks and waited. And waited.

We knew a storm was brewing so Tomek and I stayed up playing Playstation and kept checking so as not to miss what might happen. It was after 4am when the three of them strolled back into the hotel. Koeman walked over to where Haan and the others were sitting. "Good evening," he said graciously, "and goodnight." They walked straight to the elevator and went to their rooms. Haan and the other officials finished their drinks and did the same. Tomek and I decided to get some sleep, but quite frankly we were disappointed nothing had happened. We returned to Rotterdam the following day and thought it was over, but we were wrong. Haan had been told to deal with it.

After training he pulled the three players to one side: "You're going to train with the reserves for the rest of the week because of your night out in Kazakhstan." Taument and Vos took the news on the chin, but Koeman couldn't believe it. He was furious. He stormed into the dressing room, grabbed his jacket and said: "Me? Train with the reserves? Is he serious? I'm going home. See you later, lads. I've no idea when I'll return."

I turned on the TV that evening and I couldn't believe what I was watching. A live TV show was being presented from Koeman's house! "Ronald, the coach said you got in very late after your night out in Kazakhstan. Is that true?"

"Well yes, but Haan and the chairman were up drinking until 4am..."

It had to be Ronald who won the confrontation and the reaction from the Feyenoord fans suggested he had. A couple of days later we played a friendly and there were many flags in support of Koeman in the stadium. Some supporters wanted Haan to be sacked. I don't know who apologised first, but Koeman returned to the squad. It was a real eye-opener.

Koeman became manager of Feyenoord in 2011 and is now in charge at Southampton. He is a true legend. I was proud to play alongside him and one day he said to me: "Jurek, would you stay a bit longer after training?"

"Of course!" I replied excitedly. He wanted to practise free-kicks and penalties. I was on the bench all the time for the first-team, so I treated that session with Koeman as my biggest game of the season. Maybe, at that time, it was even the game of my life. How many other people could say they'd had one-on-one training sessions with Ronald Koeman?

I was 100 per cent focused when he was preparing to take a free-kick or a penalty. It was a huge honour for me, a brilliant experience, and he was even happy with some of the saves I made. We started to talk after it and I told him he had a very strong shot. I was thinking about his winning goal for Barcelona in the 1992 European Cup final at Wembley against Sampdoria when he hit some of those shots, but he made a confession to me: "I had power and I could also put backspin on the ball. It was a killer mixture, but now I can only spin the ball. When you get older, you lose your power and I've lost mine. It's like driving an old car – if you accelerate too fast it can end badly. That's why I no longer shoot at full power – I simply don't want to test my breaking point."

Koeman later admitted to me and the lads he had come to Feyenoord to see out his days until he retired so following the example he was setting would be a mistake: "If you see me somewhere drinking beer, don't take that as an example. I'm not a role model any more. It's my last professional season, I can relax a bit now." In his last game for Feyenoord we finished second in the league and qualified for the Champions League.

Koeman sat in the dressing room afterwards and his eyes were full of tears. "It's over," he said, but a moment later he had perked up. "Lads, I don't need to think about how fast the summer will go. Now I can have as many holidays as I want!"

Tortured goalkeepers

Ed de Goey wanted to move abroad and Feyenoord knew this, which is why they signed me, but no-one knew when it would happen. I was supposed to be his successor, but when I saw how the Feyenoord supporters cheered him I was sure that he wouldn't leave Rotterdam. I cannot say a bad word about him. Ed is easygoing, a great professional and – as is every goalkeeper – a maverick! He is a homebody and also a terrible sleepyhead! During away games I was his room-mate. It took him just five minutes after lunch to fall asleep and when he sleeps he snores!

Jan told me that de Goey was precious for Feyenoord but also that Haan wanted me in goal immediately after he was sold. This could have happened after I arrived in Rotterdam in 1996, but the chairman stopped any move as he wanted to sell de Goey for a good price and thought he would get more if Ed stayed for another season.

It might sound weird, but I was satisfied that I was on the bench, even if it wasn't nice not to be playing. As speculation grew about his future there were people who complained about de Goey's form, but I felt that the competition I was providing for his place improved him and he also felt I wasn't the type of player who would be an asshole and sabotage him. De Goey played fantastically that season.

I worked with Pim Doesburg at Feyenoord and he was an outstanding goalkeeper coach. He had a specific approach –

he liked to torture goalkeepers, but not literally! We always worked hard and it paid off. Sometimes I even asked him for extra training sessions ahead of my day off. He always praised me for that.

'You're the number one!'

At the end of my first season at Feyenoord I was considering my future. I'd heard that HSV Hamburg were interested in me and it seemed that Ed wasn't going to leave Rotterdam. I thought about my options when I was on holiday, but on my way back to Rotterdam I got a call from Jan: "Congratulations! You're number one at Feyenoord. De Goey has signed for Chelsea!"

I felt a great pressure immediately. Could I make it? Could I replace such a great goalkeeper like Ed? Why did he leave us so suddenly? As second choice I didn't have to worry about anything; now I had to replace the irreplaceable Ed! The obvious conclusion came to me immediately: 'I won't make it!'

"When Feyenoord sold de Goey, I had a lot of work to do. Doesburg wanted Feyenoord to sign John Karelse from NAC Breda. But Jorien van den Herik, Feyenoord's chairman at the time, signed another goalkeeper – Hungarian Zsolt Petry – without saying anything to Doesburg. I went to the chairman and reminded him what we spoke about earlier – that Jurek had to play in the reserves for a year and then would be de Goey's successor."

Jan de Zeeuw, agent

When I returned to Rotterdam, Haan told me straight away that I'd be number one because I deserved it, but I started to wonder why they had signed Zsolt Petry. He was 31 and had played for Hungary at international level since 1988 so he wasn't an ordinary keeper. You don't buy those kinds of players to sit them on the bench, so should I have been concerned?

Haan explained to me that he was afraid of the risk. He wanted a good back-up option as I was 24 and had never played a first-team game for Feyenoord. He then admitted that Zsolt and myself had blank pages – whoever performed best in pre-season would be number one. I still didn't believe I could make it. Petry had more experience than me. He had played in Belgium. He spoke quite good Dutch. How could I be picked ahead of him?

We both trained hard that summer and for me it paid off. Haan decided to trust me: "You're a better goalkeeper. You will be my number one," he told me ahead of my Feyenoord debut, a Champions League qualifier in De Kuip against Finnish champions FC Jazz. We were leading 5-1 when one of the Finnish players put a cross in. I shouted 'keeper' and came to collect the ball, but I collided with an FC Jazz player and spilled it. One of the opposition strikers had no problem putting it into the empty goal. I heard boos in the stands. The supporters probably thought they'd have fun with their new goalie!

After my Champions League debut I played my first game in the Eredivisie. We won 3-0 against MVV Maastricht. I played quite well even if I didn't have too much to do. Then we travelled to Finland for the second leg. I think the guys were relaxed after the first leg as we played poorly, but that meant I had a busy night and I played well.

"Dudek is the only Feyenoord player operating at a high level," said one of the commentators.

We won 2-1 and the coach started to trust me more and more. After the next three games in Eredivisie we flew to Turin to play against Juventus in the Champions League. We played really badly and lost 5-1. I made a terrible mistake in that game. I conceded another one after another mistake and I thought 'I'm done. It's over'. Luckily, it wasn't. Haan knew I had made mistakes, but they weren't result-defining. We would have lost anyway. He consequently stuck with me and played me in the first XI, but when we lost 4-0 to Ajax in October 1997 – our third defeat in a row having been beaten by Willem II in the Eredivisie and Manchester United in the Champions League – Arie Haan was sacked. Leo Beenhakker replaced him as first-team manager.

'Jerry Springer' in charge

Beenhakker was from Rotterdam and was a vastly experienced coach. Among others he had managed both Real Madrid and the Netherlands twice. I have to say he was a great educationalist and an authority for the lads at Feyenoord. We called him 'Jerry Springer' – after the American talkshow host – because Leo made lots of briefings and told us interesting stories about his football philosophy!

It was a better time for Feyenoord when Leo got the job. He improved the atmosphere in the dressing room and we started to win games. Leo explained to us we had to take responsibility for our performances and efforts. It paid off. We won against Juventus at De Kuip, but we couldn't reach second spot in the group, which would have given us a place in the next round of the Champions League. We finished third behind Man United and Juventus but I really liked the Champions League games, especially the two away games against Juve and United. I exchanged shirts with Angelo Peruzzi and Peter Schmeichel and they are the most precious ones in my collection.

Straight after becoming Feyenoord manager, Leo called the captain Jean-Paul van Gastel and asked him to invite the team to a dinner. He wanted to improve team spirit and we went to an Argentinian restaurant. Everyone was joking and laughing, so we decided to continue the 'integration night' and went to 'Ski Hut' – a bar themed as a local for skiers. It was funny in there, even the barman did crazy things like sing folk songs while standing on a table. It wasn't the only time we partied there with the team.

Some of the lads drank a beer or two too many and we only left the bar at dawn. It was really hard to get up for training the next day. I was tired, but as I had got injured the day before I knew that instead of training I would be in the physio's room. Van Gastel came to me after the training session had finished. He was extremely tired – he could barely stand – but he wanted to know where I had been. I told him the truth, that I was injured, but he wouldn't accept it.

"An injury? You hurt your elbow? I feel pain everywhere. If we party together until dawn, we train together when we get up. If you know you're injured and you won't train don't come with us for a party again." It was a memorable lesson. Jean-Paul was right. I realised I needed to become a team player and I never made that mistake again.

Mr Zoetebier

At the beginning of 1998, Leo signed Dutch goalkeeper Edwin Zoetebier. A new rivalry started. Zoetebier was signed from

Sunderland, where he didn't play a single Premier League game, and from the moment he arrived he made it clear why he was in Rotterdam: "I came to Feyenoord to be the number one and win every possible title." He also added that he wanted to play in the national team.

Zoetebier thought that if you played for a team like Feyenoord you had to be an automatic number one in the national team. You have to be as bold as brass to say things like that, especially with Ed de Goey, Edwin van der Sar and Sander Westerveld as competition. I knew straight away it would be a hard time for me as well given his arrogant personality, but many people didn't like his arrogant declarations. Rotterdam is a city of people who don't like clever dicks and that went in my favour, but it was a circus working with him.

We were warming up before a game. I threw the ball to Doesburg and he shot immediately. I made an effective save. Doesburg repeated the routine with Zoetebier. Goal. He commented immediately: "You shoot into the top corner when I'm in goal but for your boy you make it easy." The atmosphere was terrible. Away from the pitch we got on fine, but on it he kept niggling away at me: "You can't kick a ball properly. This is the great Feyenoord, it's not a club for you!"

I had to rise above him. Instead of working hard himself, Zoetebier was continuously talking, making out that everyone else made errors whereas he was this perfect goalkeeper who never made a mistake. In the end I confronted him: "I know your problem, but I do not care!" and then looked towards the sky to ignore him whenever he tried to talk to me. He finally figured out that his mind games were not working, but still he showed me a lack of respect.

In the summer of 1998 we played our last friendly against Nottingham Forest. Zoetebier was sure he would play, but he didn't get a chance. We won 3-2 and I was to blame for one of their goals. Zoetebier was so angry that he didn't play, and after my mistake, that he didn't attend a team dinner. The other lads didn't like it. They felt he should have shown me more respect, but finally I felt like I'd won, that I was number one at Feyenoord. And I was.

Champions!

We were Eredivisie leaders at the halfway point of the 1998/99 season. During the winter break we had a training camp in Sicily, but it went badly because of the weather. It was raining all the time so we weren't able to play on any football pitches; instead we trained on an athletics track! Our friendlies were cut short because of the terrible conditions. Even though we were five points clear, it made us nervous about the second half of the season... but we ended up playing brilliantly!

We had plenty of luck against De Graafschap, though, for whom Tomek Rząsa was playing. Tomek was brilliant that day. He scored a goal and assisted with another, outclassing Ulrich van Gobbel. I think it was after that game when Beenhakker convinced him to join Feyenoord. It meant that with five games to play we would win the title if we beat NAC Breda and before the game we received a detailed plan of our title celebrations!

15.00 – the game begins
17.00 – a ceremony for winning the title
17.15 – lap of honour
17.30 – a thank you to supporters from the middle of the pitch

17.35 – walk down to the dressing room
18.15 – a trip to the city centre
18.45 – a reception from the mayor in the town hall
19.15 – celebrating the title at the town hall with supporters
22.30 – a dinner with our wives and a party until dawn

When I read that I started to think maybe we should win the game first before planning to celebrate! Maybe it distracted us because we didn't win – the game finished 2-2 – but our closest rivals, Vitesse, lost an away game to NEC Nijmegen 3-1 to give us the title. De Kuip went crazy with joy! We started to celebrate like I had never celebrated before. It was my first trophy since that cup I won for LZS Gierałtowice. I never thought that I could achieve a thing like winning a title and I imagined it in a completely different way than it happened. I thought that in such a professional dressing room like Feyenoord it had to be a constant discussion about training sessions, matches, tactics etc, but there wasn't too much of that kind of talk. Plenty of our experienced players – Jean-Paul van Gastel, Julio Cruz and Paul Bosvelt for instance – were at their peaks and van Gastel won us games like I later found out Steven Gerrard would at Liverpool.

Van Gobbel takes it too far

We went to Rotterdam Town Hall after winning the title. The mayor congratulated us. We greeted the supporters from the balcony and the party began. The atmosphere was fantastic. I couldn't believe how many thousands of people were there. I was handed a big bottle of champagne to open and lots of it went over the supporters standing below us. They didn't care!

The master of ceremonies was former Feyenoord player and then stadium announcer, Peter Houtman. He came to me with the microphone: "Here's that Pole...."

Thousands of fans started to chant: 'Dudek, Dudek!' Like every player, I had to sing a song. I said: "We sing together our favourite song, 'Hand In Hand Kameraden...' and they all sang with me. It was spine-tingling. Everyone was having a brilliant time until van Gobbel was given the microphone. He had polished off a couple of glasses of champagne already: "My turn now – you're Jewish if you don't jump."

Everybody started to jump, but we knew it was the start of a problem. Feyenoord supporters hate Ajax. For historical reasons, the Ajax fans identify with the Jewish community. They display Israel flags at games to show this. Everyone in the Netherlands, indeed everyone who follows Dutch football, knew that van Gobbel was being derogatory towards Ajax and their fans. It caused a right furore. There were headlines in the newspapers the following day saying things like 'Discrimination' and 'Great scandal'. Feyenoord officially apologised to everybody that felt hurt because of that incident and banned van Gobbel for two weeks. He couldn't play anyway, because he was injured, but maybe it was for the best as our next match was away to Ajax!

Straight from the town hall we went to a restaurant with our wives for the official club party. The madness began. We cut off our suit sleeves and legs. No tie survived that night! Our wives sang 'Kampijone, kampijone' on the stage. It was crazy and unforgettable. When Leo saw us partying, he said that we'd be the champions next year as well. He had no doubts that we were a real team on and off the pitch. It would have happened too, but unexpected circumstances occurred and, in addition, some of our important players got injured. That's why Feye-noord didn't win the title in 1999/2000.

A parrot in the dressing room

We played Chelsea in the Champions League in 1999/2000 and for the first time in my life I played with a British Mitre football. It was very hard. When I kicked it on one occasion, I twisted my left ankle! I couldn't believe it! We had a young 19-year-old keeper called Ronald Graafland on the bench. He was a talented lad, but had no experience in big games. Leo asked me during half-time if I wanted to continue. I knew he counted on me, so I said I'd play as I didn't want to hurt this young kid by letting him play in such a big game. The masseur bandaged my ankle into a brace. It hurt a lot, but I managed to play the whole game. We lost 3-1 and I blamed myself for at least two goals even when nobody held me responsible. I had to have two weeks of rehabilitation because of the injury.

We didn't play as well in the league and Leo called a team meeting and asked all of us to tell him what we liked and what was unnecessary. A lot of opinions were exchanged but although Leo said everything should stay in the dressing room, it was all over the papers the following day. He went mad.

"Unfortunately we have a parrot here," he said and pulled a bag of peanuts from his pocket. "I hope the parrot will be happy now," and handed the peanuts to our centre-back Kees van Wonderen, effectively accusing him of leaking the dressing room discussions.

Later on we were in the games room. I was playing pool with van Vossen and Tomasson; Tomek Rząsa was standing next to us, watching our game. Van Wonderen was sitting in the corner when Paul Bosvelt came into the room. Paul was injured at the time and worked hard in the gym. He almost looked like a participant of World's Strongest Man or an MMA fighter. He went straight over to van Wonderen and said: "It looks like you said a little bit too much to the papers yesterday."

"Did I?" replied van Wonderen.

"Who did it? Maybe me?" added Bosvelt.

"Have you got a problem with that? I can say whatever I want," came the answer.

Paul came closer and pushed van Wonderen, calling him a parrot. Kees was skinny. I didn't expect that he would hit Bosvelt. He seemed to be calm. Paul looked formidable, but he didn't usually flaunt his strength. We just watched, petrified, as they fought like two pit bulls. They demolished tables and we were scared to try and separate them.

Van Vossen, who was a close friend of Bosvelt, was screaming all the time: "Paultje, don't do it!" He thought that Paul would kill Kees, but he was also a fighter and he didn't give up easily. Van Vossen was scared and asked us for help.

They cooled down for a moment and we immediately separated them. Van Vossen grabbed Kees and I got Paul, saying: "Paultje, it's alright now. Calm down, calm down…"

They were still fighting, but thankfully only with words, leaving Paul with a black eye, while Kees had a broken nose. The mess in the games room looked like a trashed saloon bar in a Western movie!

After being told of the incident, Beenhakker spoke with the Feyenoord chairman and came to the conclusion that if the team were to fight for each other on the pitch instead of with each other off it he should step down. So he did.

Henk van Stee, the Academy coach, took charge for the next five weeks and implemented tight discipline. We qualified for the Champions League, but the chairman decided he lacked experience and hired Bert van Marwijk instead. Not all of the players showed him enough respect though.

During a game of 'monkey in the middle' – a training exercise where two players stand in the middle of a circle and try to intercept the ball – Jon Dahl Tomasson ended up in the middle when he didn't think he should have been. Seconds later he flew into a challenge on the manager! Van Marwijk was lucky – if he hadn't jumped Jon would probably have broken his legs – but instead of giving him a dressing down it ended with Tomasson telling the manager to play on! I don't think Jon would have done the same with Johnny Metgod, who was the assistant for Beenhakker and later for van Marwijk. Metgod had great authority with the players and I trusted him a lot. He had played for Real Madrid, Nottingham Forest, Tottenham and Feyenoord and when Arsenal showed an interest in signing me he gave me my first English lesson, explaining the words necessary for goalkeepers in England. This ended up being very useful!

Among the stars

In December 1999 I got an invitation to play in a special match for the Dutch Football Association. They were celebrating the 100th birthday of Dutch professional football and we had to play at the Amsterdam ArenA. I was supposed to play in the International All-Stars team, alongside Włodzimierz Smolarek, versus the Dutch All-Stars. Except I didn't want to go to Amsterdam. I didn't think I belonged in that company.

There were so many fantastic players there. For the first time in my life I could play against Marco van Basten. Johan Cruyff, Ruud Gullit, Arie Haan, Ruud Krol and Wim van Hanegem were to play too. Hans van Breukelen and Edwin van der Sar were the Dutch goalies. Absolute madness. Their coach was the sainted Rinus Michels, the creator of total football, a legend among the legends in Dutch football. I felt overawed, but I eventually realised I should accept the invite. I'm glad I did.

I was very excited when the game came around. It was something unbelievable for me. I even saved a van Basten shot! I was the youngest on the pitch and I got to play with and against those stars for 45 minutes. It's worth mentioning that every player wore the shirt of the club he played for in the Netherlands and that for the first time I wasn't booed at Ajax's stadium!

Every player got a commemorative Cartier watch with the KNVB symbol engraved on it for playing in the match. Even now, it is one of the most valuable pieces of football memorabilia I am lucky enough to own. Every time I look at it, I see all those wonderful players I played with. It was a special night.

Award winner

Every year the Dutch Football Association holds a player awards gala. In 1999 they invited me as I was nominated for the Best Goalkeeper Award along with Edwin van der Sar and Sander Westerveld. I was paralysed with nerves when I sat with them on the same table. I wondered if I'd be able to speak!

Frank Rijkaard came onto the stage to present the Best Defender Award. He looked at Westerveld and winked at him. I was sure that Rijkaard knew the results and Sander would be presented with an award. I immediately relaxed. There would be no surprise. He was a great goalkeeper, was in form and there were rumours he could move abroad to Liverpool.

Jan van Beveren came on to present the Best Goalkeeper Award. Van Beveren was a Dutch international in the 1970s. He lived in the USA for years and then I heard the following in his curious accent: "And the Best Goalkeeper Award goes to... Jurek Dudek from Feyenoord!"

Dutch people have problems with the pronunciation of 'Jerzy' so I was Jurek to everybody there.

Before I knew what was happening van der Sar was shaking my hand and congratulating me and then so was Westerveld. When I was walking up to the stage I had tears in my eyes – I was so stunned that I couldn't say a word. I was choked, but I gave the standard 'I am very surprised and I want to thank the lads' speech. I tried to speak in Dutch, but it was probably all rubbish! When I came back to the table, I realised that being in the spotlight wasn't as hard as I had expected.

The following season I got the award again, but it wasn't as emotional for me as the first time was, even though I received that award from legendary Dutch keeper Hans van Breukelen.

I experienced greater emotion when I was invited to another gala. 'De Telegraaf' newspaper had 'De Gouden Schoen' (the Golden Boot) for the best player in the Eredivisie. They voted for me. It was August 2000 when I travelled to Hilversum for the ceremony at a big television centre. I felt so nervous that I drank a bottle of wine with Jan and Bobo while all the prizes were awarded, except the most important one. The director of the show suddenly asked me to come backstage and told me to get into a plane on a rail! He told me to hold on tight and explained what would happen. It reminded me of my presentation at De Kuip. I wanted to ask for a parachute, just in case!

FAMILY AFFAIR: Here I am with my mother Renata, father Andrzej and younger brother Dariusz

INTERNATIONAL AMBITIONS: As a young man in my bedroom wearing my Poland kit

JERZY'S JERSEYS: Wearing some of my early goalkeeper kits and training tops in Poland

DUDEK AT DE KUIP: Signing for Feyenoord in 1996 was a big move for me and took my career to the next level

FAMILIAR OPPONENTS: I saved this penalty from Chelsea's Frank Leboeuf in the Champions League in 2000. Sadly, Feyenoord lost the game 3-1

BIG MOVE: Gerard Houllier brought me and Chris Kirkland to Liverpool in 2001 to start another important chapter in my life

ANFIELD ADVENTURE: Liverpool became my new home and (right) I made my debut against Aston Villa in September 2001

HERO TO ZERO: Assistant manager Phil Thompson congratulates me after a penalty save helped us earn a 1-0 win at Derby, but my mistake infamously allowed Diego Forlan to score for Manchester United at Anfield – prompting a message of support from team-mates like Chris Kirkland

GOLD TRAFFORD: It felt good to keep a clean sheet and get a 1-0 win at Manchester United in 2002

READY AND WAITING: Poised for action at Charlton in 2002 – despite getting stick from the crowd at The Valley

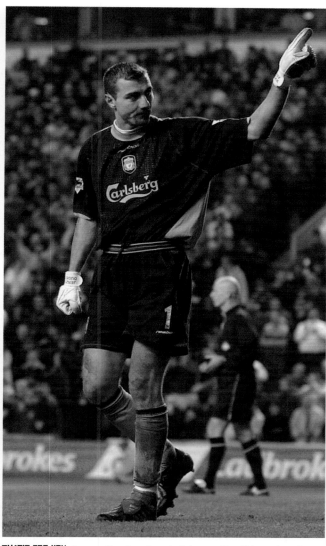

DERBY DELIGHT: Wayne Rooney clatters into me as we beat Everton in April 2003

THAT'S FOR YOU: A penalty shoot-out victory, after I'd made a few crucial saves (below right), against Ipswich in December 2002 was a reward to our supportive fans who sang my name as we took another step towards the Worthington Cup final

SAFE HANDS: Making a save from Manchester City's Nicolas Anelka

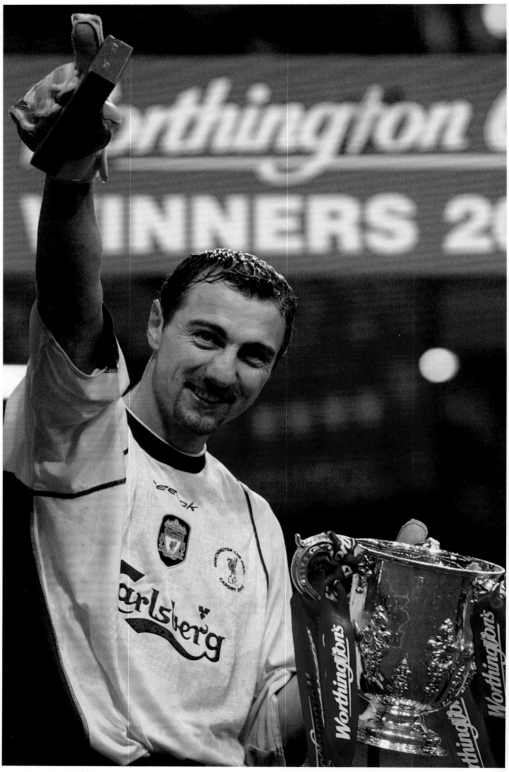

CUP OF JOY: The Worthington Cup final in March 2003 was one of my best days at Liverpool

MAN OF THE MOMENT: Steven Gerrard and Michael Owen scored the goals as we beat Manchester United 2-0 at the Millennium Stadium in Cardiff and I picked up the Man of the Match award

HELPING HAND: With goalkeeping coach Jose Ochotorena, who arrived with Rafa Benitez in 2004

RAFA'S WAY: Benitez had a hands on approach to coaching

KEPT AT BAY: Arjen Robben couldn't beat me here in 2005

TURMOIL TO TRIUMPH: Despite a few tricky moments in the 2004/05 season by the start of May we had overcome Chelsea in the semis to reach the Champions League final

This plane broke through a paper decoration and took me onto the stage in front of 800 people. The lights were so bright that I realised why rock stars wear sunglasses. The show began – with me centre-stage – and the host said: "We have a message for you. It looks like you've received a letter, but we don't know who wrote it. Do you want to read it?" I said that if it was written in Dutch I wouldn't feel too comfortable to read it fluently so the host started to read it aloud before saying: "Jurek, it'll be better if you finish it."

I faltered as I read it in Dutch, but I felt more and more proud with every word as I began to realise who the letter was from: The Pope! Jan told me later that the organisers of the show asked him what would make me happy, so they contacted people close to the Pope when Jan mentioned the esteem I held him in. The Bishop of Rotterdam helped to set it up and in the morning they received a letter from Pope John Paul II who congratulated me on winning the award! Initially I thought it was a prank set up by people not knowing the importance of the Pope, but when I saw the stamp and the official headed paper I had no doubts that it really was a letter from the Vatican. I still can't believe that they could get such a thing!

After the emotions of reading the letter it was comparatively relaxing to receive the award, but also a hugely proud moment.

I was honoured to meet Pope John Paul II before Poland's friendly against Italy in Warsaw a few years later in November 2003 when I was a Liverpool player. I was asked if I'd like to be part of a 10-man Polish delegation that had been invited to visit him. I didn't sleep much the night before.

I had to compose myself the next day when I was summoned to walk forward and felt choked, but managed to utter: "Good morning the Holy Father." I bent at the knee and kissed his ring before showing him the Poland shirt I was clutching. It had 'WOJTYŁA 1' – he was born Karol Wojtyła – on the back and I quickly added: "We are here in Vatican City representing Polish football. This is our humble gift. The Holy Father is always our number one!"

The Pope looked at the shirt and nodded his head. He made the sign of the cross but didn't say anything. He looked visibly tired, his poor health was clearly having an impact. I also did an interview with a Polish priest who worked for Vatican Radio. I was answering his questions when he surprised me: "Do you know how many Liverpool supporters are in Vatican City? When you play a game for the Reds everyone prays for you and the team. The Pope is your biggest fan!"

I almost started to cry. I'm sure my legs wobbled from the emotions I felt when I heard that. It's hard to describe the happiness I felt when I was leaving Vatican City and what it meant to have met the Pope. A day later we beat Italy 3-1 in what was one of the best team displays of Paweł Janas's tenure! Some people said it was because of the Pope's blessing.

Back in Hilversum I was the first ever non-Netherlands player to have won De Gouden Schoen. Previous winners included Cruyff, Rijkaard, Gullit, Vanenburg, Metgod, Overmars, de Goey and van der Sar. That's quite some list!

I was asked to name a person who could hand me the award – in previous years even movie stars had done so – but I invited my coach Bobo Kaczmarek to do the honours. It was he who trusted in me and because of him my career flourished. I have met many people who have helped me, but it was Bobo who opened the doors to the world of professional football for me.

"You can't buy the emotions which I experienced in Hilversum that night. Jurek's fate arranged it somehow that his next step was connected to his previous one. If he hadn't played for Sokół, he wouldn't have travelled to Rotterdam. Coincidence? I'd say destiny! I think that his success was written in the stars. God watched him and dotted the i's and crossed the t's."

Bogusław 'Bobo' Kaczmarek, coach

Bobo came to the stage with De Gouden Schoen. He told me beforehand that he didn't want anybody to ask him any questions. I tried to calm him down, saying: "Coach, everybody speaks English here. So do you. Don't worry."

But he wasn't convinced. He wanted me to translate everything from Dutch into Polish. But the host started to talk to Bobo in English: "Where do you come from? Where did Jurek play earlier?"

"Sokół Tychy."

"And where do you work now?"

"Now GKS Katowice."

"Ok, so what happened with Sokół?"

"Sokół Tychy doesn't exist. Sokół Tychy bankrupt."

"Bankrupt, because you took all the money?"

"No, no…"

All the guests started to laugh.

An invitation from Wenger

In December 1998 Jan told me that Real Madrid were looking for a goalkeeper as Bodo Illgner was injured. We asked Leo Beenhakker for advice. He had worked at Madrid and knew the club perfectly. Beenhakker advised me to forget about Real:

"There's too much pressure on results. The chairman is chaotic and disorganised."

A year later, in 1999, there were rumours about Barcelona being interested in signing me. They were looking for a replacement for Dutch goalkeeper Ruud Hesp, but there were different opinions among the Barcelona board. I also heard something about Manchester United being interested, but Alex Ferguson cut the rumours down saying that I was too short and he needed a taller keeper. Then he signed Fabien Barthez, who is shorter than me...

The most substantive offer eventually came from Arsenal, who were looking for a long-term replacement for David Seaman. In May 2001 myself and Jan flew to London. Arsene Wenger sent an official invitation and the Feyenoord chairman knew everything about it. We went for a look at the club facilities and to discuss the terms of a possible contract. A London black cab driver, who drove us to the Arsenal training ground, called the club and asked them to open the gate quickly as we knew there could be journalists, photographers or fans waiting outside.

Wenger showed me the training facilities. They were impressive. Everyone had to change out of their shoes for sports shoes with synthetic soles to protect the floor. As guests we got special shoe protectors. Inside, it was immaculate – cleaned like it was a hospital. I saw a beautiful, comfortable dressing room and two swimming pools. On the first floor there was a dining room and the club had their own chef and dietician. I also saw an indoor astroturf pitch under construction and plenty of the training pitches around. It impressed me a lot.

After an hour we received a call to say the vice-chairman David Dein and Mr Wenger were expecting us at Highbury.

We travelled there, I had a walk on the pitch, and then I went to a VIP lounge.

Wenger was inside and made a point of saying: "Look at our pitch. It's very tight, not like the one in Rotterdam where you have plenty of time to think and play the ball with your defenders. Here in England you're already under pressure from your opponents. You need to be careful as it's easy to make a mistake."

Wenger described everything about Arsenal in detail. I really liked Highbury with its sense of history and the famous marble floors. There were many journalists outside, not only from England, but from the Dutch media as well. Negotiations went well. Jan asked Dein what we should tell them. We agreed a version of events that we could confirm an individual contract for five years had been agreed. All we had to wait for was a transfer fee to be arranged between the two clubs.

Goodbye and hello again

I returned to Rotterdam and then flew away for a holiday. I was thinking about moving to London and what I would need to do so I took English lessons for three weeks to give me the basics of the language. The newspapers continued to speculate – head-lines like 'Is Dudek leaving?' were being published – and it was a weird situation while I waited for the transfer to be sorted out. I really wanted to play in London but I was still a Feyenoord player so I had to be careful with the things I said. I didn't want to say something careless and upset the supporters because I respected them a lot.

Jan finally called me and said that Feyenoord chairman Jorien van der Herik had broken off negotiations. Dein told

Jan that Feyenoord wanted €10 million for me whereas Arsenal wanted to pay about €6 million. Meanwhile, van der Herik had constantly said there was nothing official from Arsenal even though I knew that Wenger wanted me in his Arsenal team. He called Jan every day, even during his holiday to Tunisia, to try and get the deal moving along. In the end, no agreement was reached and the transfer fell through. My move to London was off and Arsenal signed Richard Wright from Ipswich Town instead. I was very frustrated.

I had to go back to Rotterdam for the first pre-season training session. It was a hard test for me. After the last league game of the previous season, because they thought I was leaving, the Feyenoord supporters had carried me off the pitch. I had also said goodbye to everybody at the club and even had a farewell training session where I was presented with flowers and gifts. It was awkward to go back, but I realised I had to return with the right mentality and forget about the Arsenal transfer. A lot of people assumed that I would throw my toys out of the pram and try to put pressure on van der Herik to sell me by maybe refusing to play, but that would have been disrespectful to the Feyenoord fans and also my manager. So, when I returned to Rotterdam, I said that I was ready to play for the club and give my all like I always had done.

I got a great reception from the supporters for that and van Marwijk also said that he really counted on me. We also had a Champions League campaign to think about, having finished second in the Eredivisie in 2000/01, so I started to prepare for the first league game against Sparta Rotterdam. What I didn't realise, though, was that there was another famous club that had closely been monitoring my situation...

THIS IS ANFIELD

I heard that I was being watched by Liverpool scouts, but I couldn't believe it at first. Why did they need a goalkeeper if they had Sander Westerveld and had just won three trophies? Nevertheless, I felt under pressure in every friendly I played for Feyenoord that summer knowing that Liverpool were interested, especially after the rumours were confirmed. Liverpool really wanted to buy me.

I played three Eredivisie games against Sparta Rotterdam, Roda Kerkrade and Ajax. After the Ajax game at De Kuip I met with Liverpool manager Gerard Houllier and his assistant Phil Thompson. Houllier made it clear he wanted to buy me and asked: "Do you want to come to Liverpool?"

"Yes," I replied without hesitation, but I advised them they would face a tough battle with the Feyenoord chairman given the Arsenal negotiations. Houllier smiled and said: "Don't worry about that, leave it to us. The important thing is that you want to join Liverpool."

Liverpool would be another big step in my career, a step I really needed to make, but I told them clearly: "Earlier this summer I was thinking about playing for Arsenal. It fell through. I was disappointed and I don't want to repeat that feeling. Unless everything is set up between the clubs first, I'm not taking this move seriously."

Jan called me a couple of days later: "Have you decided if you want to join Liverpool? If yes, we can start work to finalise the deal; the clubs have agreed a transfer fee." Massimo Moratti, the chairman of Inter Milan, also contacted us, but it was Houllier who proposed the best deal. I told Jan to proceed with negotiations with Liverpool. I had to go for it. If not, I thought, I would regret it in a couple of years.

Poland had a World Cup qualifier against Norway on the Saturday but I asked our manager Jerzy Engel to give me a day off on the Thursday because I had to sign an initial contract with Liverpool. He agreed and I travelled to the Sobieski Hotel in Warsaw where I had a meeting with one of LFC's officials. A hotline between Warsaw and Liverpool was set up to get the deal done.

Liverpool's deputy doctor arrived in Warsaw – the normal club doctor was with England Under-21s – to do some basic medical tests, but they also needed to do knee and elbows scans. The Polish national team doctor, Stanisław Machowski, helped them to do that and everything was fine – I'd never had a serious injury during my career at that time. I returned to international duty and was asked to appear at the pre-match press conference. Inevitably they asked me about Liverpool – I told them I was only concentrating on the Norway game – and the press said that I was nervous and showing signs of tension ahead of an important game. If we won we would qualify for the World Cup, Poland's first since 1986.

Coach Engel asked me to forget about the transfer until after the game, but Mirella called me and started to talk about our very sensitive uncle Janusz: "Jurek, he's crying. He heard them say on the radio your Liverpool move is off as you've not passed the medical. What's going on?"

I was shocked, but it quickly emerged that the doctor hadn't done a blood test on me so I asked Dr Machowski for help. We'd had blood tests done with Poland so the doctor instructed my agent Jan to go to a Polish health clinic and from there, with the help of a lady whose name I can't recall, the results were faxed across to Liverpool. That box was ticked and after some last-minute issues regarding bank guarantees from Feyenoord the transfer was finally confirmed on August 31.

> *"Houllier called me: 'Can you hear the sound of champagne corks popping? I'm in a restaurant in Paris'. He pissed me off with that! 'I'm in the Netherlands and I've not slept a wink!' He started to calm me down: 'Don't worry. Everything's done'."*
>
> **Jan de Zeeuw, agent**

Jan called Mirella first to settle her nerves and then phoned me: "Don't watch the TV, do not listen to the radio. You are a Liverpool player and you're registered to play in the Champions League!"

I was relieved and finally I could focus on the Norway game, due to be played the following day. My parents visited me in the team hotel. We were chatting and drinking coffee when my mum took something from her bag: "Look what I've brought for you. Do you remember it?"

She handed me the Liverpool scarf which had been hung over my bed for a couple of years. I had completely forgotten about it. It was a souvenir from the junior tournament in Germany, where we had lived with German families. I was 17 at that time and it was priceless to me. Nobody in Poland had such a thing as a Liverpool scarf back then. I took the scarf to two Górnik Zabrze games, but I was scared that someone would take it from me so I hung it over my bed instead. I didn't even dream that I would play for Liverpool when I was a teenager so this felt like a fairytale!

'We already have a keeper'

I met one of my new Liverpool team-mates, John Arne Riise, in the hotel elevator on the Friday. It was strange that the opposition were sleeping in the same hotel as us, not that I could speak to John anyway. He didn't want to and I knew only maybe 40 English words. Some Polish journalists asked him about me, but he didn't have a clue who I was: "I have a new team-mate? Why? We already have a keeper."

It looked like John hadn't been following the news and Houllier later told me that he phoned Riise after we had beaten Norway 3-0 to qualify for the World Cup and asked him about me: "That's our new keeper?" he asked, sounding surprised. "He played really well!"

Houllier also phoned Engel and asked him to let me miss the next game away to Belarus as we had already qualified. He wanted me to train at Melwood for a week to prepare for my Premier League debut against Aston Villa. Engel refused, which enraged Houllier so he threatened not to let me join up with Poland early for a future training camp. He even said in one TV interview that Engel was threatening my career by making me travel to Belarus. I hadn't even travelled to Liverpool and already I was embroiled in a club versus country row. We lost 4-1 in Minsk and it wasn't my best display.

Two goalies in one day

I flew to Liverpool from Amsterdam with Jan and thought about my first flight to the Netherlands in 1996 when I arrived at Feyenoord with one bag containing two pairs of boots and one set of gloves. Five years on I was going to Liverpool after being transferred for almost £5 million. It felt like I'd come a long way.

Amazingly, of all the people I could have bumped into at Schiphol Airport, I bumped into Sander Westerveld – the goalkeeper Houllier had bought me to replace. Sander had been at Liverpool for two seasons and was in goal for the five trophies they had won in 2001.

Westerveld was on his way back from a Holland match alongside his girlfriend and spoke to me immediately: "If you're here then it looks like all the rumours in the papers were true – Houllier has signed a new goalkeeper." He then spoke to Jan about various things at Liverpool and I decided not to interrupt. "See you at training tomorrow," said Westerveld as we said goodbye.

Later that day I signed my contract and received a work permit until 2007, although I didn't need this after 2004 when Poland joined the European Union. I had dinner with Houllier and Thompson that evening. Houllier started to talk about a Liverpool team with no superstars, but hard-working and down-to-earth players. He believed he could get the best from them and achieve a lot. This conversation uplifted me. I realised how nice Houllier was, that he cared about his players. He spoke about them like a father about his kids. "Go and get some sleep, I'll see you at training tomorrow," he said after the meal.

I arrived at Melwood the following day and only then did I realise that Liverpool had bought another goalkeeper! They had signed 20-year-old talented English youngster Chris Kirkland from Coventry City for £6 million – a higher fee than they had paid for me! Naturally I was concerned, but Jan convinced me that Kirkland was just an investment for the future. Houllier told him I would be the goalkeeper for two years and Chris would learn from me during that time.

Myself and Chris wore Liverpool shirts and held scarves as we posed with Houllier for the presentation pictures. We then attended a press conference and straight away I was asked about Kirkland being signed for a higher transfer fee. To be honest, I didn't have a clue who he was! They didn't show a lot of Coventry games on TV in Rotterdam! I answered diplomatically: "Of course we will both fight for the place on the pitch. I came here to play, but it is the manager's decision."

Houllier introduced me to the team and said to captain Jamie Redknapp and senior player Gary McAllister: "This is your new team-mate. Take care of him. I hope he'll be a good asset to the team."

After the training session I travelled to see Anfield with Jan. I really wanted to see the famous Anfield Road, check the pitch, familiarise myself with such a legendary stadium, my new place of work. When we were getting close to it though I saw plenty of abandoned houses with broken windows. It didn't look the most inviting of places. I started to wonder which area we were in. It was Anfield and moments later we saw the stadium. I must admit to being surprised by the area, but I could feel the sense of history at Anfield.

My Anfield bow

My debut was at home to Aston Villa on the Saturday, but when I came onto the pitch for the warm-up I was surprised. The stands were almost empty. It was completely different in Rotterdam. At De Kuip there are thousands of supporters in the stands and you can feel the atmosphere and hear the songs, but as I ran down towards the Kop it was almost empty. I didn't know what was going on.

Pegguy Arphexad, a Frenchman who was now the third-choice goalie behind myself and Kirkland, was on the bench for the Villa game and told me during the warm-up the two words I had to know in English football. I had to shout 'away' if I wanted the defenders to clear the ball and 'keeper' when I wanted to collect it. We went through that during the warm-up.

As we lined up in the tunnel beneath the famous This is Anfield sign I could hear *You'll Never Walk Alone* being sung. I wondered who was singing it! But when we ran out onto the pitch all four stands were full. I couldn't believe it. How did it happen that the supporters packed the stadium in only 10 minutes? I later found out that English fans sit in the pubs around the ground until the last moment drinking their pints and only get into the ground for kick-off. Clearly that is their tradition, but when I was warming up it felt like I was playing an away game with Feyenoord! I also learned my first lesson about English football when I came for a high ball and was clattered from the side by one of the Villa players. That wouldn't happen in the Eredivisie.

We lost 3-1 but the gaffer said I played fine, none of the goals were my fault and that the defenders hadn't helped me too much. He also added that he thought I was mentally strong and that gave me confidence, something I was lacking off the pitch.

The problem solver

The first few days in Liverpool were the worst ones of my life. I felt really lonely. I was in a new place with a new language, which I couldn't speak, and had to learn everything from the beginning. I lay on the hotel bed and began to wonder if I could make it in Liverpool. Would I be able to play at this high level? Why did I move from Rotterdam? I had everything there; here I had nothing.

I called Jan and started to joke with him about whether Feyenoord could return the money for my transfer to Liverpool if they'd kept the receipt! Jan reminded me of my beginnings in the Netherlands. It wasn't easy there either and he told me that I should start to convince myself that I could settle in England soon. Things got much better when Mirella and my son Alexander joined me. At least I could talk to somebody while I got to grips with English.

I appreciated Houllier's kindness to me a lot, but there was also someone else who helped me settle – the club's player liaison officer Norman Gard. There was no problem that Norman couldn't solve. If any player needed something, we went straight to Norman. I couldn't imagine my stay in the Netherlands without Jan and Tomek Iwan and I also couldn't imagine life in Liverpool without Norman! For instance, I needed a suit for my debut against Aston Villa. Norman sorted it out within 30 minutes! A tailor came to the club, measured everything and I had a suit waiting for me the next day. When I was looking for a house, Norman travelled across the whole Liverpool area with me and gave me advice. He helped me with a million other things too for which I will always be grateful. When Houllier hired Norman, he knew that the players should be focused only on playing football and resting so that's why the club needed a man who could sort out the other problems. Norman was brilliant in that role.

The Melwood shanty town

I wasn't impressed with Melwood the first time I arrived at Liverpool's training ground. I remember being confronted by a big concrete fence – it was about two metres high – with barbed wire on the top. There was also a big, imposing metal gate which all the kids would stand in front of hoping to get an autograph or a photo. Inside, there were two perfect training pitches, but with all due respect to Liverpool you could feel the history of the place. It felt like nothing had changed there since Melwood was built in the 1950s. There were buildings that looked like they were from a shanty town!

I had joined a world-renowned club, the most successful in England, but the training facilities were better at Feyenoord. We had a modern dressing room, massage rooms and a jacuzzi there. At Liverpool, and I mean no offence, the facilities were similar to Concordia in Poland. I'm a down-to-earth guy, but when I got to Melwood for the first time I thought it was a wind up – that someone was filming me for *Candid Camera* and moments later they'd take me to the real Liverpool FC training complex! Houllier must have seen the shocked expression on my face and took me to his office. I was amazed he had one there!

Houllier wanted to improve things and we moved into a new complex at Melwood a few months later. It was perfect. It had all the facilities, devices and modern day equipment that a professional footballer needs and the rules to go with it! You cannot walk around Melwood in football boots or running shoes. You get fined for that! We wore flip-flops instead. We each had our own locker in the boot room and the dressing room is huge – about 40 players could get changed in there at the same time. There are two massage tables – we had to put our initials on the board before training if we wanted a massage – plus a gym, swimming pool, a sauna, steam room, a jacuzzi for eight people, four baths, a huge shower room and both physio and masseur rooms.

There were three full-size pitches, a smaller-sized pitch and an astro-pitch, but it was the attention to detail of the main pitches – which Houllier could see from his office – that was his hallmark. The grass on those pitches was identical to the grass at Anfield. It was like they were moving the Anfield pitch between locations.

The other thing that struck me in the early days of being a Liverpool player was the amount of rules we had to stick to that were laid down by the manager. It's always a dictatorship. One man rules, others have to live with it, but that system only works if it is based on good rules. For instance, the later you were turning up for training, the more your fine went up. If you were over 15 minutes late it was £100, but if you missed a session completely the boss would hand out individual penalties of up to £5,000! It all depended on whether he accepted your excuse. If he didn't you were goosed! Our fines half went towards team bonding sessions, such as meals or a day go-karting, with the other half going to charities. Let's just say some of the lads were very charitable!

The first piece of advice I received when I got to Melwood was 'leave your phone in the car'. Houllier felt they damaged team spirit and imposed an eye-watering penalty of £1,000 if we were caught using one. He also had a sign with a phone crossed out put up at the entrance! It wasn't just the players who were banned from using them either. If you had guests at Melwood and they used a phone, the player they were with would be fined.

When Rafa Benitez replaced Houllier the ban was lifted, but all you could hear in the Melwood dressing room was the sound of text messages being received or phones ringing. It began to get on some people's nerves and in the end the players asked Rafa to reinstate the ban! He agreed, but dropped the fine to £150. He also imposed a rule which meant you were fined £100 if you brought a guest to Melwood at any time other than on the designated days of Monday and Thursday. I think Djibril Cisse got stung the most when his whole family came to Melwood to visit on a Sunday. I think that cost him more than his haircuts!

Houllier was also particular about the clothes we wore. For example, we had to wear a red polo shirt when we were on the bus and a white one during dinner, breakfast and the after-breakfast team walk. We had a tactical briefing at 1pm and then had to put our suits on to travel to the ground. For Champions League games there were three different coloured shirts we had to wear for different things. It was very confusing and anyone who wore the wrong shirt received a £100 fine. Maybe that sounds harsh, but it created discipline. That said, a couple of the lads – myself included – regularly wore club tracksuit tops, no matter how hot it was, so Houllier didn't know what colour t-shirt we had on. It was better to have £100 in our pockets than his!

A friendly rivalry

I knew only several dozen English words after my arrival in Liverpool, but I spoke Dutch perfectly after five years in Rotterdam so at least I could speak with Westerveld, Sami Hyypia, who played for Willem II Tilburg for two years, and Jari Litmanen, who had played for Ajax and had a Dutch fiancée. The three of them helped me a lot with everything, especially Sander, which some people may find surprising under the circumstances.

I told Sander straight away that I hadn't come to Liverpool to take his place, even though I had. He knew the situation and he didn't blame me for anything, but had a problem with Houllier who was constantly telling him that Liverpool didn't want to buy a new goalie... but then bought two!

Despite being relegated from first choice to fourth choice, Sander was prepared to help me and translated basic words you need as a goalkeeper from Dutch to English. At the beginning I trained with Westerveld and Arphexad because Kirkland was injured, but when he returned to training we started to get to know each other. In fact, we got on very well. Chris was very friendly and that ensured that we would only fight for a place on the pitch.

I got injured in February 2002 during a 6-0 win away to Ipswich Town. Pegguy replaced me that day and Chris played against Galatasaray in the Champions League and in the Merseyside derby against Everton at Anfield. I felt better before the return game in Istanbul against Galatasaray, but Houllier – who was instructing Phil Thompson on how to run the team from home as he recovered from illness – decided I would not play: "Get well properly," he told me. "You have plenty of time. We won't risk you."

Chris played well in Istanbul. We drew 1-1 and he made some outstanding saves so the journalists started to write that Kirkland deserved to play; that he had worked hard for his chance. I started to wonder if I'd ever return in goal. I hadn't made any mistakes for six months and suddenly my rival had to play on a regular basis after just one good game? It was a signal for me to be on alert with regard to the English media, to be curious about what they wrote and cautious with what I said.

I spoke to Jan and he reminded me of the Zoetebier situation I faced at Feyenoord. He also said Houllier's selection for the next league game at Fulham would prove if he was influenced by the media or not. I started the game and Chris was back on the bench.

I played really well and I stayed in goal until the end of the season. The journalists also stopped pushing for Houllier and Thompson to play Kirkland because he got injured again. Chris was still growing, and growing fast, but his vertebrae didn't develop as they should have done. I felt sorry for Chris when I saw him again with the doctors and physios. He couldn't physically move after training because he had such agonising back pain. It was harsh on him.

While Kirkland was doing his recovery work, nobody had a problem that I was in goal, but when he returned to full training the situation changed immeasurably. The papers said he needed to play, but he hadn't fully recovered and got another injury. All of a sudden it went quiet again. I understood why. The English national team had a real problem with their goalkeepers. 2002 was a World Cup year and they had high hopes for Kirkland so the English press were promoting him. My form was good, though, so it was completely unfair on me.

Liverpool paid a high price for the endless rivalry whipped up by the media. It put pressure on us both, which had to be visible during our displays and, because I was the number one at that time who wasn't English, all the criticism was directed towards me.

A different man

Gerard Houllier didn't look like a Premier League football manager; rather like a father trying to take care of his kids. He asked me what I thought about the lads after I'd been there for a short while: "They're all fine. I'm surprised that none of them turn into right divas, even such a great player like Michael Owen. He's very down-to-earth and friendly."

It was little more than a month after my arrival at Liverpool when Houllier fell ill during a home game against Leeds United. An ambulance took him to hospital at half-time. We found out later that it was a life-threatening situation. He had suffered a burst aorta and required serious heart surgery. We knew he had been taken to hospital, but weren't aware during the second half against Leeds about how serious it was. Tommo kept us focused on the match, which we drew 1-1. Houllier's life was saved on the operating table and he was forced to take five months off to recover.

Tommo stepped forward and took charge of the team. Some would describe him as a 'character coach' – the type of coach who motivates players, gees them up. Tommo did this well. As Houllier got better, Tommo would get instructions from him and pass them on, but he coached us well during those five months and finished every pre-match briefing by reminding us who we were playing for: "Lads, this is important. Remember how much you got from Gerard. You play for him."

He turned the pages on the flip-chart board and showed us the message: 'WE PLAY FOR THE BOSS'.

"He almost sacrificed his life for you, for the club," said Tommo before turning to the next page.

'DO IT FOR THE BOSS' it said it block capital letters. It was a good way to motivate us.

Phil was a former Liverpool player who had gone from standing on the Kop to playing for the Reds almost 500 times. He had captained the club to league titles and when they won the European Cup final against Real Madrid in Paris in 1981. Importantly, he was also a centre-half who was very, very good at setting up our defensive play. We kept loads of clean sheets, including against Borussia Dortmund and Roma, both home and away, in the Champions League, which at the time was split into two group stages. We were playing better and better.

When Houllier got slightly better, he called me before and after every game. Once he asked me how I felt and I had barely answered when he said: "The lads like you. You play well. We needed a goalkeeper who can win a match for us. This is what Westerveld lacked."

I was connected emotionally with the boss after that. Those phone calls meant a lot to me, even if I knew he called the other lads too. He uplifted me and after those conversations I had a great belief in what I was doing. I had settled well in the team thanks to Houllier's fatherly approach and I felt great. I had a similar connection with Leo Beenhakker at Feyenoord. He joked with me and spoke with me every day, saying: "That's my Pole!" or calling me "Our Polish cat!"

Leo motivated me so well I could move mountains for him and it was the same with Houllier at the beginning of my time at Liverpool. After a while we heard rumours that Thompson would take charge of the team full-time and Houllier would be a club director of football responsible for transfers. It was a realistic solution for his health condition. But, to the surprise of many, Houllier returned to the bench in March 2002 for the Champions League clash against Roma at Anfield. We needed a win to progress to the quarter-finals and seeing him back on the touchline lifted the noise inside our stadium to another level. The Anfield magic worked. We beat Roma 2-0 to go through. It was a brilliant return for Houllier, but we soon realised he had become a different man.

I had only known him for a short time before he was taken ill so it was harder for me to measure it, but the lads who had worked with him for longer than me were surprised at how he had changed when he returned full-time. Houllier became aggressive and suspicious. He lacked the calmness and patience he was famous for.

We finished the season in second place in the Premier League behind Arsenal. We gave them a fight, winning nine of our final 10 games, but Arsene Wenger's side were even better, winning their final 13 games in a row. We finished on 80 points, seven behind them, but the frustrating thing was that in many other seasons 80 would have been enough points to win the title. We were also very disappointed to go out of the Champions League in the quarter-final to Bayer Leverkusen. After beating them 1-0 at Anfield we lost 4-2 in Germany. We should have done better. On a personal level my first season at Liverpool was a good one. I played really well and felt relaxed, which boosted my confidence. My transfer from Feyenoord was voted the best in the league and I received lots of good reviews. I headed off for the World Cup feeling great, but what I didn't realise was that the 2002/03 season at Liverpool would be one of the most challenging of my career.

FROM CALAMITY
TO CARDIFF

My problems started when I returned from the 2002 World Cup in South Korea and Japan. Despite three weeks on holiday, I was mentally and physically tired. The rivalry with Kirkland started again. I worked really hard during pre-season in Switzerland, I was exhausted as never before. Our day started at 7am with a 45-minute run. We came back to the hotel for breakfast and I went straight to bed to get at least an hour of sleep before training at 11am. At 5pm we had another session and there was no reduced rate for the players who played at the World Cup. I tried not to complain, only to work hard, telling anyone who asked that I was fine.

Joe Corrigan, our goalkeeper coach, told me that Chris had recovered from his injury and was making good progress. I told him calmly: "It's your problem. You have experience with working with goalkeepers, you're responsible for us and you need to ensure we have the best conditions to work in. The first-choice goalkeeper needs to get self-confidence instead of wondering what would happen if he makes a mistake."

I hoped that Houllier would see that I lacked freshness and let me rest. Most of the international players had a break because of injury; I didn't. Physically and mentally, I was shot, and I wasn't the only one. The gaffer had also brought five new players in – El-Hadji Diouf, Salif Diao, Bruno Cheyrou, Alou Diarra and Patrice Luzi – but most of them didn't play and their arrivals created uncertainty among other key players who feared for their place in the team. We weren't playing well, but we were still winning and after 12 games we were top of the league with nine wins and three draws. It was Liverpool's best ever start to a Premier League campaign, but my problems started in game 13.

We travelled to Middlesbrough on November 9 and I made the first serious error of my Liverpool career. With eight minutes to play I came for a cross but collided with Alen Boksic. I dropped the ball, it hit Sami and Gareth Southgate put it into the net. We lost 1-0. Houllier defended me, saying the collision was bad luck and it had only cost us a point, but there was worse to come. We crashed out of the Champions League later that week after a 3-3 draw away to FC Basel when we needed to win and then after a 0-0 draw against Sunderland we lost 3-2 at Fulham, a week before Manchester United visited Anfield. It turned into a nightmare for me.

I felt great during training in the lead-up to the game – we'd beaten Vitesse Arnhem in my first game back in Holland in the UEFA Cup on the Thursday night – and the same in the warm-up, but during the game I was distracted. It was a 12.15pm kick-off on a Sunday and, as usual, we kicked towards the Kop end for the second half, but it was a very bright day and the sun was glaring into my eyes in the Anfield Road end penalty area. I kept thinking to myself 'should I wear a cap, or not?' instead of focusing properly on the game. I decided not to wear a cap when suddenly Jamie Carragher completely unnecessarily headed the ball back to me and it inexplicably slipped through my hands and legs on the edge of the six-yard box. Diego Forlan, United's Uruguayan striker, pounced upon my error and rolled the ball into the empty net. I remember lying on my back staring up towards the sky, scarcely able to believe what had just happened and thinking Houllier would definitely drop me now. Forlan scored again moments later and, although Sami got one back, we lost 2-1.

> *"I commentated on that match for Canal+. For the first time I didn't know what to say. As a footballer, I know what a catastrophe it is when you make such a costly mistake, but I knew Jurek and I was sure that he would learn from it and come back stronger."*
>
> ### Dariusz Dudek, brother

Part of the problem was that I had taken the criticism for Poland's poor displays in the World Cup personally and that had exhausted me mentally. Now I had made a massive error in the biggest match in English football and I really took it to heart. I sat in the Anfield dressing room afterwards and I cried. I asked myself why it happened to me. I was gutted. The lads were trying to cheer me up, but it had no effect. I was the last player who left the stadium that afternoon. I wanted to go home, lock myself in, close the curtains and open a bottle of vodka to forget what had happened. Never before had I drowned my sorrows in alcohol after a match, but this was different. I'd never felt worse.

My friends from the Netherlands and Poland came to see that game. Two footballers, Krzysztof Bizacki and Mariusz Śrutwa, and film director Jan Kempinski were in the crowd. All the hotels had been fully booked so I rented a big house from a former Liverpool player that weekend but after the match I phoned them to say I wouldn't be attending the dinner we had planned, even though the restaurant was booked. Mirella talked me around and eventually I agreed to go, but I felt low at the dinner and miserable at the post-dinner house party until Bizacki said to me in his Silesian style: "Oi, Dudi, what are you worrying about? Did you forget about that goal you conceded during the Hutnik game?"

Remembering how I put the error he referred to behind me helped me to relax – as did drinking about a barrel-load of beer! Bobo and Jan arrived two days later, as did Marek Saganowski with his wife, and helped me to get over it. I realised who my real friends were in the days after that Manchester United game. My team-mates and the Liverpool supporters helped me massively too. They gave me support like I could never believe three days later.

Getting back on the bike

We were due to play Ipswich at Anfield in the Worthington Cup on the Wednesday night and all the speculation was that I would be dropped, but Houllier said I should face up to what happened by playing: "If you make a mistake like that, you have to play again immediately. You have to show you're strong, you're not giving up for some stupid reason. It's like riding a bike. If you fall off you have to get straight back on or you'll always fear that you'll fall off again."

So even though I didn't want to play I got back on my bike against Ipswich and was confronted by something truly amazing. 'Jer-zy Du-dek' sang the Liverpool supporters over and over and over again. It was the first time the fans had sung my name at Anfield. I realised that night why *You'll Never Walk Alone* is the club's motto. There is no other club in the world with supporters like that. They had my back and I was desperate to repay their faith, even if I thought it was ironic that I'd had to make a terrible mistake before I heard my name sung in the stands! As it happened I had to face two one-on-one situations that night and saved both. We drew 1-1 and the game went to penalties. I didn't save one in the shoot-out, but we won 5-4 after Ipswich's Jamie Clapham hit the crossbar so we went through to the quarter-final.

I was moved after the game when Salif Diao took his match shirt off to reveal a t-shirt underneath with 'Dudek – You'll Never Walk Alone' written on it. Chris Kirkland also had the same thing written on his t-shirt and he wore it again to show his support for me on the front cover of the official LFC magazine. In the interview inside he said: "Jerzy is a fabulous goalkeeper and a great guy. He is incredibly strong and incredibly talented and we all know he'll bounce back." The LFC magazine also ran an article that showed in my first 50 games for Liverpool I kept 26 clean sheets, more than any other goalkeeper, including Ray Clemence and Bruce Grobbelaar. It was really positive for me to get such support. I felt revitalised, but Houllier said I would be rested after that match and I was.

> *"Houllier phoned me and said that we had to talk immediately. I arrived in Liverpool and went straight to his office. He screamed at me for two hours. He was furious that Jurek was overtired after the World Cup and I didn't tell him about it. He had issues with almost everything. Houllier concluded by saying that he would let Jurek rest so he was out of the team."*
>
> **Jan de Zeeuw, agent**

Our next game was Charlton Athletic away and Chris started. One of the things he found difficult was to calculate the distance between a striker and the ball and this meant he sometimes rushed out a little too late, leaving him at risk of injury as in English football forwards will challenge goalkeepers with their feet. Twenty-five minutes into the game that's exactly what happened and he was caught in the face by Kevin Lisbie. I think he may have been knocked out cold. Houllier told me to warm up but as I jogged down the touchline at The Valley the Charlton fans started singing "We want Dudek, we want Dudek." It was a mental test for me, they wanted to destroy me, but I responded by turning towards them and waving my arms like I was conducting an orchestra. They laughed. Chris was able to continue so I gave them a thumbs up and a smile before I sat down. I was determined not to let such things faze me.

New Houllier

Chris remained in goal, but there was no improvement in results. Liverpool went 11 Premier League games without a win – one of the worst runs the club had ever had – until a 1-0 victory at Southampton. I returned to the team at Crystal Palace in the FA Cup in January when Chris had to be stretchered off after suffering a serious injury. I played well for the rest of the season with my only serious mistake coming in a 3-2 win against Tottenham, but although we won the Worthington Cup by beating Manchester United 2-0 in Cardiff on what was a special day for me, we finished fifth and failed to qualify for the Champions League. The media attacked Houllier and I felt sorry for him, but he couldn't handle the criticism and deflected it onto the players. That didn't go down well in the dressing room.

During our poor run he decided to employ a London-based French psychologist. I laughed at the idea at the start, as did a lot of the other lads, but he soon found a common language with us and I changed my opinion. He made us consider how to work with the team, what is important, how we should react to defeats, how to stay positive, how to avoid provocation from opponents. It was really interesting. The psychologist also forced the foreign players to stand up and describe themselves in English. It was a test of bravery for some. As a result the atmosphere in the team was improving, there were funny moments and different lads started to talk with each other, which had been a problem before.

The psychologist asked us to bring in a picture of the best moment in our football career. Most of the lads forgot to do it, but two of them brought the same photo of them lifting the UEFA Cup for Liverpool in 2001. "You see? You've got common good memories. It's brilliant that you remember them; you need to make more." He later asked us to turn to the team-mate sitting next to us and tell him that we love him!

It was comical, and embarrassing, but it got us laughing and, combined with an exercise to promote trust, it helped.

Results improved so Houllier asked the psychologist to do some pre-match briefings. I remember one, just before the League Cup final against Manchester United, when he gave us an example of a flock of flying geese: when one of them is weak during a journey others fly with it to mobilise it for the rest of the journey before the whole flock joins. He said the team should work in a similar way – stick together if one of us is going through weakness. We won 2-0 that day, but it all started to unravel when the press discovered that the psychologist was also working with Arsene Wenger at Arsenal and was getting paid a huge amount of money. The next time he turned up at Melwood in his Bentley we stopped believing in his psychological powers! He was a nice guy, but a bit weird! His pre-match team talk is far from my best memory of the Worthington Cup final though.

Cardiff

Gerard Houllier approached me before the Worthington Cup final against Manchester United in Cardiff: "Jerzy, you are going to play and you will be the best player on the pitch."

"Boss, that feels like you are putting pressure on me."

"No Jerzy, no pressure. You can win the cup for us; be the hero."

The final was three months after my bad day against United at Anfield and I had been back in the team for seven games. The word 'avenge' is a little too strong, but to play the same team in a cup final gave me an opportunity to make amends for that awful day in December and I was desperate to do so. The

Millennium Stadium in Cardiff is a truly fantastic venue for a cup final. The stadium is right in the heart of Cardiff city centre and the route the coach travels to the ground via takes you past Cardiff Castle.

It was my first cup final for Liverpool and as the team coach approached the stadium I could not believe the number of our supporters on the streets. In the build-up to the match I had never experienced such intense hype before. The Liverpool people were living for that game and it felt like the whole city had turned out in Cardiff carrying flags, banners and scarves. The streets by Cardiff Castle and the Millennium Stadium were lined by Liverpool fans. We had a police escort but the coach had to crawl very slowly to get through the sea of people. It was, as they say in Liverpool, 'chocca!'

I was sitting on the coach and obviously I knew I was about to play in a cup final, but I realised at that moment just how big the club is and how much it means to the fans to win trophies. Of course, for the fans it is better if you beat a rival like Manchester United or Everton, but the main thing that matters to them is winning silverware. They would have still been there lining the streets in their thousands if we'd played Sheffield United rather than Manchester United. Liverpool supporters live for trophies.

I had played in the Millennium Stadium twice before. My first game there was for Poland against Wales in 2001. We won a World Cup qualifier 2-1 – Wales were awarded a goal even though the ball wasn't fully over the goalline – and I had been there in August 2002 with Liverpool for the Community Shield against Arsenal. We lost 1-0, but I had a decent game and really enjoyed playing there again. For whatever reason, I always felt at home in the Millennium Stadium. It was a special stadium for me.

The atmosphere for the United game was exceptional. It was a derby with two sets of passionate fans, but the roof was also closed due to the bad weather and that made the noise levels even louder. I thought the roof might come off when Stevie scored the first goal of the game near the end of the first half. We knew United would come back at us though and that's exactly what happened. I had to make four important saves before Michael ran clean through and made it 2-0. Game over – and the noise levels were deafening.

In a game like a cup final you don't care how you keep the ball out of the net, only that you do. Finals are all about the end result, not individual performances. If I made 10 saves but we lost, what does it matter? I'd rather make no saves and win, but obviously it is a good feeling to make an important contribution in a big game.

The first save from Juan Sebastian Veron was the most important in terms of making me feel good and lifting my confidence – the first save in any big game always is – but you have to keep your concentration for the full game.

The celebrations began at the final whistle and it was announced that I was Man Of The Match. I was surprised! I knew I had played well and helped the team to win, but to be presented with the Alan Hardaker Trophy for being the best player on the pitch in a cup final between Liverpool and Manchester United was very special for me, especially after what had happened three months earlier at Anfield. Houllier came over to me: "I told you that you would be Man Of The Match!" At that time, it was the proudest moment of my career.

'You're my players, you'll be gone with me'

As I mentioned earlier, Houllier changed after his operation and winning a trophy didn't make a difference. He was a great scholar, having worked as an English teacher, but he became angrier and would vent his fury on the players. He asked myself, Sami, Ginge and Vladi to come to his office one day.

"Why are you here?"

"Because the results are not acceptable?"

"No. Because you are the players I brought to the club and had your contracts extended, but you repay me with average displays."

"I'd give up all my money to play well for you..." I assured him, but he hit back with: "Really? I pay you good money to win games for me. Do you know what will happen when they sack me? The new manager will come in and get rid of you all. You're my players, you'll be gone with me."

He started to scream at Vladi: "Every time you go away for international breaks you come back injured." To be fair, he was right! It must have happened three or four times and I remember coming back from an international break with a knock myself and going into the masseur's room for treatment. Vladi walked in. Again!

"If the boss arrives, I'm f***ing out of here, Vladi," I said. "I don't want to see him yelling at you again!"

Vladi, who had a problem with his big toe, smiled back at me: "Neither do I..."

'You have to win it for me'

We only won three of our opening seven games in 2003/04 and after a 3-2 defeat at Charlton we were due to play Arsenal –

which is always a big game for Liverpool – at Anfield. Houllier called me in for a chat on the Monday.

"Jerzy, how do you feel?"

"Good, boss."

"Good? You were very poor yesterday!"

"Poor? None of the goals conceded were my fault."

"If you'd played well, we'd have won 2-0."

"If someone blames me for those goals against Charlton he can blame me for every goal conceded during the season."

Houllier got angry: "Do you think I want to be saying this? I know you well and I know you should have saved all three of their goals."

There was no point arguing with him. The boss is always right! But the following day, during a training match, he stopped the game after 10 minutes and shouted at me: "What are you doing? Wake up. You stand around like a pole rather than a Pole."

I had no idea what he was talking about. The action was happening at the other end of the pitch. What was I supposed to be doing? He chose to call me out in front of my team-mates for no reason because he knew I wouldn't react whereas others, who maybe needed a kick up the backside, would have argued back at him. It wound me up and I was pretty much unbeatable in that training match, but afterwards Corrigan told me Houllier wanted to see me in his office. "Again? What does he want from me? Tell him to leave me alone!"

I went to his office and he started harshly: "Do you need me to nag at you every day? Do I really have to do it on a regular basis to keep you in form?"

"I really don't have a clue what you are talking about, boss."

"You need to wake up. Do you know who we play on Saturday?"

"Of course, Arsenal."

"What do you think about it?"

"I think it should be fine."

"Good. You have to win that game for me, do you understand? Not win it if you can, you HAVE to win it for me. End of story."

I couldn't think about anything else for the next four days. What if we didn't win? Or if I made a mistake? Would the boss hang me for it? Would he get sacked? It created unnecessary anxiety. I played well, but we lost 2-1. Things got tougher and tougher for Houllier after that. The press and fans were becoming more and more critical and the pressure got to him more and more.

A clash with the captain

I had a big fall-out with Steven Gerrard in December 2003, a couple of months after he had been appointed as captain.

In November we had lost 2-1 at home to Manchester United again. Both goals were given to Ryan Giggs, but the first one was actually touched past me by Ruud van Nistelrooy. I got my foot to the second one, but Giggs' shot still went into the net. Once again I was heavily criticised and Houllier responded this time by dropping me.

There is no goalkeeper who is perfect. Some get over their mistakes quickly, others take the criticism personally. I paid a high price for the criticism because I had bad luck in Manchester United games.

They are matches that can build your reputation or destroy

it. I had a tougher task, because there was a potential English international goalkeeper who was on the bench, so the media storm demanded that Kirkland replaced me.

I returned in goal for a League Cup game against Bolton at Anfield and was given the captain's armband by Houllier.

I think I was the first goalkeeper to skipper Liverpool since Ray Clemence, which was something to be proud of, but it was a tough game.

Bolton's second goal came from a Jay-Jay Okocha free-kick in the 79th minute to put them 2-1 up. I lined my wall up to cover the left side of the goal and covered the right corner myself. As I did so Danny Murphy shouted: "Stay where you are, he'll put it there."

Okocha stepped up, curled the ball over the wall and it flew into the top left corner. Despite Vladi's equaliser in the 88th minute, we went on to lose 3-2 after a last-minute Youri Djorkaeff penalty.

I had no chance with Okocha's free-kick, I didn't even move, but Stevie – who was on as a substitute – started yelling at me: "How the f*** didn't you save that?"

Even if I'd dived I'd have had no chance – Okocha placed it perfectly – but Stevie carried on: "How can you concede goals like that when we've worked our bollocks off to get back into the game? It's your f***ing fault if we lose this."

That pissed me off: "You've said too much. Don't you ever f***ing shout at me again in front of the supporters."

Then Igor Biscan stepped in, saying: "Danny told him to cover the other corner..."

Stevie stormed off at full-time but when I got into the dressing room he was having a right go at Joe Corrigan, saying I should have saved the free-kick and it was my fault. Joe didn't say a word. He didn't defend me.

Maybe he didn't want to argue with the club captain, but as a member of the coaching staff and a former goalkeeper I believe he should have backed me up by saying it was a shot that I couldn't have saved. I went mad.

For the first time in my career I lost control and started yelling into a team-mate's face, producing more English swear words than I care to repeat!

"Calm down Stevie! How the f*** was I supposed to save it? You're the captain now. You should think positively, back your team-mates. You have no right to blame me. I'll hold my hands up and admit it when I f*** up, but I'm not taking stick for a goal I could do nothing about. To f***ing scream at me on the pitch in front of the supporters is out of order."

The lads were telling me to calm down. "Tell your new captain, not me," I snapped back at them.

A few of them later said they didn't recognise me that night, that they didn't think I was capable of being so angry. I saw the highlights on the TV when I got home and the pundits were praising Okocha. Nobody held me accountable. The next day Joe told me Stevie was looking for me.

"Listen, I wanted to apologise for yesterday, Jerzy. I said too much."

"Okay, well I will also apologise to you for all those 'f*** offs' I said!"

Stevie went on to say he understood why his criticism had angered me so much as he knew the emotions I'd been through after the Manchester United games. We became good friends after that and never had any issues again.

Last warning

A month before all this, we had travelled to Romania to play Steaua Bucharest in the UEFA Cup. It was a filthy night. We played on a rain-soaked pitch in freezing conditions and drew 1-1. Normally, after a game, we did a warm down on the pitch so it was no surprise when we heard: "Outside in three minutes lads," from Sammy Lee, a former Liverpool player who was one of our coaches.

"You kidding?" said Stevie. "We're going nowhere. Look at the lads, they're all freezing. Djimi is shaking so much he looks like he's been wired up to the mains. We'll do stretches in the dressing room instead."

Lee wasn't having it. He started to argue with Stevie when Houllier walked back in: "What's going on?" Stevie explained that we didn't want to go back out into the freezing rain so Houllier thought for a moment before telling Tommo, Lee and all the rest of the staff to leave the dressing room.

"This is what I like to hear," he said. "Sometimes you have to take the responsibility. You don't want to go? Fine. Stevie, lead the stretching in the dressing room. It'll be the best for you all."

This was the moment when I believe Houllier lost the Liverpool dressing room. He undermined one of his coaches and gave the power to the players. Sammy even came back into the dressing room and apologised to Stevie while we were doing the stretches! That said a lot.

Increasingly, Houllier had been trying to 'motivate' players by making examples of them in front of the other lads. After another game he started going through the team.

"Where's that player from Leicester City? Emile? Emile Heskey? Where are you? Remember when you used to get the ball, run through the defence and score goals? Where is that player now? Am I missing something? We paid a lot of money for you..."

Then it was Salif Diao: "Do you remember where you came from? Sedan. And do you know the difference between Sedan and Liverpool? I don't think you do. You don't appreciate the fact you play for mighty Liverpool now."

Stephane Henchoz had problems with his Achilles tendon. He was doing all he could to get back on the pitch and had been a great servant for Houllier, especially when Liverpool won five trophies in 2001, but now he was on the receiving end of the manager's anger.

"How long are you going to be injured, Stephane?" asked Houllier. "You're taking your time to recover on purpose because we're not playing well."

"I've just come back from the doctor. I've had another injection," he replied. "He says I've got tendinitis but this might help..."

"I know what I'm seeing."

Then it was my turn. He went back to the start of my Liverpool career and listed every mistake I'd made, month by month.

"November 2002, Middlesbrough. December 2002, Manchester United. March 2003, Tottenham." He chucked in a couple of other teams and yelled: "You think because you were Man Of The Match when we won the League Cup you can act like a star? You're making mistakes which cost us points."

"That's not too bad for the three years," I snapped back, smiling as I did so.

"You think it's funny? Let me tell you this. If Chris had been fit he'd have played in the League Cup final."

Then he turned to Danny Murphy: "And don't think I haven't been watching you. You train like a grandad. Are you going to retire soon?"

But then he paused for a moment. Danny was part of a 'titled' group at Liverpool, I suppose you might call it a group of players the manager favoured. "But Danny, I liked your reaction against Bolton." Danny had scored in that game and, realising he was a player he wanted to keep onside, he tried to soften the criticism.

Traore also got stick from Houllier: "Since you got your contract extension you've stopped trying in training – you're lazy."

He concluded by addressing the whole group and displaying his paranoia: "I know what you're up to. You're waiting for me to be sacked. You're playing badly to get rid of me. You'll be sorry. The new manager will put most of you in the reserves. You won't be laughing then."

I had a knee problem at the time. I was playing after taking painkilling injections but I wasn't getting better so I needed treatment.

I was doing exercises in the gym later that day when Houllier approached me, asked how the knee was and then spoke to me in a friendly tone.

"I hope you're not upset about what I said in the dressing room. Some of the lads needed a shock. You know what I mean? I had to shake them up. Are you angry with me?"

Houllier had destroyed my self-belief with his rant. He had flagged up my individual errors in front of the lads. He'd slaughtered me. But now he was acting as if nothing had happened. When I first got there Houllier and Tommo would play 'good cop, bad cop' with Tommo handing out the rollickings – he threw out more f-words than I thought possible to get into one sentence – but when Houllier tried to be both good and bad cop himself it was comical.

All over for Houllier

Things kicked off again during a training match at Melwood. Stevie was in central midfield and Tommo was shouting for him to move to the left:

"Stevie, go left, cover the space."

"Don't tell me how to play in midfield."

Tommo carried on. "Stevie, Stevie, go left."

"F*** off. Stop f***ing shouting at me. I know how to play in midfield and I can't focus when you're chipping away at me."

The row carried on and Stevie went over to the touchline. Tommo stayed calm and said he was just trying to pass on advice, but Stevie was wound up. He got so close to Tommo that they were almost touching noses.

"F*** off. Don't tell me what to do."

We were all shocked at how Stevie was talking to him. Tommo wasn't just the assistant manager, he was a Liverpool legend. We thought a fight would break out until Houllier stepped between them and told Tommo to walk away.

"But boss, I was just giving him advice."

"Phil, stay on the sideline and be quiet."

It was another clear example of who was really in charge at Liverpool. The team was being run by someone who was supposed to be a player, not the boss, and it set a bad example.

The following day El-Hadji Diouf arrived for training 15 minutes late. Tommo collared him.

"Dioufy, 15 minutes. £100 fine. Give the money to Joe."

"F*** off," replied Diouf immediately.

Tommo looked visibly shocked: "Sorry? What did you say?"

"F*** off."

"You're telling me to f*** off?"

"Yes. Stevie did it yesterday and today it's me. F*** off."

It was over for Gerard Houllier. He'd completely lost the team. Discipline had gone out of the window and respect for the coaching staff had been lost by some players. It was obvious that Houllier wouldn't be able to turn the team around and incidents like these proved why.

We won nothing in 2003/04 and finished fourth after a 1-1 draw against Newcastle United on the last day of the season. It was enough to qualify for the Champions League, but the writing was on the wall. A few days later, when I was on holiday, I discovered that Gerard Houllier had been sacked.

Quite frankly, I wasn't surprised.

RAFA THE PERFECTIONIST

There were two clear contenders to be the new Liverpool manager: Jose Mourinho of Porto and Rafael Benitez of Valencia. Both had just won their domestic titles in Portugal and Spain, Mourinho having led Porto to the European Cup and Benitez having guided Valencia to the UEFA Cup. They were considered to be the best young managers on the continent and inevitably they were destined for the Premier League. What nobody knew then was just how big the rivalry between Chelsea and Liverpool would become after Mourinho took charge at Stamford Bridge and Benitez arrived as our new manager.

Benitez was appointed on June 16 while we were on holiday and brought several Spanish coaching staff to Liverpool with him. Unfortunately none of them spoke English. Benitez spoke a bit of English, and improved every day, but it made communication difficult at the start, especially as managers are responsible for everything in English football, whereas elsewhere in Europe only the day-to-day coaching is the manager's responsibility.

He realised immediately he had lots to do, and not just on the pitch. In my opinion, we began 2004/05 with a weaker team than we had a year earlier. Owen, Heskey, Murphy and Babbel left, Cisse arrived and, before the transfer window closed, Benitez brought in Xabi Alonso, Luis Garcia, Josemi and Antonio Nunez. We had a lot of tactical sessions during pre-season. The new manager preferred a completely different style of play to Houllier and had a vastly different method of communication with the players. He wanted us to discuss and assess his decisions rather than force them on us.

Benitez felt that if we had some input into how we should play we would carry his tactical plan out better, but he saw there was a lack of knowledge within the squad tactically. He felt we played too intuitively, relied too much on certain individuals to score goals and that the fitter players were doing the running for some of the others. He wanted us to think on the pitch more, to create more thought-out chances by establishing a new methodical style of play. He also told the younger players, some of whom hadn't been on Houllier's radar, that they would be given a chance in first-team games.

I remember Patrik Berger watching the reserves train and saying to me: "These are the most talented young players in England, but they have no future. Which manager at a big club will invest in their development at the expense of results?" But now Benitez was giving them a chance. Darren Potter, Johnny Welsh, Neil Mellor, Richie Partridge, David Raven, Zak Whitbread and Mark Smyth all got at least one game. Stephen Warnock, who didn't play once under Houllier, made 30 appearances and got in the England squad!

Benitez changed the mentality of the young lads. They may have generally played in the League Cup and been on the bench in the Champions League, but it motivated them to work harder as they believed they could have a future at Liverpool. Of course, you could argue that if he'd had a huge transfer kitty like Mourinho at Chelsea he'd have overlooked them and bought players instead, but those players all showed progress, as did most of the rest of us. Benitez spoke about football all the time – he's a workaholic – but his desire for perfection would pay off.

> *"Houllier was an open person. When Jurek brought family to Melwood he came to say hello and chat for a bit. Benitez was the complete opposite. I spoke to him only a few times and when Jurek was injured he would barely say a word to him. It was a different way of working from a different personality."*
>
> **Jan de Zeeuw, agent**

Tips from the top

One of the big changes for me was that Benitez wanted his goalkeeper to be closer to the back four. He demanded bravery, for the goalkeeper to dominate the penalty area and for my starting position to be much further forward. I had to change my style of play and it took most of the season to adapt.

Where a goalkeeper stands in the penalty area depends on how deep the defenders are. Benitez wanted the back four to play a high-line with a 'sweeper-keeper' behind them. It meant there were fewer opportunities to make eye-catching saves and a requirement to run 14, 15 or 16 metres out of the box to deal with balls in behind the defence. His view was that goalkeepers should nip danger in the bud before a shot could even be made.

I asked Rafa during one training session how high I have to play as it felt like I would end up having to make interventions on the halfway line! "How many goals have you conceded when someone has lobbed you from long range?" he said. "None? Maybe one? It happens, but think how many goals you'll prevent by not letting them shoot at you in the first place."

Journalists tend not to see a goalkeeper rushing out to clear danger as an important contribution compared to making a spectacular save from a shot, but it is. A goalkeeper who can carefully read a game by quickly measuring the distance between himself, the ball and his defenders is more important to a team than one who can't make those judgements, but is a good shot-stopper. I finally got my head around that style of goalkeeping during the second half of 2004/05, but our defenders had a tougher task because they couldn't figure out Benitez's zonal marking system!

Try as he might, Benitez couldn't get the lads to adapt to zonal marking. At one point we seemed to concede from set-pieces in every game. We begged Benitez to return to our man-to-man marking system, but he stood by his decision and explained it was the best way. Still we were struggling and it began to make us nervous. Even Benitez started to doubt if we'd ever get it right, but he was stubborn and during one training session said: "It is a matter of two games. Get it right twice and you'll keep getting it right. Zonal marking is like a jigsaw. When all the pieces fit each other they will stay together."

He was right. It worked. We started to understand his system and began to concede fewer goals. Benitez worked on free-kicks and corner kicks at both ends of the pitch a lot. We also started to score goals from corners and free-kicks more regularly, Sami Hyypia's goal against Juventus in the Champions League from a Luis Garcia flick-on being a good example of something we had worked on. He was also keen for us to get crosses into the penalty area. The more we worked with him, the better we got, but our eye-catching technical style worked better in the Champions League than it did in the Premier League that season.

A new approach

Joe Corrigan left the club with Houllier and Benitez brought in a new goalkeeping coach, Jose Ochotorena, who had played for Real Madrid and Valencia among others. I had heard a lot of positive things about Spanish goalkeeping coaching and I was really looking forward to experiencing it during training. Ocho didn't leave me feeling disappointed. As soon as I started to work with him I felt like a better keeper.

Tactically he was very good. He got me to repeat matchday situations, like crosses into the box and shots from different angles, and got rid of senseless exercises. Everything was geared to situations that can happen during a match. I had to learn certain things about how he worked at the start, but he communicated them well. I enjoyed working with Jose. He showed me how to attack a ball when it was coming into the box. He worked on my starting position and how to judge when to come out to collect the ball. He also tried to help me deal with the English media and the constant stick they were still giving me.

"Say nothing for now," Ocho said. "Be patient. You don't

know how the season will finish. We'll sit down after the season and analyse everything. We'll think what to do next."

"But when I was in Holland, everyone praised me," I'd reply. "Michał Żewłakow [who played for Anderlecht] told me his coach urges his keepers to watch my games. The English media don't praise me; they only wait for my mistakes."

Ocho calmed me down: "You can't judge the weather by what you see out of the window when you wake up. You wait until you go to bed to judge if it was a good day."

It proved to be good advice, given what happened to me in the last game of the season in Istanbul and when I returned to Melwood after the summer Ocho welcomed me back: "Remember what I told you about remaining calm? You never know in football what the next day will bring. That's why you have to work hard and patiently to achieve success. You need luck, but fate will always reward hard work."

Not everyone was keen on Ochotorena's methods, though. Chris Kirkland complained about them during our pre-season tour of the USA. I tried to explain what his methods were designed to achieve, but Chris was adamant that goalkeepers in England should work differently. Benitez stepped in.

"Chris, Jose is the best goalkeeping expert in Spain. Answer me one question: how many English goalkeepers play in Europe?"

"None, that I can think of."

"And what about England?"

"A few."

"In Spain, almost every goalkeeper who plays in La Liga is Spanish. In Germany most of the goalkeepers are German. In England maybe a third of the teams have English goalkeepers. That says everything about English goalkeeping coaching."

Chris was still my rival when Benitez took charge. At the beginning I was first choice, but at the start of October he told me I'd had a chance and now he wanted to see what Chris could do. I only played in League Cup matches until mid-December when, after we had lost the Merseyside derby 1-0 at Goodison Park, Benitez called me into his office and told me that after assessing Chris for two months he had concluded that I should be his number one. He praised my professionalism, as I had continued to work hard in training, and said he liked my positive attitude. Shortly after the Everton game, Chris suffered a back injury. He had been blamed – unfairly in my opinion – for the winning goal but that injury ruled him out for the season and he never played for Liverpool again. It meant Benitez needed to sign a new keeper in the January transfer window.

Patrice Luzi, a French keeper, was still in the squad, but Benitez didn't appreciate his somewhat dismissive attitude towards training so Paul Harrison, a 20-year-old Scouser, was promoted to second choice. Paul was very ambitious, but he had no first-team experience so Benitez signed Scott Carson from Leeds United. Scott was only 19, but had played in the Leeds first-team and was highly regarded. We got on well, he became my new room-mate for away games and, as I will explain later, he helped me during the Champions League final penalty shoot-out by making hand signals from the touchline. He was also in a local casino on a night when some of my team-mates made a lot of money!

A big gamble

Liverpool had plenty of invitations to go for team nights out and during the 10-day break between our final Premier League game against Aston Villa and the Champions League final in Istanbul we were invited to the newly-opened Leo Casino at the Queen's Dock in Liverpool. The boss there was a huge LFC fan, laid on free food and drink and told us to play as much as we wanted as he had reserved the entire downstairs room just for us.

I'm not a big fan of casinos. I've only visited them a few times but, after working out what I could afford to lose, I sat down at the blackjack table where Milan Baros, Igor Biscan, Didi Hamann and John Arne Riise were already playing. Milan was on a lucky streak. After every fifth hand he would go over to the roulette table and bet £1,000 on black. Eight out of 10 spins ended up on black. Luckily for him the Reds weren't betting on red that night!

Blackjack is very tactical and it wasn't long before the £1,000 I had brought to the table had all gone. I was jealous that the other lads were doing well when I wasn't, but I was still pleased for them. Baros was about £7,500 up, but Didi – 'Kaiser' as the lads called him – was displaying a blackjack tactical master-class like he played it for a living in Las Vegas. People say that Rafa was good tactically, but you should see Didi in a casino! When Ginge felt unwell – the official reason was because of the food! – and had to leave the table with about £3,000 in chips still on it, Didi said he'd carry on for him. By the time Ginge returned to the table there was a cheque for £10,000 waiting for him! In the end we had to try and convince Didi to stop playing before the casino went bust! He left the table with over £30,000 that night with the lads making over £50,000 between them. Gambling is risky, you can lose a lot of money, but we integrated very well that night and it paid off in Istanbul.

THE ROAD TO ISTANBUL

My Champions League 'final' started after the group stage when Liverpool were drawn to face Germany's Bayer Leverkusen in the last 16. The Polish media focused on the potential battle between myself and Jacek Krzynówek. It was billed as a head-to-head between the two of us.

Jacek was the best Polish player at that time and my very close friend. He had been playing for FC Nurnberg, but despite his form for the club they were relegated from the Bundesliga and he moved to Leverkusen where he played in an attacking side with Dimitar Berbatov and Andriy Voronin. Leverkusen had been in the same Champions League group as Real Madrid and had finished top after beating them 3-0 in Germany and earning a 1-1 draw in Spain. During that 3-0 win Jacek had scored a memorable goal – a thunderous left-footed shot from

30 yards that flew in via the post and Iker Casillas – and the media were keen to focus on the meeting between the two of us.

I tried not to pay attention to such stories before important games. The newspapers asked: 'Will Krzynówek score against Dudek? How many shots will Jerzy save against Jacek?' Everyone knew that me and Jacek were friends and that's why there was so much excitement about it. The best Polish player meets the best Polish goalkeeper – that's what the media back home said. We both knew that everyone would look at us and that can be a distraction going into big games.

Because we were so experienced we didn't take too much notice of the media storm. We tried to focus on the game and even called each other twice a day to talk about it and joke that at least one Pole will play in the next stage of the Champions League.

Thankfully it was to be me, not Jacek, who would reach the quarter-finals.

To be honest, we were much the better team in both legs. We played well at Anfield in the first game, even though we were without the suspended Steven Gerrard. A quarter of an hour in, Luis Garcia opened the scoring, then Riise made it 2-0 with a free-kick and when Didi scored with another free-kick in the 90th minute it looked like we were through, but then came a bad moment for me. I screwed up. Berbatov's shot from distance bobbled in front of me and I spilled the ball instead of keeping hold of it. It fell to Franca and he put it into the net to score a crucial away goal.

It gave Leverkusen a chance to advance in the return leg. Their form at the Bay Arena was very good in European competition and we had been knocked out of the Champions League there in the quarter-final in 2002, losing the second leg 4-2, having won the first game 1-0.

Our away form wasn't especially good at the time either so even though we had won the game 3-1 the media attention was on me and the error I had made.

I had played well until the 92nd minute but that was generally ignored. I was heavily criticised for that goal and there were just a few people who remembered my earlier important saves. I felt better the following day, however, when I was watching a Polish TV programme and one of the experts said that there is some kind of schizophrenia in England regarding how goalkeepers are viewed.

"They only think if the goalkeeper screwed up or not," he said. "Nobody thinks 'did he have a chance to save it?' Nobody notices that the keeper saved his team earlier with some crucial interventions when he has made a mistake."

I was waiting for the second leg. 'Thanks to me' – as the media put it – Bayer could progress to the next round on away goals by winning 2-0. It meant that I was exceptionally focused before that return leg. So too were the rest of the team, but it meant a lot to me to get a result.

By half-time Garcia had scored twice and the tie was over. Leverkusen had needed two goals to go through at kick-off – now they needed five and that wasn't going to happen. Milan got a third on the night for us and although my friend Jacek found a way past me a couple of minutes before the end after Rafa had taken off Steve Finnan, Carra and Didi to give them a rest, we had progressed comfortably with another 3-1 win. My mistake for Franca's goal had not proved as costly as people had predicted.

That put us into the last eight and normally you would hear talk that nobody is thinking about reaching the final at such a time. Benitez did things differently though! Rafa told journalists after the game that Liverpool's players had to believe quickly that they can reach the final, because if we did then we could do it.

We heard this and started to talk about it in the dressing room. Some of the lads were impressing Benitez with a smile and saying: "Yeah, of course we'll be in the final, boss. And we'll win it!"

But then one of the lads said: "Does anyone know where the final is this year?"

"I don't know," replied someone else, "but we need to check it!"

That type of banter is typical of dressing rooms. Having a laugh, even at something the manager has said, eases the tension and helps players to relax. Having that type of atmosphere inside a club is as important as everyday training sessions.

All the jokes stopped immediately when we were drawn against Juventus, though. Everyone in the Liverpool dressing room knew how tough those games would be. Benitez constantly repeated that it was a game between two well-known teams and anyone could win it, but we knew it was going to be very, very difficult.

They had only let two goals in during the Champions League all season and had players like Buffon, Cannavaro, Thuram, Nedved, Del Piero and Ibrahimovic.

There were also issues for the club to handle off the pitch as it was the first time that Liverpool and Juventus had met since the Heysel Disaster in 1985 when 39 Juventus fans were killed before the European Cup final following the collapse of a wall after fighting in the stands.

The first leg at Anfield arrived at the start of April and it was a tough time for me. I had suffered from sickness for a full week, then there was the death of Pope John Paul II and I also got injured during an international game against Northern Ireland. I had wanted to play in that first leg, it was such a big game, but Benitez said no. He said he preferred to leave me on the bench for one game rather than to risk a more serious injury which could prevent me from playing for a couple of weeks. Now I can thank Rafa for that decision, but at the time I was upset.

Although I was on the bench I really didn't have a clue what was happening on the pitch. My thoughts were completely somewhere else. I was thinking about the Pope. He had died on April 2, three days before our match, and even though I was sitting on the bench for a Champions League quarter-final at a noisy Anfield, his death was dominating my thoughts. I didn't want to be there.

Just before the game I had spoken with Dr Mark Waller. I explained that Rafa wanted me on the bench, but I didn't feel mentally prepared to even do that because of my emotions. I almost cried when I said that to the doctor. I was waiting for Dr Waller's answer and he said, without any emotion, that he understood the situation I was in but this was a decision for the manager. I had gone from wanting to play to not even wanting to be on the bench – my head was all over the place – and I must admit that I was angry with Rafa at the time when he said that I had to remain as a substitute.

"I prefer you on the bench than one of the youngsters from the reserves," he explained to me. "They have no experience.

If you needed to get on the pitch, even injured or not mentally right, you would do more than them."

Scott Carson, who had only started two games for Liverpool since arriving from Leeds, played instead of me and even though Rafa had reassured me I spent that game questioning myself all the way through it. 'What the hell am I doing here?' I was thinking to myself.

The game itself went pretty well. A lot of European teams had problems playing at Anfield because of the very hard and fast pitch we had. The grass was thick and the ball moved at least twice as fast as at other grounds they were used to playing at. Some players can't even control the ball on fast pitches. It comes as quite a shock to them and you could tell from the way Juventus were playing that they were struggling to adapt.

We were 1-0 up before they had got used to the pitch, Sami volleying the ball in after a flick-on from a corner. We continued to play really well and 15 minutes later we scored again, Garcia getting another big European goal with a great strike that flew past Gianluigi Buffon from distance.

Juventus gradually got to grips with the pitch and Cannavaro scored an important away goal in the second half. I thought Scott made an error for the goal, but luckily for him there was far less criticism in the media compared to what was said about me after we had played Leverkusen at Anfield.

It meant that we had a 2-1 lead to take to Turin and with the second leg only eight days away I realised that I needed to regain my focus and start to mentally prepare for the trip to Italy immediately, as Rafa had said that once I was fully fit I would be back in goal. Beating Juventus 2-1 was a big night for Liverpool and the fans at Anfield, but for me it was an emotional time following the death of Pope John Paul II, a man I looked up to.

Don't look at the stadium!

I flew to Turin with my head full of English media speculation. I constantly thought about the stories in the papers that Benitez was looking to sign another goalkeeper and that it might be my last season at Liverpool. I tried to forget about it, to focus on training to ensure I put in a good performance against Juventus, but when your name is in the papers it is hard to ignore because people ask you about it.

I don't read the newspapers, but my friend called me and asked if all the stories were true. I also saw talk of Liverpool being interested in signing a new goalkeeper on the TV. You can't live like a hermit and completely steer clear of the news. One way or another you find out what is being said anyway. Later in my career I stopped caring about such stories in the way I used to when I was younger, but it is difficult. Once you hear something said that could affect your future, you keep it on your mind.

I tried to analyse the situation. If Benitez was going to sign a new goalkeeper then I'd want to sit with him and talk about my future.

There's always a bit of truth in every rumour and Rafa hadn't denied anything so the more I thought about it the more I felt that something must really be going on. But, because Liverpool had so many important games to play – we were playing every weekend and midweek at the time – I didn't have a chance to discuss the situation.

Before the second leg against Juventus I also recalled that my

Champions League debut was in Turin when I was a Feyenoord player in 1997. We lost 5-1 and I made an error. I thought to myself that hopefully this wasn't a bad sign. Because of their away goal Juventus only needed a 1-0 win and a lot of people thought they would get it. I wondered if my Champions League career would finish at the Stadio delle Alpi, the same stadium where it began.

I even recalled one sentence from Paulo Coelho's *The Alchemist* about there being signs to follow for each of us. Did I have mine in Turin? Everything started there and everything is supposed to finish in the same place!

I prayed for the media not to dig up the story that my Champions League debut had been at Juventus as speculation that things could go full circle for me and my last appearance in the competition could also be on the same ground wasn't something that I needed at this time.

I never saw the story written and I had been feeling quite relaxed until we started the landing procedures over Turin. It reminded me of the flight to Turin in 1997. The pilot's words as we approached the airport sprang to mind. "Look out of the windows. On the left-hand side you can see the beautiful stadium of Juventus."

Everyone looked to the left to see it and the stadium looked fantastic, but because we lost 5-1 I became superstitious about it. I decided that it was bad luck to see a stadium I was about to play in if the plane was about to pass it, so I had a plan when we flew back to Turin with Liverpool. During the flight I put my headphones on and closed my eyes. As the landing procedures began, a stewardess came over to me about five times to ask me to switch off all the electronic devices, but I didn't have any switched on. I showed her that the headphones weren't plugged into anything; it was simply my way of isolating myself from everything because you can't have the window blinds shut when you are landing.

Once we landed, I thought to myself 'Okay, I haven't seen the stadium, so it has to be fine! We can get a result here'. And we did...

Talking rubbish in Turin

The second leg in Turin was the first one which wasn't sold out for the away fans. Liverpool fans will travel anywhere to watch their team but there were about 700 tickets left for the away enclosure at the Stadio delle Alpi. Many of the fans were afraid to go to Turin; they didn't want to risk meeting the Italians. They simply couldn't predict what would happen. The media had obviously recalled the Heysel tragedy and spirits in Italy were still running high. The atmosphere around the game was heated and we could all feel the tension.

During the first leg at Anfield, officials from both clubs had declared a reconciliation. There was a mosaic on the Kop that said 'Amicizia' (friendship) and before the game Ian Rush, who had played for both clubs, Michel Platini – who scored the winning goal for Juventus on the night of the Heysel tragedy – and Phil Neal, Liverpool's captain in 1985, were on the pitch as a banner was carried down to the away fans in the Anfield Road end. It said 'Memoria e amicizia' – in memory and friendship.

It was a gesture of friendship, but many Juventus fans turned their backs to the pitch and refused to look at it. The Italians clearly showed that they didn't want to be a part of it and I saw faces full of aggression when we travelled across Turin to get to the stadium. The tension had been raised; we knew it was going to be a difficult atmosphere to deal with.

Benitez prepared unique tactics for the game. We practised them all week during our training sessions at Melwood. Obviously, it was a top secret plan – no-one could find out or the element of surprise would be lost. It was a very defensive plan, with three centre-backs supported by two wing-backs, three midfielders and two strikers. We also had Stevie and Didi missing through injury, but Xabi and Djibril were both ready to make their comebacks after being out for several months with broken bones.

I was designated to take part in the pre-match press conference and Benitez gave me some instructions: "Don't say anything about the tactics, because those Italians will find out immediately how we want to play. Maybe Capello will send someone to listen. Tell them you don't know who will be in the midfield. Keep repeating that we're going to play a 4-4-2 and that Igor Biscan has been in brilliant form over the week during training."

In England there are plenty of generalisations during press conferences. We'd talk about how we'd play our hearts out, that it'd be a tough game, all that kind of stuff. Rarely were we asked to talk about tactics, but the Italians are so inquisitive and we knew the questions would be asked so I went to the press conference and did exactly what Rafa wanted me to do. I talked rubbish!

The manager took a bit of a risk with the tactics as we weren't used to that system, but Juventus only had to score one goal to get through so we tried to stop them.

Benitez constantly said to us that Italian sides will always continue to play guarded, methodical football. They don't force the pace, they wait patiently to score and get the minimum result that they need.

That's why we had to play calmly and with restraint. We had to stay close to them, deny them space and prevent their strikers from shooting on goal.

His plan worked. We carried it out as instructed and contained Juventus so well that they only had two clear-cut chances during the entire 90 minutes.

Zlatan Ibrahimovic had one of the opportunities in the first half, but he headed the ball over my goal from close range. The other chance came to Fabio Cannavaro in the second half and I had to make an important save. From a free-kick on our right he met the ball at the far post and headed it goalwards from about two yards out. The ball struck the post then rebounded back off Djimi in the direction of the goal. I had a split second to react, but I managed to get down low and scoop the ball off the goal-line with my left hand.

Cannavaro and the Juventus players claimed the ball had crossed the line – they celebrated to try to persuade the referee it was a goal – but thankfully the linesman was well placed and saw that it hadn't gone in.

The game finished goalless and we progressed into the semi-finals, just as we had wanted. As we flew home I thought to myself how glad I was that my Champions League career definitely wouldn't be ending in the place it had begun. Now we had a semi-final to plan for and it just happened to be an all-English encounter against Chelsea. If we were going to win my favourite competition it was clear that we would have to do it the hard way.

Mourinho's mind games

Chelsea were on the verge of winning their first league title since 1955 and were setting their sights on a first Champions League victory. We knew we were the underdogs and had already lost to them three times that season, twice in the Premier League and once in the League Cup final. All of them were tight games. Maybe we had a lack of luck.

We had lost 1-0 at Stamford Bridge in October – a game I didn't play in – and were beaten 1-0 again at Anfield on New Year's Day. We were incredibly unlucky to lose that match. Joe Cole had scored Chelsea's winner in London and it was his goal that won this match, but only because it took a massive deflection off Carra that completely deceived me.

Our next meeting was in Cardiff for the League Cup final. Chelsea were big favourites for the trophy, but we were very close to winning. Ginge scored in the first minute and it looked like we would hang on to win 1-0 until Stevie inadvertently headed an own goal past me with 10 minutes to play.

I usually played well in finals and it happened again during that Carling Cup final. I'd go as far as to say it was one of my best games ever. Before the own goal I had to make a number of stops including a double save from Eidur Gudjohnsen and William Gallas. Two minutes before the game went into extra-time I had to make another double save, both from Damien Duff, but I got injured while doing so. As I made the second stop Duff's studs badly cut the skin on my tibia. The doctor came on and when he rolled down my sock I saw two white bones. I was shocked. There was no blood, just flesh and bone!

I really needed to go off to have stitches, but Benitez had already made three substitutions so the doctor started to bandage my leg up. "What are you doing?" I angrily asked him. "You've been fantastic Jerzy," he replied, "brilliant! Keep it going. You can do it!" So even though I ended up needing nine stitches after the match I carried on, but as soon as I stood up I could feel my sock getting wet. By the end of extra-time my boot was half-filled with blood!

The score was 1-1 until the opening minutes of the second half of extra-time when Didier Drogba bundled a long throw-in into the goal at my near post. There was nothing I could do about it. Chelsea scored again five minutes later when Mateja Kezman stabbed the ball over the line after a Frank Lampard free-kick. Antonio Nunez did pull one back for us a minute later but we couldn't get an equaliser and Chelsea won the cup. I had been hoping for penalties – although my leg was so sore I'd have been lucky to save any of them – but instead we had a third defeat from three games against Chelsea.

Having seen how tight the games were, with few goalscoring opportunities arising during those matches, most people expected the Champions League semi-finals to be tactical games, but first we had to face a battle off the pitch – Mourinho v Liverpool in the media!

Mourinho impressed me with his intelligence, the way he spoke with journalists. He is a master of social techniques, but also an arrogant man who is full of self-confidence.

He uses his personality to deal with journalists, to play mind games, to try to strike psychological blows to gain his team an advantage. Everyone knew that Mourinho really wanted to have Stevie in his team, but Stevie was loyal to Liverpool so the Chelsea manager tried to stir things up. He claimed that Gerrard would end up playing for Chelsea; that he wouldn't be a threat in the semi-final; that Liverpool had no chance to win.

Maybe he thought that if something went wrong for Stevie in the semi-final, as it had done in the League Cup final in Cardiff, he could put negative thoughts into the Liverpool supporters' minds to see how they would react. If he could get the fans to turn, maybe boo their own captain, our key player, it would be to Chelsea's advantage. We knew that we wouldn't be able to overcome Chelsea without the backing of our supporters, especially at Anfield. We needed their support.

The Liverpool supporters are fantastic. Even if you make a mistake they stick with you. You could hear them shout 'c'mon mate, you can still do it lad'. Or they'd sing your name in support. 'We've got a big Pole in our goal' was the song they sang for me. When you hear Liverpool fans singing your name or shouting encouragement it motivates you to try and pay them back by playing well and winning. It inspires you to do better. But, if those supporters go to a game having read rubbish in the papers that questions the loyalty of a player, it can plant a seed in their minds if something goes wrong.

You can't explain everything so if Stevie made a mistake in the semi-final would the Liverpool supporters remember what Mourinho had said and think 'is Gerrard playing badly because he's already a Chelsea player?'

It's a pressure you cannot get away from and with the Chelsea games being so high profile it became a bigger story. It created a distraction. Nobody wondered who would score the goals, but if Gerrard had signed for Chelsea or not. Stevie was under huge pressure and we could sense it so when a journalist asked me before the tie whether I thought he was going to move to Chelsea it pissed me off. "It is just Mourinho who is playing his mind games," I said. "He talks rubbish about Stevie just to unsettle us." As it happens, Mourinho's mind games didn't work. Stevie brushed it all aside and showed what fantastic character he has in the semi-final. He proved that he could handle the pressure and so did the rest of the lads.

Can you hear me Sami?

As anticipated, the first game in London was really tight. There was no big difference between the two teams and it ended with a fair goalless draw. We went to London with the same mentality that we showed in Turin – to limit goalscoring opportunities, to keep our shape, to be resolute. We did it so well that, in truth, I didn't have a difficult save to make all night. In fact, we came the closest to scoring in the first half when Milan flicked Stevie's cross towards goal only for Petr Cech to make a brilliant diving save.

We were very disciplined so it was a huge disappointment when Xabi was booked just before the end, for a supposed foul on Gudjohnsen, ruling him out of the second leg. Xabi was distraught at what had happened as he hadn't touched Gudjohnsen and now he would miss the biggest European game at Anfield in years. We were all gutted for him and afterwards Stevie told the press that we were now even more motivated to get to Istanbul so that Xabi could play in the final. The whole dressing room felt the same so I also spoke to the media about the incident.

"What happened has made us all the more determined to make sure we finish the job at Anfield for Xabi. He looked distraught and the whole mood went quiet, even though we had played so well and come away with a good result. We all really felt for him. He was so down, visibly upset, and those were difficult moments for us all. We will try to do it for him and make sure there is a Champions League final for him to look forward to. That would be the perfect answer."

Chelsea secured the Premier League trophy on the Saturday between the two semi-finals when they won at Bolton so we knew they would be coming to Anfield on a high. It was also pointed out that Mourinho had never been knocked out of Europe as a manager – his Porto side had won the UEFA Cup in 2002/03 and the Champions League in 2003/04.

A couple of my friends travelled to Liverpool from Poland and the Netherlands to watch the match. Their seats were in the Main Stand, almost directly in line with the Kop end goalline, and that's where all the controversy was. Liverpool traditionally kick towards the Kop end of Anfield in the second half of games as it was famously said by Bill Shankly that the fans in that stand suck the ball into the back of the net, but John Terry had won the toss and chose to make us kick towards the Kop in the first half. Maybe that was a mistake. We had started the quarter-final against Juventus quickly and part of Rafa's plan was to do the same. We had scored a first-minute goal against Chelsea in Cardiff so we hoped to catch them out again before they could settle.

We attacked as planned and in the fourth minute Stevie played Milan through on goal. He flicked the ball over Cech and was brought down for a definite penalty, but before the referee could blow his whistle the ball had fallen to Garcia and he flicked it goalwards. William Gallas raced back to the goal and hooked the ball away, but Luis and the fans on the Kop were already celebrating.

Had the ball crossed the line? Was it a goal or not? I was at the other end of the pitch so I had no idea! But the linesman signalled to the referee that it was over the line and the goal was given. Anfield exploded. What a noise!

After the game I asked my friends about it, knowing where they had been sitting. They were adamant that the ball had crossed the line before Gallas cleared it. The linesman had given the goal and my friends agreed so that was good enough for me, but as it proved to be the only goal the controversies remained and still do now!

Supporters love controversies and conspiracies so the media naturally plays on these to ensure such incidents continue to be talked about.

There was a computer simulation on Sky Sports and in the papers that suggested the ball hadn't completely crossed the line and it shouldn't have been given. But who cares? I thought exactly as our supporters did. It was a goal. Period.

There was one thing I wondered about, however. The TV replays showed the situation only from three camera angles and none of these were on the goal-line. Why didn't they have a camera angle on the line? It would have proved everything. Chelsea talked about Liverpool being lucky, but arguably it was fortunate for them that the goal was given as ironically it gave them more of a chance of getting back into the game. The referee, Lubos Michel from Slovakia, later admitted that if he hadn't given the goal he would have given us a penalty for the foul on Milan and sent Cech off.

You can never be certain, but we'd have probably scored from the penalty spot and Chelsea would have had to play almost the whole game with 10 men on the pitch. Now they were a goal behind, but they still had 11 men to try to score the away goal that would have sent them through.

Once again we defended well that night and restricted Chelsea to just a few goalscoring chances. I remember one free-kick taken by Frank Lampard. I didn't have a good view of it as he struck the ball from 25 yards. It seemed to come from nowhere at me but I dived to my right and somehow pushed it past the post for a corner kick. We also had another problem to deal with – the noise from our own fans!

The atmosphere at Anfield was absolutely unbelievable that night. It was the loudest I have ever heard. There was talk in the build-up that Anfield would be like this, but to actually be in the centre of it was something else. They recorded the volume level at 122 decibels that night, which is quite something when you consider a jet plane taking off has a volume of 144 decibels! We were defending the Kop end in the second half so I had a wall of noise behind me that felt like an extra man, but in stoppage time it almost played a part in Chelsea getting the goal they needed.

When the Anfield scoreboard ticked on to the 90th minute we knew we were close to realising our dream of going to Istanbul, but then the fourth official raised his board to show there would be six minutes of additional time added on. The Liverpool fans responded by booing at first, followed by a cacophony of ear-drum-piercing whistles for the rest of the game.

Mourinho had thrown his big German defender, Robert Huth, up front in stoppage time to try and unsettle us so they were now hoofing long balls into the box. By the final minute John Terry had been sent forward as well so when a clearance fell to Lampard he simply lobbed a diagonal cross into our penalty area. Terry got up above Finnan at the far post and headed the ball back across goal.

I had a great view of the ball. I was confident of getting to it first before Kezman, the only Chelsea player in the centre of the penalty area. It drifted across the edge of the six-yard box, seemingly taking an hour or two to do so, and I screamed to Sami that I was coming off my line for it with the intention of grabbing it. But because of the incessant noise coming from the stands, Sami didn't hear me!

He jumped to head the ball clear at the same time as I arrived to catch it and as he did so Kezman used his shoulder to give Sami a nudge. The result was that we both collided in mid-air so all I could do was try to punch the ball. I didn't make good contact with it. I was only able to punch it softly and the ball fell to Gudjohnsen at the far post with myself and Sami on the ground.

It fell perfectly to him. He was less than six yards out with just Djimi and Carra on the goal-line and Drogba steaming in at the far post. He had to score. He couldn't miss. But I must admit that in that split second I thought to myself that even if he gets this on target one of our defenders would block it. Someone would clear the ball. We were in that frame of mind in the Champions League. We felt like no-one could score against us. But this was a hairy moment!

Gudjohnsen chested the ball down and lashed a half-volley towards goal. It flashed past Djimi at the near post, flashed past Carra at the far post and flashed past Drogba as he desperately tried to get a touch, the ball going inches wide of the post. You could feel the sigh of relief in the stands. Moments later the final whistle went and the celebrations were fantastic. It almost felt as if the noise levels got even louder and I remember *You'll Never Walk Alone* ringing around Anfield as we celebrated on the pitch.

We had won the 'battle of England', our little Champions League final...

TURKISH
PARADISE

We had two Premier League games to play before we could think about the Champions League final and we really needed to win them both.

We were in fifth place, three points behind Everton who had a game in hand, with only the top four qualifying for the Champions League. UEFA had also changed the rules that meant the Champions League winners no longer got automatic entry to defend the trophy, they had to qualify through their domestic league.

The day before our game at Arsenal, Everton won their game in hand. We could now only finish ahead of them on goal difference, which was close, but we had to beat both Arsenal and Aston Villa and hope they lost their other two matches.

We lost 3-1 at Highbury. It meant our only hope of getting

back into the Champions League was to win it in Istanbul then try to persuade UEFA to change their rules. We beat Villa 2-1 in our final league game – Rafa rested me, Sami, Stevie, Didi, Finnan, Milan and Luis Garcia for that one – and then we had 10 days before the final.

We had to use the break wisely to prepare as much as we could for the final and having had a similar break before we played Bayer Leverkusen in February our fitness coach, Pako Ayestaran, had a plan.

Pako prepared a perfect training programme before the Leverkusen game. He used the extra time we had brilliantly. Pako arrived at Liverpool with Rafa and the job he did was phenomenal. He had us thoroughly prepared for that game against Bayer, we were much fitter than them on the night, and our victory was proof of that. Pako used the same model, the same drills, the same sessions to prepare us for Istanbul.

Rafa, as you would expect, looked at things tactically. As the week went on he started to give us more and more information about AC Milan.

Their results in Serie A had been poor in the weeks before the final. A 1-0 defeat to Juventus was followed by draws against Lecce, Palmero and Udinese. Benitez thought that they looked physically weak, that they were vulnerable to conceding goals late on in games and liable to make defensive errors. He was right.

The night after we had beaten Chelsea we had also watched Milan's semi-final second leg against PSV Eindhoven in Holland. They had won the first leg 2-0 in Italy but after 65 minutes PSV were 2-0 up and looked more likely to go through. Massimo Ambrosini scored for Milan in additional time, but even after that they conceded another goal so only ended up going through on away goals.

Having watched that game, and seen the information Benitez had given us, we were actually happy that we would be playing Milan in Istanbul rather than PSV. We were slowly – very slowly – starting to believe that we could beat a side that had famous players in it such as Maldini, Cafu, Stam, Seedorf, Pirlo, Kaka, Crespo and Shevchenko. Perhaps we got a little overconfident, though.

In hindsight, we ended up going out onto the pitch with a false attitude about their real capabilities.

I was bombarded by interview requests and questions from Polish journalists before the Champions League final. I knew I would be the third Pole after Zbigniew Boniek (1985) and Józef Młynarczyk (1987) to play in the European Cup final. It was big news to have a Pole in the final after an 18-year gap.

I calmly said, to everyone that asked, that Milan are the favourites and we are the underdogs so we have nothing to lose.

Everyone asked me the same question. "The game goes to penalties. You save a couple of them and become a hero. What do you think about this kind of scenario?"

I always answered with a bit of contrariness: "I wish for Liverpool to win after 90 minutes. I'd be happy with even 1-0 and without me making any kind of impact. We just want the European Cup!"

Ian Cotton, our press officer at Liverpool, admitted that it was the biggest media interest that the club had had to deal with in 20 years. Liverpool were in the Champions League final for the first time since 1985. Everyone wanted to tell the story.

All the players were getting bombarded for interviews by

the media. Benitez realised it was becoming a distraction so one week before the final he organised a press conference and invited any journalist that wanted to attend.

He made every single player available to do interviews that day, but made it clear to the press that afterwards there would be no more media access. We had to focus on the final, isolating ourselves from the external world, without any distractions.

Bowling and reading

Police officers and security staff were everywhere when we arrived in Istanbul. I guess there were twice as many of them on duty than for other Champions League games. It was the first Champions League final to ever be held in Turkey and they were taking no chances.

The most important buildings had security checkpoints at the entrance and when cars stopped in front of them police even checked underneath the vehicles to be certain there were no suspicious objects.

Such massive precautions make you realise how big an occasion a Champions League final is and in the middle of this tense atmosphere we had to prepare for the game!

On the Tuesday morning, the day before the game, Rafa organised a surprising activity. Instead of going for a walk in the hotel grounds, he took us ten-pin bowling!

We played in teams of two so it was me versus Cisse. Djibril played quite well, but I beat him. I could have played better and beaten him by a bigger margin I think, but I had to be cautious. I was afraid that I could pick up a hand injury as the bowling ball was quite heavy, about 12 kilograms.

Can you imagine the irony, and the media interest there would have been, if Liverpool's goalkeeper got injured ahead of a Champions League final during a game of ten-pin bowling!

After the bowling we had dinner and then a rest in our rooms before travelling to the Ataturk Stadium for a training session on the pitch, which was open to the media.

Milan trained before us. After they had finished I bumped into Jon Dahl Tomasson, who I had played in the same team with for Feyenoord, and Clarence Seedorf in the tunnel. I chatted to them in Dutch.

"What's up? How's the pitch?"

"It's fine," Jon replied, "Wet, fast, good for the game."

"So what about tomorrow?" I asked Seedorf.

"We have a good, technical team."

"So do we."

"It should be a good, fair game on a great pitch."

I started to tease them. "Let's play fair, but we have to win."

Jon had won the European Cup before and Clarence had probably lost count of how many times he had kissed the cup with Ajax, Real and Milan!

"Let us win lads. We need some silverware. You should be satisfied enough with getting to the final!"

They just smiled and walked away.

Jon was right. The pitch was wet and soft. The ball moved smoothly. We couldn't believe how well everything worked in that training session: passes, crosses, shots, one-twos – they all came off.

Benitez was really happy because of that. I would even say he was proud of what he was watching. I knew that because he didn't say a word, he was so surprised with how it was going too!

Personally, I felt very well, in good form. I was confident in my penalty area. I dreamt that the following day I would feel the same. I couldn't envisage feeling in a different way on the day of the game.

I slept well on the eve of the final. I didn't have any problems switching off or getting to sleep because I had been reading a very interesting book. If a book draws me in I can't put it down or break away from it. Reading takes my mind off things, isolates me from the world, and this is helpful ahead of a big match.

I remember feeling annoyed that night when I had to put my book down to go for the team meal.

I didn't have a bookmark so I folded the corner of the page – I apologise for this lack of respect! – and headed down for the meal looking forward to continuing to read it when we had eaten.

What was I reading? *The Remembrance and Identity* written by Pope John Paul II. One of my fans sent it to me with an inscription: 'Voltaire once said: Books are just like people. Not many of them are important for us. The rest simply disappear in the crowd.'

It's a very wise sentence. I read the book before going to sleep and the following day until the evening. Thanks to that I slept well and I felt good.

I was focused and relaxed and I also bumped into an English couple, who happened to be in Istanbul as tourists, in the hotel lobby. They were staying in the hotel and told me that the week before they had visited Krakow and said that they enjoyed it. I appreciated that. It made me feel proud to be Polish and reminded me again that I was going to be only the third Pole to play in a European Cup final. I was determined to make my country proud of me.

Be quiet Luis!

We were standing in the tunnel of the Ataturk Stadium waiting to go onto the pitch for the Champions League final and all I could hear was the voice of one of my team-mates. Luis Garcia was anxiously screaming at us all.

"Don't touch the cup! It's bad luck! Don't any of you dare! Don't even look at it! Don't you even dare look at the cup!"

The European Cup was on a podium at the end of the tunnel by the side of the pitch. Both teams would walk out together and pass either side of it, something Luis had a bee in his bonnet about. In fact, he was screaming so loud that I wanted to punch him! "Chill out Luis! We start the game in a second and you're talking bullshit?"

We all have our superstitions and not touching a trophy before you have won it is one of Luis's. He spoke about it after the final. "I prayed to God: please make it that no-one touches the cup, because if that had happened we wouldn't have won it." I have laughed about this with Luis since the final, but at the time it was very annoying!

> *"We watched the game with Jurek's brother-in-laws. I excused myself and went to the other room. I lit a votive candle and grabbed the rosary beads which I received from Jurek. He brought it to me when he returned from the Pope's visit. I started to pray."*
> **Renata Dudek, mother**

As we walked out of the tunnel to a wall of noise we all passed the European Cup. Luis turned to me and gave me such a glare that I looked to the left side of the cup straight into the stands. I didn't believe in that particular superstition, but unfortunately one of them became real.

I have a couple of friends that are real sport fanatics. They travelled with me almost everywhere, for Liverpool games, Real Madrid games or if I was with the national team. If they couldn't sort out tickets I was always trying to help them. They always have a special flag with them – a big white and red one with 'TYCHY' [the town very close to my Szczygłowice] written on the front.

They have taken that flag to all kinds of sporting events – the Olympic Games, ski jump competitions and they also brought it to Istanbul. I received a call from Łukasz Jachym – he is one of those crazy fans – while I was in the hotel the day before the game:

"Hi Jurek, can you come down to reception, please? I have brought one of the guys over here and security don't want to let us in. It'll just be for a moment. We'll take two pictures and we're off."

I went to see them after dinner. We took the pictures and before I said goodbye I made a gesture. I started to hit my heart with my right fist. Łukasz started to moan: "What have you done? Didn't you see [Polish heavyweight boxer Andrew] Golota's fight? He did exactly the same. He was walking into the ring, pointed to the supporters and hit his heart with his fist. And what happened? Fifty-three seconds later, he was knocked down!"

I instantly replied: "Why the hell are you telling me that?! Stop saying such rubbish. There are no knockouts in football.

I have at least 90 minutes in goal tomorrow. See you later and keep your fingers crossed." I went back to the hotel and completely forgot about it until a minute after the final had kicked off.

The game had barely started when Milan scored the opening goal. Pirlo curled a free-kick into the box towards Maldini, who was near the penalty spot. He connected with it well, on his right foot, and volleyed the ball downwards. It zipped off the turf and flew past me into the net. I looked at the clock on the scoreboard. The goal came after 53 seconds. What did I think about next? About bloody Golota and that f***ing gesture! 'Watch yourself, Łukasz!' I thought to myself. 'I'll be after you and your mate when I come back to Poland!'

I had to get back to thinking about the game. I couldn't save Maldini's shot. The ball bounced up off the pitch far too quickly for me to have had any hope of getting to it.

I always blame myself when a goal goes past me. I always tell myself that I could have done something better and I was furious that we were 1-0 behind in the first minute. I wasn't even questioning whether any of my defenders could have marked Maldini better.

Emotions had replaced realistic judgement. 'Man, you have to save those, especially at the beginning of the game! You have to save the team in those hopeless situations!' But let's be honest, I was too short to save that ball. There was nothing I could have done about it.

Milan were in control of the game. Shevchenko had a goal disallowed for offside and the Italians scored again in the 39th minute. Kaka ran through the middle, played the ball through to Shevchenko and he passed it across goal to Crespo who turned it past me from six yards out. Two-nil. We thought we were in trouble at that point but there was worse to come a minute before half-time.

Kaka played another brilliant through-ball for Crespo to run on to and as I raced towards the edge of my penalty area to narrow the angle he flicked the ball over me to make it 3-0. What a total nightmare.

There were a number of reasons why we were three goals down by half-time but one that perhaps doesn't get mentioned too often is the condition of the pitch.

We had trained on it the night before and the surface was greasy and soft underneath, but when we arrived for the final and checked it we discovered it was dry and hard, like it hadn't seen rain for a month.

I thought to myself 'wait, this is a Champions League final, the pitch has to be wet and well prepared!' But I knew it wasn't just from the steps I took while walking onto it before the game.

The pitch disturbed our game, it slowed the ball down. Instead of playing quick passes we suddenly needed time to create the attacks.

It was a completely different pitch than the one we trained on the day before and we didn't adjust to that very well, whereas Milan did.

Don't get me wrong, Milan played magically. They did all those tricks, no-look passes, perfect through-balls, clever lobs and they hurt us three times, but there was no question that we had been unsettled by the pitch not being in the condition we had anticipated.

As it sunk in that we were three goals behind I recalled the whole week of preparations. All the talk that Milan are physically weak, that only Liverpool can win the final. And what now? Everything was gone.

Milan had showed us how an experienced team handle the important games. They weren't three-nil up because we were playing particularly badly; they deserved to be three goals up because they were playing fantastic football. We simply couldn't stop them.

"Our son was preparing for his Holy Communion so I couldn't travel to Istanbul. I watched the final with our friends from Szczygłowice in the pub. Jurek asked me to take the camera and record it so he could watch it after the final. There were about 50 people there. We all knew each other, like a big family. We were devastated during the half-time interval. I really wanted Liverpool to win, to make Jurek happy, for him to be successful."

Mirella Dudek, wife

"It was a deathly silence at home. I started to ask: 'Mother of God, Lord Mercy, please help. If not the people will start to pick on my child again.'"

Renata Dudek, mother

"It was terrible. We opened champagne with my sister-in-law. 0-3, what are we waiting for then? I cried, because I felt sorry for Jurek. Two-year-old Julia, Mirella's niece, started to smile, dance and scream 'Jurek Dudek!' when she saw Uncle Jurek on the TV. She didn't want to go to sleep earlier. She kissed the screen, she was the only one in the whole of Szczygłowice who was happy because she didn't have a clue what was going on."

Krystyna Litwin, mother-in-law

A horrible half-time

I looked towards the thousands and thousands of Liverpool supporters who had travelled all the way across Europe to watch us in the Champions League final when I was heading to the dressing room at half-time. I thought they would probably kick our asses, but they were calm.

The fans probably knew that reaching the final was the best we could do and were thinking that AC Milan was a game too far. Maybe they were just stunned!

I was furious. Ocho came over to me in the dressing room and started to talk: "Keep your head up, don't worry. There is the second half!"

I angrily yelled back: "Don't worry? We're losing 3-0!"

Everyone was broken. We were all gutted. And with AC Milan playing so well there was potential for it to get worse. Benitez knew he must change something. He started with Traore. "Djimi, thank you very much, go and take a shower." He also told Pako to go and get Didi warmed up. Didi would be coming on for Djimi. It would be our second substitution as Vladi had been brought on during the first half when Harry Kewell got injured.

Meanwhile, Finnan was with the physios and started to complain about his thigh: "My right thigh hurts a bit. I've no idea how long I can play with it. Maybe 20 minutes? I'll do my best." Dave Galley, our physio, gave Steve's thigh muscles a massage. Then he whispered into Rafa's ear that Finnan was grumbling about his thigh. He told him that he might only be able to play for another 20 minutes. Rafa immediately changed his plan.

"Okay then. Steve, thank you for your efforts but we cannot

risk you. Djimi, you're back in the game, get dressed again."
When Finnan heard that he went mad. He almost attacked
Galley. "What on earth did you say to him?" he screamed.
"Substitute me? Maybe I can play the whole game. This is the
Champions League final. I want to play!"

Benitez stayed firm. "We can't risk you. The decision is made."

Although we were three goals down and staring down the
barrel of being humiliated on our big night, it was a funny situation for Djimi.

He had to come back from the showers and start looking
around the dressing room for his socks and shorts! Finnan,
meanwhile, was still angry at what had just happened.

It was chaos. When Didi came back into the dressing room
with Pako after getting warmed up, Benitez wanted to say
something about the tactics, but then we heard the ref's whistle,
the signal that we had to come back out onto the pitch.

"Let me think for a moment," said Rafa. "Carra, you play on
the right of the defence, Sami in the middle and Traore on the
left. Riise at left wing-back, Smicer on the right. Didi, you hold
the middle where we have the most problems."

At that moment there was a complete silence while we took
stock of the changes. We waited for Benitez to hear some more
instructions, but we really had to go. Then, Alex Miller, one of
Rafa's assistants, spoke up.

"I know what you are thinking. Clear your heads. Don't you
dare think that this could be the worst defeat in Champions
League final history. Forget it! They are so confident about their
lead. They think they've won. Try to use it against them! If we
score in the first 10 minutes we're back in it. Milan won't react
and you'll have lots of time to score another one. Then they'll

panic! We've still got a chance, but you need to forget what happened in the first half..."

To be honest, Alex came across as being desperate. I'm not sure any of us believed we could get back into the game. As they admitted after the game, the lads mostly thought about not getting beaten 5-0 or 6-0. But, when I think about it now, even though we started the second half slowly, I think Alex's desperate words subconsciously boosted us, especially after we pulled a goal back.

Just after half-time I saved a free-kick from Shevchenko. It wasn't as spectacular a save as the one I made in extra-time, but it was an equally important moment. We were losing 3-0 and if we had conceded another one it really would have been game over. Not many teams come back from 3-0 down, but 4-0? I wonder if Liverpool have ever come back from four goals down in their entire history.

As Shevchenko lined up the free-kick from just over 20 yards out I looked for a gap in the wall, but there wasn't one. He was running up to strike the ball and I couldn't see it. I didn't know if it would go over the wall or to either side of it. The ball was tapped towards him and as it was, Milan Baros and Didi rushed out to try and charge it down.

Suddenly, I saw the ball flying towards me at pace. I'd barely dived to my left when I got one of my hands to it and pushed it wide. Thankfully, it was the whole of my hand, not just my fingertips. If I'd only got my fingertips to it then it would have been a goal for sure. He hit it that well.

When you watch replays of that goal, one of the English commentators, Clive Tyldesley, says: "Good save! I don't know how much Jerzy Dudek saw of that but he threw himself away to his left to deny Andriy Shevchenko." I can answer that question of how much I saw of the ball now – not much! I was so lucky to make that save!

A moment later the Miracle of Istanbul began. Our six magical minutes started when Maldini gave the ball away on the edge of our box. We began a counter-attack which ended with Ginge swinging a cross into the box. Stevie rose high, swivelled his neck as he met the ball and sent a powerful header that flew past Dida as he scrambled across his line. Three-one, with 54 minutes on the clock.

The Liverpool fans were mainly in the end behind the goal I was now defending and as Stevie ran back towards the halfway line he gave a 'come on, make some noise, we can do this' gesture with his arms towards them. We suddenly had a glimmer of hope. Our skipper had pulled one back and we still had over half-an-hour to play.

Our fans responded by upping the noise levels. The AC Milan fans, behind the goal at the other end, had been whistling when we had possession but now they were a little quieter. Now we were getting much more possession of the ball.

Having Didi in the middle of the pitch had changed things. Kaka could no longer run the show with Didi there and it was Hamann who set up our second goal two minutes later. He passed the ball to Smicer on his right-hand side who took one touch and fired a low shot goalwards which Dida tried to save but the ball sneaked past him and nestled in the bottom corner. Three-two!

Vladi ran back towards the halfway line screaming and shouting with his arms raised aloft. The noise behind me was phenomenal!

We left the dressing room fearing it could end up five or six-nil. Now we had scored two goals in three minutes and it was the Milan players who looked stunned. I remembered what Alex Miller said – "they'll panic if you get two goals back" – so now we'd get to find out if he was right.

We were completely on top at this point. The Liverpool fans were getting louder and louder and the Milan players were sinking deeper and deeper towards their own goal. It felt like we had to make it count, that Milan were vulnerable, and if we kept pushing forward we could get another goal. So that's what we did.

Carra surged forward with the ball and played it in to Milan Baros on the edge of the box who flicked it into the path of Stevie, who was about to shoot when he was caught from behind by Gattuso. The referee pointed to the spot but didn't show Gattuso any kind of card.

Now came the nervous part. Xabi Alonso had to convert the penalty. Xabi had never taken a penalty for us before but he had been chosen by Rafa as the designated taker, although I think Luis Garcia was asking for the responsibility until Carra stepped in. Xabi stepped up and hit it low to Dida's right but he guessed correctly and saved it. The ball came back to Xabi and he fired the rebound into the roof of the net. Three-three!

Nobody could believe it. The Milan players and fans were shocked. Six minutes ago they were cruising to victory, probably already thinking about parading the European Cup in Milan when they returned to Italy; now they had blown a three-goal lead and it looked more likely that we would get a fourth goal to win it rather than them. That never happened though.

We used a lot of adrenaline and energy to get those three

goals back and we couldn't sustain it. Maybe we even subconsciously thought 'we're back in this, we can't let it go again' and sat back a little. Maybe it was just the tiredness kicking in but there were only a couple of goalscoring opportunities before the full-time whistle. Vladi had a shot saved by Dida and Djimi cleared a shot from Shevchenko off the line after I hadn't dealt with a cross as well as I had intended to.

Then came extra-time and THAT save, the one I'll always be remembered for.

> *"When Liverpool scored the first goal I thanked God for that. It was the same with the second and the third one, but before the penalties I stopped. I knew that he could make it!"*
>
> ### Renata Dudek, mother

As I have already said, I knew it would go to penalties after I made that double-save and when the final whistle in extra-time blew I realised that I had to focus on saving the AC Milan spot-kicks. But that is easier said than done when you've got Jamie Carragher screaming in your face!

Be like Grobbelaar!

It was total chaos on the pitch after extra-time had finished. A combination of tiredness, tension and disbelief that we'd somehow turned the game around made this a very intense period. A couple of lads came over me and said some words of praise: "Great work Jerzy! Now focus on the penalties. It's your game, you can win this for us!"

Carra was the most excited. He pushed me, got right into my face and shouted at me.

"Jerzy, try to do something to put them off. Do you remember Grobbelaar? Be like him, he irritated everyone! Do the wobbly legs! Move around on the goal-line! Distract them!"

"Okay Carra, okay, okay! But leave me alone, let me focus on the penalties!"

"Remember! Do something. You have to do something! Remember Grobbelaar! You have to!"

I just kept saying "okay" to Carra as I really wanted to speak about the penalties with Ocho but I kept what he said in mind. Maybe it was worth a try.

I had a notepad in Rotterdam where I wrote down how different players took their penalties. I read somewhere that similar notes were made by the famous Dutch goalkeeper Hans van Breukelen, who was in the PSV Eindhoven goal on the night they beat Benfica on penalties in the 1988 European Cup final, so I decided to copy him and make notes for myself.

My notepad contained information on whether different opponents would take powerful or skilfully-placed penalties. If they used their right or left foot. Which side of the goal they tended to aim for or whether they would shoot straight down the middle.

I'd used the notepad during my time in Holland but at Liverpool I didn't need it. Rafa was very keen on attention to detail and before the final all the information about AC Milan's penalty and free-kick takers was put on a board in the dressing room. There were also video clips for me to watch of their players taking penalties and set-pieces.

Saving penalties is something Rafa had actually worked with me on throughout the season.

"How would you describe penalties?" he said to me. "Top,

low, middle?" You need to look at it differently. He advised me to mentally divide the goal into six squares. Starting from the top right would be squares one, two and three and from the bottom left would be squares four, five and six. I would then look at videos of opposition penalty takers and work out which 'square' they were most likely to strike their penalty towards. It took me four months to truly get my head around it and every so often Benitez would test me.

"Where is Lampard shooting? Which number?" I answered "six" – the right low corner of the goal – but everyone except myself and Rafa had no clue what we were talking about. We had our own penalty code.

While we were waiting for the shoot-out, which would be taken at the end of the Ataturk Stadium where all six goals had been scored – in front of the AC Milan fans – Ocho took out a list detailing the penalty-taking habits of their players. It was written in our code with each AC Milan player having a number next to his name. It felt like that list was as long as a toilet roll!

"I'm not going to remember all this," I said to Ocho. "You need to help me." I tried to convince him to stand behind the goal to give me instructions, but obviously the referee wasn't going to allow him to do this, so I came up with another plan instead.

"Before each penalty I'm going to look at you. Stand up and raise your hands. If you raise one hand, I'll go left, if you raise two, I'll go right. That's all you can do from the distance, but it will help me."

I'm not sure if many people noticed this, but it was actually Scott Carson who would raise his hands to signal which way I should dive. Ocho would look at his notes and tell him which arm to raise as each of their players walked down towards me. But it wasn't an easy call for Ocho to make. Some players vary their penalties so I could see some consternation in Ocho's face every single time he had to make a decision on which way I should dive.

It reminded me of when ski jumping coaches have to wave a flag to signal when their ski jumper should start his descent down the slope. He is waiting for perfect wind conditions before he waves that flag, but it's a test of nerve as to when he does so in the time allotted before a jump must be made.

The ski jumper puts his faith in his coach to make that call and that is what I did with Ocho. Scott's arms would effectively be my flag.

Spaghetti legs

AC Milan would take their penalties first and the first man to step up was Serginho, their Brazilian winger, who had taken and scored the first penalty in their 2003 Champions League final penalty shoot-out victory against Juventus at Old Trafford. He was one of three specialist penalty takers that Carlo Ancelotti, AC Milan's coach, had on the pitch, so naturally he selected him to go first.

Before he took the penalty I grabbed the ball and tried to look into his eyes. Then, as I handed it to him, I said: "Same as usual, mate? You'll shoot to the same side as you usually do, right?"

I don't know if he understood me. I had no idea if he spoke English. It was just a game to try and mess with his head. Even if he didn't understand me, I wanted to confuse him by talking at him. I wanted to dominate the penalty shoot-out, to give the impression that I was in charge, even to the referee! I wanted to show the AC Milan players that I ruled on the pitch, not them or the referee.

I needed to show I was confident, relaxed and make my opponents feel uncomfortable. That's why I reacted flippantly to the ref when he told me to get back onto the goal-line. "I'll go when I'm ready, ref, I'm in charge here."

I had spotted the signal from Scott and now I had no interest in anything else other than the ball and the penalty-taker. Nothing else. I was focused like never before in my life. It was like I was in a trance. After my save in extra-time it felt like I had received a shot of confidence and I also had what Carra had said to me in the back of my mind.

When Serginho placed the ball on the spot, I started to move my hands. I wanted him to pay attention to what was going on in the goal. When he looked at me, I moved. I stopped when he stopped. He looked again, so I raised my hands and started to move them like I was communicating in semaphore. Then, while he was preparing to take his run-up, I moved right and left on the line. Maybe he got confused at seeing me do this. Perhaps it created uncertainty in his mind.

Usually the player knows where he wants to shoot before he steps up to take a penalty. The decision is already made. But after my antics on the goal-line I wonder if it made Serginho change his mind?

As he took the kick I dived to my right as planned, but I didn't need to make a save. Serginho sliced the ball high and wide. "This is it!" I thought, "Keep it going."

Didi was our first taker. He was the most experienced player in our squad and calm in these situations. As he stepped up I wondered if Dida would try to distract our players in the same way that I was doing. Two years earlier, AC Milan had beaten Juventus on penalties in the Champions League final and Dida had saved three penalties in the shoot-out.

However, he was heavily criticised for being allowed to get away with moving a long way off his line before the kicks were taken. I don't know if he was thinking about that in Istanbul, but he stayed completely still with his arms at his side until the very last second when Didi was taking his run-up.

Didi showed great composure. He struck the ball powerfully to the right of Dida, who dived that way, and it nestled in the bottom corner. **One-nil** for us and I knew that if I could stop the second penalty we could be in a very commanding position.

Andrea Pirlo was next. I looked towards our bench and Scott had one hand raised so I was meant to go left. I stared at Pirlo. I tried to look directly into his eyes. Then I started dancing on the line. I waved my arms, squatted down, jumped up and moved from left to right. Pirlo ran towards the ball slowly. He was trying to provoke me to dive early so he could then slot the ball to the other side, but it didn't work.

As he slowly stepped forward, so did I, taking a couple of steps towards him but without diving. Pirlo couldn't delay his penalty any longer and he struck the ball to my right. I dived the right way and saved the penalty, but I'd taken so many steps by now I was about three metres off the line!

Dida started to scream at the referee. He was demanding it should be retaken.

In that split second I thought to myself that if I looked at the ref it would be an admission of guilt, that I knew I was too far off my line and would be giving him a reason to tell Pirlo to retake the penalty.

So instead I turned away from him, raised both of my arms in the air and then looked towards the AC Milan fans behind the goal. It may have looked like I was being arrogant, but that wasn't my intention.

When I turned back towards him I heard the whistle which meant he had allowed the penalty to stand. Dida was still furious, so as I walked past him to the part of the pitch where a goalkeeper must wait while his team-mates are taking penalties I shouted at him in English: "You did the same two years ago, don't you remember?!" He made a gesture at me. "Calm down," I said, smiling at him.

You can't beat the emotions you feel at moments like that. It doesn't even cross your mind if the other person understands you. There are so many things going on in your head but really you just want to enjoy the moment no matter how tense it is.

Djibril, who came on as a substitute for Milan Baros late in the second half, was our second taker. Again Dida stayed still and Djibril sent him the wrong way, confidently slotting the ball low to his left. **Two-nil**. Now the attention was back on me and I really, really wanted to save the next one.

Jon Dahl Tomasson was next. He was my best mate when we played for Feyenoord. He must have taken loads of penalties against me in training in the past but he wasn't someone who always did the same thing. I tried to talk to him as I handed him the ball, but he didn't react. He was ice-cool. He didn't even look at me before he started his run-up.

Jon is very aggressive so I thought he might try a powerful shot, but he was also a player who could place skilful penalties into the net too. In this instance I simply had to guess which way he would choose to go. Bizarrely, as he ran up to take it, an ambulance drove past on the running track behind the goal. I wasn't aware of this at the time – it's only something that I've noticed on the replays – but even that didn't distract Jon. I dived to the left and he struck a hard shot low to the right, but fairly centrally. **Two-one**. That annoyed me. Had I dived to my right there was a good chance I would have saved it, but now it was Ginge up next.

Ginge was always one of our best penalty takers in training. He always put his foot through the ball, smashing it into the net. He never missed either and I fully expected him to extend our lead. Unfortunately the situation stressed him out. He felt under pressure.

I think he lacked confidence from the past when he had taken penalties and instead of his usual powerful shot, he tried to beat Dida with a light, precise penalty low to the right. Dida saved it. It dispirited me a bit – Milan could go level at 2-2 if they scored next – but I stayed focused.

"Keep focused! Stay focused on your penalties and do your job," I said to myself. "Don't you dare be happy with the things you have already done. What if you concede all the rest of the penalties and Dida saves his? What kind of satisfaction will you have if you saved a penalty, but lost anyway?"

I'd experienced this kind of situation in the past and I know how it hurts. A goalkeeper gets praised for saving penalties in a shoot-out but it is no consolation if you lose the game.

Kaka, Brazil's star player at the time, was AC Milan's fourth penalty taker. I decided it was time to copy Bruce Grobbelaar and do the 'spaghetti legs' that had put the Roma players off when Liverpool won the European Cup on penalties in Rome in 1984. I moved to the left, to the right, wobbled my legs and moved forward off my line but Kaka wasn't distracted. He hit the ball high to my right as I dived to the left. **Two-two**. We still had a penalty in hand though and Vladi walked forward to take it.

This was to be Vladi's last game for Liverpool. His career at Anfield hadn't quite gone as well as he had hoped it would, but he now had the opportunity to end it in the best way possible. I was quite surprised that Rafa selected Vladi to take a spot-kick, but he took his penalty with great confidence. Dida dived to the right again and Vladi went left. **Three-two**. And that meant all the pressure was now on Milan's fifth penalty-taker, who just happened to be the man I had made my miracle save from in extra-time.

Andriy Shevchenko had won the Ballon d'Or only a few months earlier. But now the pressure was on him.

If he missed, or I saved it, we would win the European Cup, but I didn't realise that as he walked towards me. He looked stressed, worried. Like a man with the weight of the world on his shoulders.

Two years before he had converted the penalty that won the Champions League for AC Milan in Manchester, but this was a totally different pressure. Sheva had to score to save their asses so it didn't surprise me that he was feeling the heat.

I had hold of the ball as he reached the penalty area and as I passed it to him I gave him something else to think about. "Andriy? Andriy? Will you shoot the same way as usual?"

As he ran up to strike the ball I danced around on the goal-line again. I waved my arms, jumped and did the wobbly legs.

I think it created uncertainty in his mind as when he reached the ball he almost stopped. He wanted to shoot to my right side but at the last second he spotted that I was diving that way so tried to change his mind and put the ball in the opposite corner. But it was too late. He couldn't adjust his body and sent the ball straight down the middle.

I was hanging in the air like someone had miraculously held me there. It was like slow motion as the ball came towards me. I raised my left hand and my left leg as I dived to my right in the hope I would get something on it. The ball hit my left hand. It landed one metre in front of the goal-line. **I saved it! I saved it! I SAVED IT!!!**

I leapt to my feet, ran right past the referee and when I saw the rest of my team-mates running towards me the realisation that it was all over hit me. So did the lads! The other 10 players who had been lining up on the halfway line, the subs and all the rest of the squad jumped on top of me. I was lying on the ground with a pile of Liverpool players on top of me! It was total madness, a sense of euphoria I had never experienced before and cannot accurately describe now.

We had won the Champions League. We were champions of Europe. After being 3-0 behind at half-time. And I had made the crucial penalty save. It was beyond my wildest dreams!

"I couldn't stand the penalties. I turned my back to the screen. When my friends started to shake me, I knew that either Jurek had saved one or Liverpool had scored. And they shook me quite frequently so I knew it wasn't too bad! After the last penalty they lifted me up and I was flying towards the ceiling! I was passed from hands to hands in the air and they started to sing. Someone

went out and plucked a big lilac bouquet for me and all the pub was chanting 'Jerzy Dudek, Jerzy Dudek!' I was achy all over. That game took more out of me than it did out of Jurek in Istanbul!"

Mirella Dudek, wife

"Szczygłowice went crazy. There were people on the street below our windows. I didn't even know that my daughter-in-law was with them. When we came to the windows, the people started to chant 'Thank you, thank you…'"

Renata Dudek, mother

'Last-minute' trip

While we were waiting for the presentation, Benitez came over to me on the pitch and, without displaying any emotion, said to me: "Tell me, Jerzy, why did you dive in completely different directions than we showed you?"

He was right. I think I dived three times in the opposite direction than I should have done according to the signals that were being made on the touchline for me from Scott and Ocho. Unlike the incredibly serene Rafa, I hadn't thought of that in the midst of all the celebrations, but I'm glad I did dive the opposite way!

They brought a stage out onto the pitch for the trophy to be presented to us on and then came the moment when, one by one, we stepped up to receive our medals and the cup of our dreams. I had a million thoughts in my head. How on earth could I explain that we won this final having been 3-0 down at half-time? I was laughing to myself thinking about it; I felt like I was in paradise!

It felt to me like God himself had helped us. Like he had looked at how badly we played in the first half and showed us mercy by guiding us on this last-minute trip to the presentation to receive the cup.

Personally, I had my own 'last-minute' moment with God at the very end of the match: 'There you go Dudek. For all those years of your hard work, patience and persistence. This is also for those who believed in you, even after the first half in Istanbul. Thousands at the stadium, millions in Poland and England'.

We had to receive an injection of impetus from somewhere – positive fluids I would call it – and for us to turn that result around was divine intervention. It cannot be explained in another way. There is no rational explanation.

AC Milan went to collect their runners-up medals first. When I saw Jon Dahl Tomasson's face as he walked past me I thought he might have punched the president of UEFA after being handed his medal!

No-one likes to lose, Jon particularly, so to have done so after being in such a commanding position at half-time must have really hurt. Somebody said that a few of the AC Milan players threw their runners-up medals away. I guess they didn't ever want to be reminded of the Miracle of Istanbul whereas we, on the other hand, wanted to lap up every minute.

I felt relaxed. I felt happy. I felt proud. It was like I'd woken up in a private paradise. Like I was now in a world where there would be sunny holidays and Sundays only, no problems at all, no duties, no rush. A world where you can smell and enjoy the freshly-ground coffee. That's exactly what I thought about while waiting for the presentation in the Ataturk Stadium.

Did I think about my haters? Would those who regularly criticised me finally get off my back? Let's say I announced an amnesty for my feelings towards them. This was a moment to celebrate a success, not think about those who doubted me.

As I held the European Cup aloft and felt the red ribbon of my golden winner's medal hanging around my neck I felt euphoric, but still I couldn't believe it. For the first time in my life I was so proud of myself. I could do anything with that medal! I was so happy that I almost did some crazy stuff!

We were all celebrating in front of the thousands upon thousands of Liverpool fans and I spotted my friends from Tychy in the crowd. I wanted to give them the European Cup so they could lift it too! This possibly wasn't the best of ideas though. It could have ended up being passed around the whole crowd! So I only took the flag with 'TYCHY' written on it and celebrated holding it on the pitch.

On the opposite side of the stadium I saw other Polish supporters who threw me the beautiful Polish flag with our national emblem on it. I draped it over my back to show how proud I was that the Champions League winners had a Polish player in their ranks.

To get the flag I had climbed over the advertising hoardings but I had a problem when I tried to return to my team-mates on the pitch. There was a melee of players and photographers and they were all surrounded by security guards who obviously wanted to stop any fans from getting onto the pitch.

One of the security guards thought I was a fan so prevented me from getting back onto the pitch! I tried to explain to him that I was one of the players, but he wasn't having it! I stepped away from him, moved a bit further down and jumped back over the advertising boards. He tried to follow me, but thankfully one of his mates recognised me and convinced him that I really was a Liverpool player who had just won the European Cup!

The gloves that held the cup

As a kid I dreamt about owning real goalkeeper gloves and I used to play in my dad's work gloves because one pair of them had a rough surface on the palm to get more grip. They were too big for me so I sewed part of my shoes into them to grasp my hand better!

I also tried to attach the surface of a table tennis bat to some gloves to give more grip but it wouldn't glue on! I drew logos, such as adidas, onto them too, but when coach Słabkowski saw this during my time at Górnik Knurów he said I should be ashamed to wear such things and got me some proper gloves which had red and blue dye on that stained your hands when it was wet!

After my 16th birthday I decided to invest in a pair of professional gloves and got a pair of 'Walter Zenga Uhlsport' that cost me 117 Deutschmarks [about £45] from a friend in Germany. It was a lot of money but I felt on top of the world when I got them.

I wore adidas gloves when I played for Feyenoord and until 2004 when I was approached by a company called Sells, owned by Adam Sells, an amateur goalkeeper who had dreamed of playing at a high level and created a brand that was exclusively for goalkeepers.

During the group stage of the 2004/05 Champions League, Adam had a premonition that I would lift the European Cup in a pair of Sells gloves. I thought he was bonkers, but when I lifted the cup in the Ataturk Stadium I thought of Adam because his dream had also come true.

"Jurek called me in the middle of the night. I started to cry: 'Son, I was praying for you. I thought you were going to lose.' 'Mum, I still can't believe what just happened...'"

Renata Dudek, mother

My new wife!

It was about 2.30am when we finally got back to the hotel in Istanbul. We had a party to celebrate and Jacek Krzynówek was with me. I invited him to Istanbul and told him that for this trip he will be my wife! Mirella had to stay in Poland so I gave Jacek the ticket I had for her. Now he was my 'plus-one' at the post-match party!

So it was me, Jacek, my agent Jan de Zeeuw and my closest friends from Poland. They had travelled to Istanbul in a little Peugeot 206 and had as many adventures on the way to Turkey as I had in the final.

I took plenty of pictures with my medal and the only thing I missed that night was smoking a cigar. They say that you have to smoke a cigar after that kind of success! I felt that something special had just happened and some of the other lads smoked cigars, but I didn't.

Around 5.30am everyone returned to their rooms. We could have partied all night, but the lads were probably afraid that they would not be able to wake up for the plane back to Liverpool in a few hours' time. There was only me and Jacek who were left in the hotel restaurant.

"Unbelievable! Can you imagine what this party would look like in Poland?" Jacek said to me. "It would be hard to take the lads back to the plane!" It was at this point that he realised how professional a team Liverpool was.

Suddenly all the lights came on. It was the manager of the hotel restaurant and he asked if we'd like to order any more drinks as they wanted to close the bar. "No problem, but if you're closing, we're going to help you with the cleaning," I joked. "It'll be faster!"

And that's how I finished celebrating the Miracle of Istanbul – helping the waiters to clean the restaurant after our party!

> *"When I woke up the following day I started to wonder if that game had really happened: 'God, is that a dream? Did it really happen?' I thought to myself. I turned the TV on and I saw the replays and highlights from Istanbul. I finally watched those penalties. I didn't recognise my husband! I couldn't believe that he had danced so crazily in the goal. Then I saw that joy and all of his team-mates running to celebrate Liverpool's success. Jurek always called after games. He did after Istanbul as well, but in all the madness I couldn't answer as I didn't hear the phone, so he called me again in the morning. We started to cry tears of happiness."*
>
> **Mirella Dudek, wife**

Welcome home!

We flew back to Liverpool on Thursday and next up was a tour of the city with the European Cup.

I have never seen scenes like it. There were probably around a million people on the streets! They were standing on roofs, up trees, hanging from road signs. It was like a sea of red running through the streets!

I was on the upper deck of the bus for about four hours and by the end of that journey – which took so long because the bus could barely move through the crowds of people – I was more tired than after the game! But it was worth it.

I will never forget how our supporters cheered us on that bus. You cannot forget a day like that. It was unbelievable.

I went up to the front of the bus and held the European Cup aloft. I smiled and celebrated with my team-mates and supporters until a moment when I saw what was in front of us. There were policemen on horses who were making a path for the bus to pass between the crowds of people.

Then, to my horror, one of the horses started to panic for some reason and struck one of the officers. Someone pushed another horse, someone fell down and it was all a bit chaotic. There were so many kids down there too. It calmed down a bit later when the horses got used to the huge crowds, but the first minutes of being at the front of that bus were terrifying! I went through more unpredictable emotions than I did during the final!

I stood at the back of the bus for much of the journey, which took us through the streets to Liverpool city centre where there were huge crowds amassed in front of St George's Hall and by Lime Street Station.

After the celebrations I was talking to some police officers and they asked me about the final, saying that I did a great job to make the saves that I did. "Thank you, but today you were the heroes," I said to them. "You controlled everything perfectly and no-one got seriously hurt." I was full of appreciation for

Merseyside Police. They did a massive job that afternoon to keep control of so many excited people.

There was no time to rest when I finally got home. I had to pack my bag as I was in a hurry to catch a flight back to Poland for my son's Holy Communion.

I had a morning flight from Manchester to Katowice via Warsaw and was sitting on the plane when the captain made an announcement: "Ladies and gentlemen, let me warmly welcome onto this flight our hero from Istanbul, Mr Jerzy Dudek. Congratulations!" All of the plane started to clap. Tears welled up in my eyes. It was simply wonderful.

Alexander's little sins

We had previously had to postpone my son Alex's Holy Communion because of the Champions League final. We moved it from Katowice to the little village Piechotne, near Kielce, where my wife's family lives.

I arrived in Katowice and travelled with all the guests by hired bus. I felt great surrounded by my close friends. I was at home, happy, fulfilled.

Finally, I had some time to reply to the messages I had been sent. After the final I received about 100 text messages with the congratulations from friends, but had been so busy that I hadn't had the chance to reply. It took me a few days to get back to them, but I think my friends forgave me for that!

Alexander was very stressed about his Holy Communion. He asked me about the confession, where you confess any sins you have committed, to the priest. I told him that when I was his age, I had the same list of sins: I lied to parents, I messed up, I fought with my brother, I behaved badly in school and outside.

He took a piece of paper and started to write things down. He confessed properly. While he was doing his confession, his daddy had to confess his sins too.

To be honest, it took me a bit longer than Alex! When I had finished confessing I saw Alex running across the – luckily almost empty – church screaming: "Daddy, why were you in there for so long? What did the priest say to you?"

I was so proud of him. Again, tears welled up in my eyes. I think all the emotions from the past week started to release. It's a period of my life I will never, ever forget.

A NEW
RIVAL

Although we had won the Champions League in the most dramatic of circumstances we had failed to finish in the top four of the Premier League and with UEFA having changed their rules so that the European Cup winners don't automatically qualify for the following season, the club had to spend the summer arguing that we should be allowed to defend our title. Eventually UEFA relented, but forced us to play in the three qualifying rounds, starting on July 13!

Despite this, Rafa gave the international players an extra week off before pre-season training, but when I returned to Melwood I had a new rival. Jose 'Pepe' Reina, a Spanish international, had been signed from Villarreal for a reported £6 million. I wasn't happy and went straight in to see Benitez, who tried to calm me down.

"It doesn't mean that I'll let you go."

"What will my role be? You don't buy a player for so much money to leave him on the bench..."

"Okay, it is true, Pepe will be my number one at the start, but I will look at him for a while to see how he settles and plays. Keep working hard, there will be plenty of games for you in the League Cup and FA Cup."

"No offence, but I'm not happy to just play in the cups. I want to play in the World Cup next summer. If I don't play for Liverpool I might not get to play for Poland. It is very important to me."

"I understand. Two days ago Scott came in and said the same. He's not happy to be third choice. I told him perhaps he will play in the cup games..."

"So I might not even play in the League Cup? The situation is clear then. There's no point talking about it if you can't even guarantee me games in the League Cup."

"Jerzy, wait. I really like your professional approach. You're a true professional. I don't have any problems with you. It's the troublemakers I want to get rid of, that's why we paid up the rest of Luzi's contract. I don't need people like him, but I want you to stay."

"Should I look for a new club or will you take care of selling me?"

"Be patient. You need to see how things go."

"I've got two years remaining on my contract. How much will the club want for me?"

"We can't let a good international keeper go to another club for peanuts."

"How much? Be realistic."

"Okay, let's wait for serious offers. Then we'll start to talk money. We'll find a good solution for everybody."

Benitez said that he wouldn't play me in the Champions League so that I wasn't cup-tied. It made sense. We'd only get serious offers from clubs playing in Europe and having been a Champions League winner in May with Liverpool I wanted to continue playing in that competition if I was to move on.

In the meantime I started to train with Pepe and he made a great impression on me from the very first minute. I realised straight away there would be no problems between us and we became good mates, like I had been with Westerveld. The atmosphere was good in training and the press asked me about him: "He's a good goalkeeper, but it's hard to rate him only on his training work," I said. "He'll have plenty of occasions to show his skills – what happens on the pitch will prove everything. It's hard to accept my current situation after the Istanbul final, but that's life."

Pepe is a great lad with amazing personality and a good sense of humour. He's very open, creative and full of interesting ideas. I prefer people like Pepe to robots who only follow orders from the manager. Pepe has many off-the-pitch attributes. He integrates with people quickly and even recommended me to Villarreal when I was considering my future: "Talk to them. I'll help you. It is a really nice club. I'll put a word in for you."

Physically, Pepe is very strong. During training sessions we were divided into groups to train with players who had similar physical strengths. Pepe, Riise and Bolo Zenden were in the strongest group. I trained with players like Sami. Pepe was also our 'social secretary'. He was the initiator of buying the gifts to be handed out during the Christmas party – I think they call it 'Secret Santa' in England – and he was at the forefront of helping Benitez to integrate the team away from the pitch. We became room-mates and supported each other through highs and lows.

If you want to see what Pepe is like then have a look on YouTube for the videos of Spain celebrating when they won Euro 2008, the 2010 World Cup and Euro 2012. He may not have been first choice for Spain, but he was the leader in the celebrations. Standing on a stage alongside his team-mates with thousands upon thousands of fans in the streets of Madrid, Pepe took the microphone and went crazy! He was a spontane-ous master of ceremonies. He got the crowd singing *Camarero* and improvised by introducing every single player one by one. It was a one-man show. And he did this three times! That is Pepe for you and I found it easier to get used to being the deputy goalkeeper because it was him I was second choice to.

Technically, there are better goalkeepers than Pepe and he made some mistakes when not catching the ball properly, but his distribution was exceptional – he could create goals himself – and he was very confident and dominating in his penalty area, something that is important in the Premier League. He would also try to help me when I was selected. I saved a penalty in a League Cup defeat to Arsenal in 2007 with Pepe's help. He told me if Julio Baptista got the chance to take a penalty he would put it to my right-hand side about a metre high. Arsenal got a penalty and Baptista struck it very hard to my right-hand side about a metre off the ground. I saved it and pointed to the bench when I did to thank Pepe. A penalty save would improve my chances of being in the team more regularly, so it says a lot about Pepe that he still passed on that advice. He's a class act.

A NEW RIVAL

In two minds

After a couple of weeks of training with Pepe I decided that I could, and would, compete with him for a place in goal. I didn't want to move from Liverpool – the fans gave me so much energy after Istanbul – I believed in myself and I enjoyed working with Ocho so I decided that I would fight for my place unless a serious offer came in.

> *"I received calls from Sporting Lisbon, Werder Bremen and Roma about Jurek that summer. I also heard rumours about Fenerbahce. I directed them all to Liverpool, but no-one came back to me after speaking to the club."*
>
> **Jan de Zeeuw, agent**

I was still in two minds over whether to stay when the season started though. I loved being at Liverpool, but Benitez clearly didn't want me. I'd been the hero in Istanbul so could I now just be a fire-fighter who waits for the moment when a fire needs fighting? If this was Poland, the media and fans would have demanded that I play, but I didn't have that support in England. Then rumours started that I was earning between £60-70k per week and Benitez wanted me off the wage bill. I wondered if someone had made this story up to try and turn the Liverpool supporters against me. I was confused, so I spoke with Ocho about what he thought Benitez was up to.

"You want to leave? No? He said he will discuss serious offers for you? I am absolutely against that. I'm going to tell him you're not for sale!"

Ocho went in to see Benitez and from that moment on there was never any suggestion that I would be sold. Despite what he had said about ensuring I wouldn't be cup-tied, he put me on the bench for the Champions League qualifying game away to FBK Kaunas in Lithuania and then Ocho told me that Benitez had decided I would play away at CSKA Sofia in the next round despite the fact that I'd missed three days training with an Achilles tendon injury. I wasn't sure I was fully ready to play, but I also knew this was my chance to prove I should be playing. Then disaster struck...

'Call an ambulance'

It's Sod's Law that just when things are starting to go well for you in football something bad happens. I was still on a high after Istanbul and about to play my first game of the season, so inevitably something was about to go wrong. And it did.

Most of the lads were already back in the dressing room when Ocho did some shot-stopping practice with me. He would run through on goal then shoot. It was a routine exercise. He ran through and shot to my right so I dived in that direction, but as I did so my right hand somehow got hooked in the grass. My arm was straight so didn't bear the tension, resulting in a dislocation of my right elbow. I didn't want to fall on the arm so at the last second I turned my body and fell on my left shoulder. If I hadn't done that, I would probably have had a dislocation fracture. Even now I wince when thinking about it.

I was in shock when I saw my elbow. It was bent in the wrong direction! I yelled for the doctor. I was convinced it was broken. I noticed the panicked reaction of the people around me. Ocho shouted for the doctor too. My whole career flashed before my eyes. 'There you go, you didn't enjoy Istanbul enough, you were thinking should you stay or should you go, now you've got a broken arm and plenty of free time to think about it'. I didn't feel any pain at that point. Ocho screamed: "No, no... don't touch anything. Call the doctor!" But I instinctively turned my right wrist towards me and I heard a 'click' as the bone went back into place. Then I felt it. "Call an ambulance!"

"I can still see what happened clearly in my head; it's like a movie. I see the bone and how it jumped from the joint. It looked terrible. I admire Jerzy for his composure and cool head. He behaved like an experienced surgeon and slotted the bone back into place. I couldn't have done it!"

Pepe Reina, former Liverpool goalkeeper

I felt like I was losing consciousness when the doctor arrived. "Docky, I've broken my elbow. Give me something to drink." "No, not now." "I'm losing you Docky, I can't hear you. Give me a drink." "I can't." "Give me a f***ing drink!" Finally he passed me a bottle and I drank half of it. He later explained that he was concerned I'd drink too much in one go and send my sugar levels rocketing. The doc cut my gloves off and helped me to my feet. I can still remember the pale faces of my team-mates as I was led away to the doctor's office and all the time the pain was getting worse. Docky gave me some painkillers but it took 20 minutes for them to kick in. During that time I punched the wall of his office with my left hand. "What are you doing?" "I'm trying to kill the pain, I can't stand it any more." I was so frustrated at what had happened to me but punching the wall was a bad idea. By the time we got to the hospital my left hand was sore as well! I phoned Mirella on the way to hospital but because I had played some pranks in the past she didn't believe me at first! It was a similar story with my parents and my agent Jan was very emotional when I told him. The first x-ray didn't go well. It was painful to do and I wanted to howl like a dog when I had to do it again, but it showed a hairline fracture on one of the bones. They scanned my ligaments and muscles too.

Jan called Rien Heijboer, a fantastic orthopaedic surgeon who used to work as a doctor for Feyenoord. Jan described everything in detail to him and Heijboer asked if I could move my fingers. When Jan said yes he said that the arm is not broken, but I should ensure the blood supply is not affected by squeezing half a tennis ball with my right hand as often as I can. I didn't have one on me at the time! But I was grateful for his advice.

I felt better the next day. I could move my arm a little and I went to see a broken elbow expert who was used to treating rugby players. He asked me to explain what happened in detail and when I said that I'd popped my elbow back into place myself he shook his head: "I have no idea how you did it, but you did a perfect job! It was a one-in-ten chance you could have done it so well. Most people still need surgery."

Within three days I could rotate my fist, but I suffered a haemorrhage in the joint capsule. My arm looked massive. I had massages at Melwood to get rid of the fluid in my elbow! I went back to see the expert a week later and he couldn't believe my progress. They thought I would be out for three months – six months if a break had been discovered – but I was now able to do exercises with the ball after three weeks and return to full training three weeks after that. Unfortunately, though, I missed out on playing in a game that I had earned the right to play in.

Monaco

We faced UEFA Cup winners CSKA Moscow in Monaco in the European Super Cup in August. My elbow injury meant I was unable to play so ahead of the game I questioned whether I should bother travelling there to sit in the stands. But then I thought to myself about the massive contribution I made towards Liverpool winning the Champions League and decided that I should be part of things, even if I couldn't play. Stevie was also injured so I wasn't the only one to be missing out. In any case, I was invited to attend a ceremony before the match – and the Champions League group stage draw which we were in – by UEFA after being nominated for the UEFA Best Goalkeeper of the Season award with Petr Cech, who won, and Gianluigi Buffon, so I travelled to Monaco with the lads.

We stayed in a beautiful hotel with a really nice view over the principality. I was amazed by it and for once could enjoy my surroundings as I didn't have the match to stress about. Ronaldinho came to say hello to me during the ceremony and I was with Michał Listkiewicz, the president of the Polish FA, when Michel Platini came over to us. Listkiewicz introduced me to him: "This is Jerzy Dudek, our goalkeeper." Platini looked at me and said: "Yeah, I know you. You're lucky that you didn't play during my time! It wouldn't have been so easy for you!" A moment later he added: "I was only joking."

I also got talking to staff from Villarreal. They were interested in my availability and asking about the condition my elbow was in as they were looking for a goalkeeper to go straight into the side for their first Champions League group game. Unfortunately I wouldn't be fit but I joked that I'd jump into their bags and go back to Spain with them. I was standing with Liverpool's chairman David Moores and chief executive Rick Parry during the conversation and after they left the chairman spoke up.

"Who were they?"

I was surprised. "Don't you know them, sir? You bought Pepe Reina from them last month."

"Oh, is that who they are? I thought they were people you knew from Poland..."

A Polish TV company asked me to commentate on the game and our commentary position was at the very top of one of the stands in the Stade Louis II stadium. CSKA took the lead, but Cisse came on and equalised to send the game into extra-time. Djibril scored again and then Luis Garcia got another to give us a 3-1 win. Two minutes before the final whistle I told Polish TV viewers I was going down to the pitch to be with the lads but when I got to the elevator I was stopped by three security guards. I explained that I was a Liverpool player and we were about to receive the cup, but they didn't care. They told me the elevator was not to be used until the Prince of Monaco had made his way to the pitch so I should go and find the stairs. So I ran down the stairs, but they took me to a different area from where you couldn't access the pitch.

I was getting desperate now and considered jumping in with the Liverpool supporters – who were all cheering me! – and then trying to get over the fence, but thankfully a steward was on hand to show me a different way and he opened some doors that gave me access to the pitch.

I missed the trophy and medals presentation – they were firing red confetti into the air when I finally got to the stage – and one of the physios, Mark Browse, asked where I'd been and why I didn't have a medal. I explained what happened and Mark gave me his medal. I felt awkward about this, but he explained the club would receive extra medals for the staff so I finally got my hands on the European Super Cup with another medal hanging around my neck. We celebrated in front of the Liverpool supporters and although I hadn't played I felt I had made my contribution by getting us to this match in the first place. You've got to win it to be in it after all!

Desperate to leave

The main problem with my rehab was the fluid that kept building up in my elbow. In the end the doctor punctured through my skin and drained 55 millilitres of the stuff. I had more fluid drained the following day. I was able to start training again after five weeks wearing a device that kept my right arm stiff and the focus was on me making saves with my right arm. I was called up for Poland's final World Cup qualifier against England in October, but I wasn't yet ready. We had already qualified anyway by winning eight of our opening nine games, but with Artur Boruc deputising for me it made me focus again on how desperate I was to play in the World Cup and whether that would happen if I wasn't playing regularly for Liverpool.

I was back on the bench when we played Anderlecht on November 1 and I was regularly asking Rafa about my future. His response was always the same: "We'll help you with that. If the club receive a concrete offer we'll discuss it." Maybe I was naïve to believe him because, to be honest, he didn't help me at all. HSV Hamburg and Benfica were interested and the prospect of moving to Portugal was especially exciting as my old Feyenoord team-mate, Ronald Koeman, was the coach there. He knew what I was capable of from the extra training sessions I had with him in Rotterdam and he tried to convince me to attempt to win a title in a different country. Liverpool were interested in Simao at the time so there was speculation that I would move to Lisbon as part of a deal in the January transfer window. As we flew out to Japan a fortnight before Christmas for the World Club Championship I did so thinking a move to Portugal could be on in the new year.

Bright lights of Japan

It was an amazing experience to travel to Japan and be involved in the World Club Championship. This competition is still not treated seriously enough and I don't understand why. We, however, treated it very seriously. Rafa planned everything to the most tiny detail and was so determined to win it.

Our flight took 12 hours, but to counter the jet lag and time difference we weren't allowed to sleep. The doctor ran up and down the aisle waking up anyone who nodded off! We also had to keep getting out of our seats and walking up and down.

When we landed in Japan we were all handed sunglasses and the coach that was taking us from the airport to the hotel had its curtains closed. Apparently the strength of the light at that time of day is far stronger in Japan than we were used to in Europe so we had to try to protect our eyes. This was the level of detail Rafa and his staff went into!

It was my first time in Japan and I was excited to see lots of things so as the coach set off I pulled back the curtain. A couple of the other lads did the same. Rafa gave us a rollicking!

"We are not here to be tourists."

"But I've never been to Japan boss..."

"We are here to do a job so do as you're told."

So the only thing we saw of Japan before we got to the hotel was through the front window of the coach! As well as he prepared things, though, I think Rafa got it wrong on the pitch. We beat Costa Rica's Deportivo Saprissa 3-0 in our semi-final with Peter Crouch, our two-metre-tall striker who had been signed in the summer, scoring twice. But despite this he put Crouch on the bench for the final against Brazil's Sao Paulo and played Fernando Morientes instead. There was no rational explanation for it. You can't say it was 'rotation' for a cup final to decide the World Club champions!

Peter had a tough start at Liverpool, he didn't score in his first 18 games, but his goals against Saprissa meant he now had four in five appearances. He was absolutely flying – full of confidence – and we could see the surprise on his face in the dressing room when he heard he wasn't playing.

We conceded a first-half goal, but Benitez waited until the 79th minute to make any substitutions. He only put Peter on with five minute to go and, although Florent Sinama-Pongolle had a late goal wrongly ruled out for offside, we lost 1-0. It was a big disappointment as it is the one big trophy that Liverpool have never won and we were all desperate to be the first players to bring it back to Anfield.

We had one-and-a-half hours of free time! It was just enough time to buy a few souvenirs. It's a lesson to anyone who thinks that a footballer has a nice life and gets to visit places in the world for free. We mostly only get to see airports, hotels and stadiums. Anyway, we had a chance to go for dinner in a Japanese restaurant – one of my favourite places to eat in Liverpool is Sapporo Teppanyaki where you can see the chef making your food in front of you. I saw something similar in Tokyo. There were plenty of smiles, energy and laughs. But I soon came back down to earth when I received some messages to tell me about the Champions League draw.

We had been in the same Champions League group as Chelsea and we both qualified, but the draw for the last 16 couldn't have been worse for me: Liverpool v Benfica. I was devastated. All the magic of a pleasant evening had gone away and I couldn't eat any of my delicious meal. I knew straight away that I could forget about my proposed move to Portugal. No club in the world would sell a player to an opponent they're about to play in the Champions League and as I wasn't cup-tied I could have played against Liverpool. The Benfica fans were also up in arms about Simao's proposed move to Liverpool so that also fell through. Ironically, after a 1-0 defeat in Lisbon, it was Simao's goal at Anfield that effectively knocked us out. Our defence of the Champions League was over and I was watching it all from the bench. I later found out that the Benfica chairman wanted five times my transfer value for Simao. So the move probably would never have happened anyway.

I wanted to punch Rafa

Benfica weren't the only club interested in me. A return to Feyenoord, now managed by Erwin Koeman, Ronald's brother, was mooted, but a transfer ban on Feyenoord due to financial issues put paid to that. The main interest was from 1. FC Köln. I received a call from their manager, Michael Meier, and in a

15-minute conversation he made it clear he was desperate for me to try to help them get off the bottom of the Bundesliga. We had played a friendly in the Rhein Energie Stadium in 2003 so I already knew they had a great bunch of supporters so I told Benitez I wanted to go there. He said it would be a good move for me, adding: "We'll definitely help you, we'll do whatever it takes to make a deal."

The negotiations started. There was an issue over whether it was a loan move first or a permanent transfer straight away. A week-and-a-half later and there was no progress. I was in touch with Meier regularly and he told me Benitez wouldn't speak to him, but was saying Köln's offer was unacceptable. They wanted to take me on loan for six months, for which Liverpool would get €800,000, then complete a permanent €3m transfer in the summer if they avoided relegation. German clubs are financially savvy – Köln knew they couldn't afford to buy me if they weren't in the top division – but Rafa refused to let me go on loan. It was a permanent deal or nothing as far as he was concerned. I tried to convince him to change his mind: "What have you got to lose? If they go down I'll come back to Liverpool and stay until my contract ends or you can sell me then. I really need to play games to be prepared for the World Cup."

He said he understood and liked my desire to be playing so negotiations with Köln continued. Three days before the transfer window closed I went in to see him again – "Relax, Jerzy, there's still time, but we want a permanent deal," – but Meier was telling me that Rafa was still refusing to take his calls! I got more and more frustrated with him until transfer deadline day when I finally boiled over. As soon as training had finished I stormed over to him and ripped my gloves off in an aggressive manner. I was so angry that the lads said later the aggression was pouring out of me. I raised my voice. The lads could see I was fuming so all hung around to see what would happen. Footballers love seeing a bit of confrontation on the training ground!

"We'll talk in a moment, Jerzy."

"No, let's talk now. What is going on with my transfer?"

"I will be honest with you, I am not interested in loaning you. If they come back today to buy you, they need to double their offer as this is the last day of the transfer window."

I was furious with him, absolutely fuming, and in my head I could hear a devilish voice saying 'punch him in the face – punch him in the face and he'll let you go to Germany'.

To be completely honest, I genuinely considered punching Rafa in the face. Then the consequences of doing so flashed through my mind. Would he let me go? Or would it just lead to a massive media scandal? Surely I couldn't stay if I gave him a smack?

I don't know how, but I managed to stop myself. Punching a Liverpool manager who had won the European Cup only a few months earlier wouldn't have looked too good on the CV I guess, but I was still angry.

"You said you'd help me. You said you'd do everything to get a deal through. You didn't mean it."

"I cannot let you go on loan. I'll get €800,000, great, but I can't spend it today and I'll be five months without an experienced reserve goalkeeper. What if Pepe gets injured next week? I'll have Scott and a kid from the Academy. Imagine the pressure I'd be under if that happened..."

"Why should I care? I haven't played all season. Scott played in the cups. You promised you would help me but now I have a concrete offer you've not kept your word."

"I cannot risk it. I repeat, if they come back in today they must pay double."

As I walked off towards the dressing room Stevie walked alongside me. "You wanted to punch him, didn't you lad? You really wanted to f***ing punch him..."

Benitez was walking a few metres behind: "Jerzy, once you get changed, come to my office please." He knew that after a shower I would have cooled off and I would react differently.

I explained to the lads in the dressing room how he'd promised to help me move but was now going back on what he said. I felt he was treating me unfairly, but that's how Rafa operated. He did everything so coldly, almost inhumanely, because he saw things as business. He had to protect his interests, but it was hard to be on the receiving end of it.

I went to his office and he said that if Köln paid €3m now and he could get a replacement in immediately he would let me go, but we both knew that wasn't going to happen. So I was stuck at Liverpool with no prospect of playing or even being on the bench. Or so I thought...

Back in the team

On the Sunday after the transfer window closed we played Chelsea at Stamford Bridge. Rafa put me back on the bench. His fear that something could happen to Pepe proved to be correct. We were 2-0 down when Pepe was sent off and I had to come on for the final eight minutes. I made a couple of saves, one from a Lampard free-kick, but we still lost 2-0. Rafa called me in the next day.

"You remember our chat from last week, no? Look what happened. Who would have gone in goal? The €800,000? Pepe will be suspended for three games so you will play against Charlton, Wigan and Arsenal. Later on you'll play two or three games in the reserves. We're still in the FA Cup, so there's maybe another two or three games to play. By the end of the season you could play in about 12-14 games."

As annoyed as I was with Rafa, I could see what he was trying to do. He realised I was well liked by the lads, a good influence in the dressing room and, because of Istanbul, was popular with the fans. Scott was only young and had some difficult moments in games when he had played so it made sense for Rafa to have an experienced back-up to Pepe while he was trying to build his own team.

I played in those three games – we lost 2-0 at Charlton and I kept clean sheets as we beat Wigan and Arsenal 1-0 – but Pepe was back in goal for the FA Cup tie against Manchester United at Anfield. We also won that 1-0.

Rafa mentioned that I would play some games for the reserves so I could stay sharp, but the only one I played in was against Blackburn Rovers in April.

Other than that I appeared in just two more Premier League games – away wins at West Ham and Portsmouth – when Pepe was rested ahead of the FA Cup final, meaning that in the season after the glory of Istanbul I made just five starts for Liverpool with only one of them coming at Anfield. I was on the bench for the FA Cup final against West Ham, which we won on penalties after Stevie scored two stunning goals in a 3-3 draw, and received a winners' medal for being part of the squad, but it was far from an ideal situation.

How Rafa worked

I happened to live in the same area as Rafa – Caldy on the Wirral peninsula – and our kids went to the same school. Sometimes we would bump into each other on the school run so not only did I get the chance to talk to him about topics other than football, I also began to understand how and why he did things by watching matches differently. I didn't give tactics a second thought before I met Rafa – I was only focused on how I would play – but I began to understand that goalkeepers need to work in co-operation with defensive systems, such as being a sweeper-keeper so you can play with a high line.

When I got injured in the summer of 2005, I had more time to observe the team from the sidelines. Plenty of things looked completely different to how you see them on the pitch. I looked at how quickly Rafa reacted to what was happeneing on the pitch, why he chose his formations and which changes he made. I always sat close to him and observed how he worked. I found it fascinating at times. I started to discover a completely new side of football and I focused on it.

Rafa is truly passionate about the game. He has a great knowledge of football. He's not a fool who comes out with bullshit theories that are all talk. He has his own ideas how to do things and usually they were justified by what happened on the pitch. His problem is that he's not a great 'people person' so always encounters problems when managing a group because he is very cold and hard-faced in how he makes decisions. He kept a distance between himself and his players – like there was an invisible wall there – but it didn't stop him from being a genius of a coach, as a couple of lads described him when I spoke with them after I left. I worked under Jose Mourinho at Real Madrid

223

and while no such thing as an ideal coach exists you'd be close to finding it if you combined his and Rafa's qualities. Mourinho had more respect in the dressing room because he was a more personable character who spoke to his players as people. It was a different philosophy, but one that helped players to accept his demands in training more than they did from Benitez.

For example, Rafa thought we weren't fit enough or tactically good enough when he arrived at Liverpool so he made us work twice as hard in training with Pako than we had been used to. In the past we would only have a light training session before a game, but Benitez would work us harder, even if we'd just had a tough match a few days earlier. Most of the lads didn't like it and Stevie was one of them.

I knew he had some issues with Rafa and twice it looked like he might leave Liverpool for Chelsea. Rafa wanted him to leave – I think he thought he could buy three or four players with the money – but deep down Stevie didn't want to go. The problem came when there was miscommunication between him and the Liverpool board. They thought Stevie wanted to go and he thought the board were thinking the same as Rafa and wanted to cash in on him. This happened twice, but somehow they managed to sort things out and Stevie stayed where he belonged. I know that the relationship between Stevie and Rafa was never the same afterwards though and because Benitez had played games with me regarding a potential transfer I was on Stevie's side, even if I decided not to say anything publicly.

Stevie once said to me that it would have been great if Mourinho could have taken over at Anfield when Rafa left. I think it was after my leaving, when I came to Liverpool as a Real Madrid player in the Champions League. I remember those words well, even if it was just a casual conversation. Mourinho has a great respect for England. His press conferences show one side of his personality and his behaviour in the tunnel and in the dressing room show the other. He shakes hands with everyone if that person behaves respectfully.

I think Liverpool could have improved under Mourinho. Stevie and Jose had a mutual respect. It's a pity that Stevie didn't come to Real. In my opinion that move would have extended his career at the top level for at least two years and he would have learned even more by playing for Mourinho.

Back to school

Just because I had issues with Rafa doesn't mean I couldn't appreciate his quality as a coach and he deserves a lot of credit for our European Cup triumph. He prepared us well and worked out Milan's weaknesses, but when things hadn't gone to plan he was capable of changing things under pressure at half-time to help us get back into the game. He made us think differently ahead of Premier League games, telling us that the traditional English 'blood-and-thunder, play with your hearts' mentality could be beaten by logical, effective football, but his preparations for Champions League games was far more detailed.

Rafa knew everything – and I mean everything – about our Champions League opponents. He drilled it into us that if we got it right tactically we could beat anybody in Europe and turned training sessions into school lessons. We had to study our opponents and answer questions on them. He would say an opponent's name – say Fabio Cannavaro of Juventus – and we had to tell him Cannavaro's strengths and weaknesses. Of course, you'd get some clichéd answers – "he's good in the air boss" – but that wasn't enough. He wanted precise answers, like if he was weaker turning to his left or right, and he wanted us to use this knowledge to help us decide how we should play against a certain opponent. I forget who the opponent was now, but the discussion between the lads and Rafa went like this.

"They often play the long balls boss."

"Correct. How do you stop it? Their forwards don't play between the lines, they prefer to head the ball.

"We need to avoid crosses coming in then boss."

"Good. So you must stop passes to the wings. Mark the wide players closely. You might not win every header but be ready for the second ball."

It was a new strategy for us all. Instead of just talking at us – players often switch off when that happens – he was getting us to think, to analyse our opponents and to tell him what he already knew. He believed that if we worked out the finer details ourselves and then he reinforced our analysis by adding information to what we had worked out ourselves it would stay in our minds better. He would then get us to put these tactical ploys into action on the training pitch.

This was the secret as to why we did so well against Chelsea in Europe. They were a better team than us over the course of a season, but we could beat them in one-off games because we knew how to counteract Mourinho's tactics: the long ball to Drogba, two wide players such as Duff or Robben or Cole running beyond him, Lampard loitering around the edge of the box for the second ball. We played them six times in the Champions League between May 2005 and April 2007 and only conceded one goal. That was down to Rafa's preparation.

BEING
HANDCUFFED

I wasn't desperate to leave Liverpool when I returned for pre-season training in the summer of 2006. I was happy living on Merseyside – it felt like home – and my family were settled so I decided that rather than push for a move I would see out the final year on my contract and make a decision about my future during the summer. Due to the Bosman Ruling I would be able to move to another club without a transfer fee having to be paid so I felt this would open up different opportunities for me, especially as trying to convince Rafa to sell me for a reasonable amount was so difficult!

New players such as Dirk Kuyt, from my old club Feyenoord, Craig Bellamy, Fabio Aurelio, Jermaine Pennant and Gabriel Paletta arrived at Liverpool that summer, but my position didn't change. I was understudy to Pepe and played just twice before

Christmas, away to Birmingham in the League Cup and, after we had already qualified for the knockout stages, away to Galatasaray in our final Champions League group game. Before that, though, I experienced something new – getting sent off!

Seeing red at Widnes

I had asked to play in the reserve team to get some football and in October 2006 we played away to Everton in the mini-derby at the Halton Stadium, home of Widnes Rugby League Club. Over 5,000 fans attended the game on a night when I received the first red card of my career.

It was a very physical game. Our Argentine defender Paletta and Everton striker Victor Anichebe spent most of the night kicking lumps out of each other and there were some meaty challenges. One of them was on me.

We were drawing 1-1 with 56 minutes on the clock when the ball was played through for Anichebe. I came off my line and dived to smother the ball, but as I did so Anichebe slid into me with both feet. He caught me in the neck with his studs. It was a bad challenge so I leapt to my feet and grabbed him around the throat. He took a dive rather than have a go back at me. The game was already simmering and this sparked a melee in the penalty area with pushing, shoving and even some punches thrown.

When it finally calmed down Michael Oliver – who is now a Premier League referee – consulted his linesman and called Anichebe and myself over to him. Anichebe was booked for the challenge and I was shown a straight red card.

I'd never been sent off before and a disciplinary hearing was held by the Premier League to review the incident. Both clubs were charged with failing to control their players and I was accused of manhandling the referee and not leaving the field promptly, even though I only touched his elbow and video evidence proved it took me just 18 seconds to get off the pitch!

In the end they banned me for three reserve-team games and one first-team match while Anichebe got away with just the yellow card shown on the night.

I still disagree with the referee's decision and the Premier League's verdict now, but going for an early shower was a new experience for me.

Ironing out a few problems

One thing I had experienced before was playing in the Ataturk Stadium and with Rafa deciding to rest Pepe I got the opportunity to play in the Champions League against Galatasaray, who had switched the match from their normal stadium, to the scene of my greatest triumph just over 18 months on. We lost 3-2 and I prefer to only think of my good memories in that stadium.

It turned out that Europe would be the story of our season.

We were drawn against Barcelona in the knockout stages and because we were out of the FA Cup we had a free weekend ahead of the first leg in Spain. Rafa decided to take us away to Portugal to prepare for the match in the warmer weather conditions we would face in Camp Nou. He also wanted to integrate us into a team off the pitch and I must admit this went really well!

If you believed everything you read in the papers at the time then it would seem that I was one of the main stars of the biggest football scandal of 2007, the crime scene being Vale do Lobo, near Faro, on the Algarve. We stayed in apartments at a luxury resort close to the sea and Rafa allowed us to go to a restaurant for dinner. The new players had to do karaoke as an initiation ceremony with the rest of us judging them so the wine was flowing.

Craig Bellamy got into an argument with Ginge. Craig has got a fiery temperament – he's not afraid to say what he really thinks – and because Riise had missed a previous party the lads had decided part of his punishment was to do karaoke.

Things got a bit heated between them and I think Sami stepped in to calm things down but Bellers was still fuming at something Ginge had said to him. Ginge might have been bigger than Craig, but Bellers wasn't afraid of a scrap and vowed that he wasn't going to let it go after Riise decided to leave early.

Rafa had told us to be back in our rooms by midnight and with the restaurant closing we were politely asked to leave. We were about to get on the mini-buses outside when I realised I had left my camera in the restaurant. It had pictures on from that night that we didn't want to fall into the hands of the press so I went straight back for it.

"F*** off," said a security guard standing at the entrance.

"My camera is inside; I just want to get it."

"F*** off."

This really pissed me off. He was being completely unreasonable and had twice told me to f*** off in front of the other lads. I didn't want to fight him – he was a really big lad – but I didn't want to lose face in front of my team-mates either. Besides, I was in the right so there was no way I was going to take a step back. Within seconds a bit of a scuffle broke out. Suddenly it was mayhem. A couple of lads rushed in to try and split us up.

I thrust my head forward towards the security guard to scare him, not head-butt him, as I was dragged away by the lads with Daniel Agger saying: "Jerzy, I've got the camera from the restaurant, let's go." Everything cooled down. The press later made out there had been a full-scale brawl with punches thrown but that was complete bullshit. It was nothing more than a scuffle.

Handcuffed and on the ground

We arrived back at the apartments a little late and I returned to the room I was sharing with Pepe. We were in good spirits and spent about half-an-hour singing! I was just about to go to bed when a thought flashed through my head. Maybe I'd had too much wine, but I decided to go back to the restaurant to apologise to the security guard.

Pepe thought it was a stupid idea, pointing out that the security guard wouldn't be standing outside a closed restaurant at this time of night, but he didn't do enough to convince me and I walked out intent on returning to find him.

As I went outside, though, I was confronted by two policemen. They looked like a couple of commandos, like they were from a SWAT team or something! I was petrified. I hadn't even said a word when they grabbed hold of me.

"I'm innocent," I said, "I'm a good lad," but it fell on deaf ears as neither of them spoke English. Suddenly I felt brave and took a cheeky course of action – I wriggled free from their clutches and legged it! One tried to grab my sleeve and the other grabbed at my arm, but I evaded them.

Unfortunately they had back-up and I was quickly floored by two other officers, a total of four of them taking me down. They used brute force to overwhelm me and I smacked my head against the floor, leaving me with a cut above my eyebrow. As they handcuffed me and pinned me down in front of my apartment like an escaped convict I thought to myself 'well, that escalated quickly – I'm in serious trouble here'.

Pepe had dashed outside and was demanding to know what was going on. He could speak some Portuguese and told the officers it was a mistake, but they said I had terrorised other people at the resort and there had been trouble at the apartments.

I was puzzled by this. Then Rafa turned up.

"They're saying you provoked a situation here?"

"But I was in my room with Pepe; he can confirm this."

"Okay, there must be a misunderstanding, but they also say you wanted to fight this gentleman outside of the restaurant?"

I looked over towards the police and noticed the security guard I had scuffled with was standing alongside them. It turned out he was the head of security for the entire resort.

Rafa spoke with the police and they agreed to release me. "I'll sort all this out; go to your room," he said.

I was confused – something else seemed to be going on – but I did as I was told and went to bed. When I went for breakfast the following morning the other lads started laughing at me.

"Sorry lads, I messed up."

"You messed up?" someone replied. "You don't know what happened last night do you Jerzy...?"

I didn't, but I soon found out.

Bellamy and Finnan were sharing the apartment next to myself and Pepe. When we had returned from the restaurant Craig was still fuming at Ginge taking the piss out of him and, according to what Finnan told me, was shouting: "I'll f***ing kill that lad, this isn't over. F*** it, I'm gonna sort him out now. Which apartment is he in?"

Finnan didn't want to tell him, but Bellers texted Agger, who was sharing with Ginge, to find out which room they were staying in before walking over to his golf bag to make a club selection.

"Which one should I use, Finny?" he said like he was talking to a caddy.

Steve thought he was joking and said: "He's about 150 metres away so a 7-iron should do the trick."

When Craig pulled out the 7-iron and stormed out of the room with it I think Steve feared the worst! We weren't alone in the resort and a German couple who had kids with them had seen what they thought was a maniac armed with a golf club. Understandably they phoned the police, but they didn't arrive until after Craig had walked into Riise's apartment, whacked his backside with the 7-iron and hurled a volley of abuse at him. He then went back to his apartment where some of the other lads, not knowing what had just happened, joined him for a party in their lounge.

Unluckily for me, the officers had arrived to try and find Bellers at the same time I had left my apartment and with the head of security recognising me from earlier they were convinced that it was me who had caused the trouble.

They didn't even try to find Craig after that so I had completely unwittingly saved his arse and prevented him from facing any serious consequences from the police. I think he said in his book he was relieved when he found out they'd tried to blame me for the trouble instead!

When Finnan explained the situation to the lads, they looked at me with sympathy: "So it was his fault? Not yours? Holy f***, unbelievable. You had such bad luck…"

Craig was labelled 'the nutter with the putter' and one of the rooms was left in a bit of a mess but it was nowhere near as big a scandal as was made out in the papers. We quickly decided to apologise to everybody and I apologised to the head of security. We also left LFC merchandise with people at the resort to say sorry. Although I was innocent, I was punished by the club, as was Craig. I was fined two weeks' wages; I think Craig was fined three or four. We all laugh about it now when we meet up, but before the Barcelona game it was no laughing matter.

Because our form in the Premier League had been patchy – we'd lost our last game at Newcastle, were 16 points behind leaders Manchester United in third place and out of both domestic cups – our season would effectively have been over if we lost to Barcelona.

What had happened in Portugal put extra pressure on us and now we had to deal with Lionel Messi and Ronaldinho. I prayed for a positive result in Camp Nou as I felt jointly responsible for the mayhem, but all the lads were desperate to win and show that team spirit in the camp was very good. You couldn't have written the script for what happened next.

Deco scored first, but shortly before half-time Bellamy equalised. He celebrated by running to the corner flag, with Riise closely behind him, and swinging his arms like he was holding a 7-iron! They still had a bone to pick with each other, but that proved we had unity on the pitch and gave us all a good laugh! Incredibly, Ginge then scored our winning goal in the second half after being assisted by Bellers and we became only the second English side to beat Barcelona in Camp Nou. The first was also Liverpool in 1976! It proved to be a crucial goal as we lost the second leg 1-0, but went through on away goals.

Milan's revenge

That win in Barcelona was a turning point in the season for us. We beat PSV Eindhoven in the quarter-finals to set up another semi-final meeting with Chelsea. This time we were beaten 1-0 in the first leg at Stamford Bridge, but a brilliant goal from Daniel Agger at Anfield sent the tie to penalties and this time it was Pepe who was the hero. He saved two spot-kicks. From February I played just twice more that season, at home to Sheffield United and away to Portsmouth, before we travelled to Athens to play AC Milan again in the Champions League final.

We stayed in what was supposedly a 'five-star' hotel in Athens but unfortunately our rooms were in the older part of the hotel. It looked like it hadn't been refurbished for about 30 years and as someone who has stayed in a lot of hotels I would say it was three stars at best. We were all really pissed off on that first night.

Our bathroom was so small that Pepe had to sit on the toilet with his legs pointing diagonally so that he could close the bathroom door. If he sat normally he would have had his legs sticking out into the bedroom and although we are good friends there are some things you don't want to see!

The horrible plastic shower curtain wasn't very pleasant either, but thankfully we were moved into a better part of the hotel for the second night.

Inevitably, the final was billed as Milan's chance for revenge, but it was a completely different game. We dictated the match this time and were the better side, but Milan took the lead just before half-time when Andrea Pirlo's free-kick deflected past Pepe off Filippo Inzaghi's chest. Inzaghi got their second goal in the 82nd minute and although Dirk got one back for us a minute before full-time, which must have made Milan nervous, we couldn't do another Istanbul and take the game to extra-time. It was a disappointing night for us all and I also knew that it was the last time I would be part of a Liverpool squad. My time at Anfield was coming to an end.

Christmas Party

One thing I knew I would miss after leaving Liverpool is the Christmas parties. We would hire a restaurant that was closed to the rest of the public and let our hair down. I mentioned earlier that Pepe introduced the 'Secret Santa' idea of getting gifts for our team-mates, and the aim was to get the funniest present to take the piss out of whoever we were drawn out to buy for.

One of the gifts that made us laugh the most was when Ginge unwrapped a giant poster of Steven Gerrard that Stevie had signed and written 'especially for my greatest fan' on it. Ginge had admitted that Stevie was his hero when he was younger and when he first signed for Liverpool he pretty much followed Stevie everywhere, so at least when he returned home now he could drift off to sleep looking into his hero's eyes! One of the gifts I got was a set of equipment for professional ballet dancers – ballet shoes, a pink tutu and a parallel bar. I suspect Carra got it for me as he had suggested that I had pranced around on my line like a ballet dancer in Istanbul, but I never did find out if he was behind it.

Craig Bellamy was, of course, the life and soul of any party and

I had a bit of an adventure with him at Christmas 2006. There's a tradition at Liverpool that you attend Christmas parties in fancy dress and some of the lads wore amazing costumes. Stevie went as a punk rocker, Dirk was dressed as Superman, Kewell came as Shane Warne, Sami was Zorro, Bolo Zenden turned up as Captain America, Robbie Fowler was dressed as Saddam Hussein, Luis was Huggy Bear from Starsky and Hutch and Peter Crouch turned up as a giant parrot! Some of the younger lads also arrived dressed as a family from Coronation Street. Myself and Jermaine Pennant went for a Star Wars theme – he was Chewbacca and I hired a Darth Vader costume including a lightsaber. It only arrived from London about two hours before the party and when we got there the paparazzi were waiting outside Aldo's Place – a bar that was owned by former Liverpool player John Aldridge.

During the party prizes were awarded for the best costumes and both myself and Pepe, who was dressed as someone from a horror movie, were two of the winners.

Having a pint with a Darth Vader helmet on proved to be rather difficult and as I was getting so hot with it on I took it off during the party.

We were having a great night but when it was time to go home the helmet was missing. I couldn't find it anywhere so went home wondering what I would tell the hire company, but it was returned the next day by a taxi driver who had taken Bellers home after the party. He told me the full story but made me promise not to tell Craig!

Bellers had stolen my helmet. Even though he'd attended the party dressed as an evil jester and had a mask he had decided that the best way to avoid the paparazzi was to leave in my

Darth Vader helmet and jump into a cab. The taxi set off and Bellers fell asleep, but during the journey he woke up with the helmet still on and felt disorientated. "What the f*** is this on my head?" he said to the driver before opening the window and chucking it into the road. The cabbie decided it wasn't safe to stop so I had to have a father-and-son style chat with Bellers the next day. "Craig, I know you were trying to evade the cameras mate, but you've ruined my costume." He had no recollection of what had happened but he gave me a couple of hundred quid and our Christmas party was finally over.

Needing a new challenge

My contract at Liverpool expired in 2007, but Benitez wanted me to stay. He appreciated my full commitment in training, even if I was only Pepe's understudy, and knew that I still lived and breathed everything to do with the team. So Rafa offered me a new contract. He said he knew how happy my wife and children were on Merseyside, how much the staff liked me and how important it was to have two experienced goalkeepers at the club.

But there was one condition: "Jerzy, when you got your last contract you were the number one keeper, but now you are second choice. So you'll have to take a 50 per cent pay cut..."

I found that hugely disrespectful. Yes, I was 34, but I was still fit, confident in my ability and goalkeepers are far from finished at the age of 34. I realised then that it was time for me to leave Liverpool. I needed a new challenge.

I knew it would be hard to uproot Mirella and the kids, but the thought of taking a pay cut to still not play any football – I had only made 12 appearances for the Reds since Istanbul –

didn't appeal to me. It was time to say goodbye and start a new chapter in my career.

Before this the media had started to speculate and one tabloid ran an article claiming that I had said Benitez was treating me 'like a slave'. It was bullshit. I never said such a thing. The word 'slave' is a very strong word and people who heard about this were unhappy with me, but I was disgusted that they had misquoted an interview I had done elsewhere to sell copies of their paper. All I said was that I was unhappy not to have been first choice for two seasons and it is hard to put your heart into things when you never play.

Rafa remained as Liverpool manager for another three seasons but despite coming close in 2008/09 he was unable to win a Premier League title. I have a theory as to why he was never able to achieve this. I returned to Liverpool a couple of months after leaving the club and had a chat with Rafa. He was moaning at the failure of some of his Spanish players to settle down. "Is it any surprise they don't settle when it goes dark at 4pm? And the food is a problem. In Spain we have nice weather, we can sit outside tapas bars and have wine with our meals until late at night. You can't do that here so how can they play well on the pitch if they are not happy off it." It made me think of Josemi.

Josemi was Rafa's first signing. He was a right-back who played for Malaga and was considered to have the physical toughness to adapt to English football quickly, but he and his wife found it very hard to integrate into the English way of life. He used to tell me that his wife couldn't find places she liked to eat at, didn't know how to spend her time during the day and was feeling more and more depressed. I think that had a knock-on effect on him and he didn't show his best form at Liverpool before returning to Spain.

Personally, I loved living in England, but I had come from Poland and then Holland. The culture is very different in Spain and having spent four years there myself I can appreciate why some Spanish and South American footballers find it hard to acclimatise to living in England. So I found it strange, after having this conversation with me, that Rafa paid a record fee of around £20 million to sign Fernando Torres from Atletico Madrid that summer.

Rafa needed a new striker; a goalscorer. Cisse had been signed for a lot of money but he broke his leg in 2004 and was unable to play in the way Rafa wanted him to when he got fit so speculation was rife about who Liverpool would sign. Rafa's scouts told him to go for Torres, who was the king of the Vicente Calderon at the time, and with us just having played in a second Champions League final in three seasons and other Spanish players being at the club he decided to move to Merseyside. I got talking to Iker Casillas about Torres and his view was interesting: "Torres is the most overpriced player in Spanish football history," he told me.

He went on to score a lot of goals for Liverpool in his first couple of seasons but ultimately it wasn't enough to win Rafa the title or any other trophy for that matter. Why not? Because it took him too long to figure out that England wasn't the best climate for his colony of Spanish players to thrive in over the course of a full season.

Best fans in the world
I grew up as a Górnik Zabrze fan and travelled to matches with

my mates – we got the 47 bus from Szczygłowice to Zabrze – so when I became a professional footballer this helped me to understand the lengths people go to when following a team and why I experienced some crazy behaviour!

At Liverpool I was lucky to feel the support of some brilliant fans. After we beat Bayer Leverkusen at Anfield in 2005, Jacek Krzynówek asked me what the doctor had given us as he couldn't believe we had the energy to have done so much running that night. I told him the only performance enhancing drug we had was the Anfield atmosphere. It was magical on the big European nights.

Liverpool supporters have huge expectations, but they can lift the team and I regard them as the best in the world. They seem to be able to get anywhere they want to get to!

We were celebrating on the pitch in Istanbul when I noticed a lad in an official club tracksuit who wasn't part of the team. He'd blagged his way onto the pitch as one of the squad players and we had no idea who he was. Stevie had hold of the European Cup and he was shouting: "Let me have the cup Stevie, let me hold it for a minute lad."

"F*** off," said Stevie, who had sussed him, but that didn't stop him from getting onto the team picture with all the lads. I think it's a badge of honour for some Liverpool supporters to do crazy things they will be remembered for!

The former Polish Prime Minister, Jan Krzysztof Bielecki, praised Liverpool fans a lot. He asked me for a ticket to watch a game against Arsenal at Highbury. I sorted it out and I realised later on that it was in the away end.

I felt foolish that I had sent Mr Bielecki in with the travelling Kop but afterwards he rejected my apology: "Jurek, don't

241

worry, it was amazing! I had a great time with your supporters and learned all the Liverpool songs."

MY LIVERPOOL
TEAM-MATES

I spent six years at Liverpool and trained with and played alongside plenty of stars and characters. I can't mention them all, but these are some of the biggest names and most memorable lads I shared the Anfield dressing room with...

Daniel Agger

Solid, classy and with a strong shot from distance, Daniel was the best golfer in the Liverpool team. When I wasn't playing I would watch his swing – I thought he could do some out-of-this-world stuff with a golf ball until I gained more experience myself. When he was a kid, Daniel had to choose between a career as a professional golfer or a footballer. Maybe he lacked a little something to become a world-class defender, but I'm sure he has no regrets as he succeeded at Liverpool. He's also up there with Djibril Cisse as the most tattooed person I've ever met. There's probably only one place on his body that isn't tattooed... but I'd rather not know!

Nicolas Anelka

Never believe everything you read. Like most Liverpool supporters I had a preconception about Nicolas when he arrived on loan from PSG that he must be a moody troublemaker who can't settle anywhere. He was nothing of the sort. Nicolas was quiet, classy and never thought he was a superstar. It made me wonder why he attracted so much negative publicity and maybe it was because he is not the type of character who would try to find a common language with the managers he worked for, or would compromise over expectations of what his salary should be. I'm not sure that endeared him to managers and as a result perceptions of Anelka never changed.

Pako Ayestaran

Pako is the best fitness coach I've worked with, but he was in the shadow of Rafa Benitez. I had turned 30 when I started to train with him and didn't think he could make me fitter but he developed drills that got the best out of individuals. He worked us hard, but everyone respected Pako so it was a sad day when he parted company with Liverpool within hours of having a fall-out with Rafa. I am absolutely sure that the physical condition of the team was worse without him.

Markus Babbel

Markus was a great player, but not long after I joined Liverpool he developed Guillain–Barré Syndrome – a debilitating condition that appears rapidly and affects the nervous system. Krzysztof Nowak, my friend from the national team, suffered the same condition and sadly lost his battle against it. Markus was in a very bad way as initially no-one could give him a precise diagnosis. He had to see experts in Germany and when he was diagnosed everyone rallied around him. David Moores gave him a new contract, even though there were no guarantees he would recover and even though he was in a wheelchair the club brought him back so he could be part of the team photo and still feel like one of the lads. Such gestures showed what a big club Liverpool is. I think all that support – along with his will-power and determination – helped Markus to recover. To see him back on the pitch again after a year recovering made me incredibly happy.

Craig Bellamy

A real character. One of the most colourful players I've played with. He had a good and a bad side – like he had one leg full of tattoos and the other tattoo-free. Off the pitch, Bellers was the coolest person you could ever meet. Butter wouldn't melt in his mouth – you'd have no idea what a fighter on the pitch or what a shit-stirrer he could be! He may have been small, but Craig was cocky and would never let an argument lie when he thought he was right. I enjoyed having him as a team-mate, but he was an unpredictable character.

Igor Biscan

Igor was a talented midfielder who struggled at first in England but his career was resurrected by Pako Ayestaran. When Pako got him fitter he really progressed at Liverpool and played well in some big games for us in the season when we won the Champions League. Igor was a great mate of mine – we spent a lot of time together away from the pitch so I got to know him well – and the lads used to joke that he was a walking weather forecast. If Igor walked into the dressing room with his head down we knew it was raining. He was used to the sun in Croatia and found the weather here depressing! Igor was also the butt of a lot of jokes in the dressing room and you could see him simmering away so we used to wonder if one day he'd turn up in the dressing room armed and come after us! Thankfully he didn't and my best memory of playing alongside him was in the League Cup at Tottenham in 2004 when the two of us, Stephane Henchoz and Salif Diao were the only senior players. They fielded a strong line-up but we won on penalties.

Jamie Carragher

The foreign players always had problems understanding Carra when they first arrived at Liverpool. It's not just his Scouse dialect, it's the pitch of his voice and how strongly he puts things across. There were times at the start when I thought 'why the f*** is he digging me out?' when he was actually just getting an opinion across that I had wrongly interpreted. Carra has a massive football knowledge – I think he's read every football autobiography and is no doubt reading this! – and he was completely underestimated by people when he was younger. He went through a tough spell at full-back when Houllier was in charge but as soon as Benitez arrived he put him alongside Sami at centre-half and they were rock solid. I'd go as far as to say Carra was one of the top central defenders in European football when Rafa was here, but he was also a master of resting. If the boss gave us a five-minute break, Carra would take six minutes!

Scott Carson

He didn't have as dazzling a career with Liverpool and England as I thought he might, but Scott developed into a better goal-keeper than Chris Kirkland. His reflexes and ability to keep the ball out on the goal-line were excellent and he was good with his feet, but Scott didn't fulfil the potential he had when coming to Liverpool as a teenager.

Djibril Cisse

When Djibril flew to Liverpool for the first time, Norman Gard asked him to dress casually to lessen the chance of him being recognised as his transfer wasn't completed and the club wanted to keep things under wraps. Norman told me what happened: "I was standing by the arrival doors at Liverpool Airport when out walked Djibril. He was dressed like a panther. He even had a matching hat. The entire arrivals lounge couldn't help but stare at him. So much for being subtle." Every newspaper wrote about Djibril the following day. He is a walking fashion house and he seemed to change an element of his hair every three days. Different patterns, different colours, different styles and cuts... you couldn't get bored looking at him. He was also super-stitious and, like many footballers with connections to Africa, had a strong faith in the magical powers of different things such as colourful wristbands. He was definitely an extrovert!

Joe Corrigan

Joe's style as a goalkeeping coach was to focus on the physical side of the game plus reflexes and goal-line drills. I had a great relationship with him, but I always felt he favoured Chris Kirkland – something I tried to understand – because he was younger and wanted to try to develop his talent more. Joe took a recording of my footwork and analysed it with Chris to help his co-ordination. We all tried to help each other and when Joe invited me to train with the young players as part of their development I agreed as I enjoyed training as much as I did playing.

Peter Crouch

Also known as 'Robo' because of his robotic dancing celebrations after goals, Peter defied the laws of physics by playing football when he was big enough to be a superstar of basketball or volleyball. He was actually the ideal example of a volleyball player – over two metres tall and weighing 80 kilos – but he was also the most difficult player to get the ball off in training. He used his body perfectly to protect it. The strange thing was that Rafa brought him in and stuck with him when he couldn't score but then as soon as he was finding the net all the time he was constantly rotated and this killed his form. I still don't understand why Rafa did that.

Czech Army – Milan Baros, Vladimir Smicer and Patrik Berger

It's a common theory that Poles are mentally similar to Czechs because we share a border and although I realised there are a lot of differences between us, I became close to Milan, Vladi and Patrik. Milan's hometown of Ostrava is about 50 miles from Knurów and I went with him to see it. He had signed for Liverpool one month before me and we became good friends quickly, helping each other to acclimatise and learn English. When Milan was unhappy he wasn't afraid of showing it and this was typical of the Czech lads. They stand their ground. I got on well with Patrik and when he wasn't playing he would get very pissed off. He would walk around swearing in Czech and while most people didn't understand the words he was using, I did. Let's just say he was very, very angry! Most players avoid showing their emotions but the Czechs don't. It's in their character to fight back when they are upset and I think they earn more respect for doing so. They also know how to drink! Vladi, who was also a good mate, visited Knurów with Milan for a charity game I organised in 2005 and after it we got seriously drunk. I'm still in touch with them and myself, Patrik and Vladi all play golf. Whenever we meet up for the Liverpool Legends games we spend most of our time trying to arrange our next golf trip!

Salif Diao

Salif was superstitious and when he got injured he returned wearing a colourful bracelet around his ankle. He told me to make one myself and assured me that it would protect me from future injuries unless it snapped. I decided not to test his theory, but after he wore that 'Dudek – You'll Never Walk Alone' t-shirt under his shirt when we played Ipswich after my nightmare against Manchester United, I realised I could count on him during difficult moments. I'll always be grateful and thankful to Salif for that.

El-Hadji Diouf

I was in South Korea with Poland at the 2002 World Cup when

the press quizzed me about him because Diouf had just signed for Liverpool and starred in Senegal's shock first-game victory against France. I didn't know what to say as I didn't know who he was! He appeared to have a big talent, but he was too much of a showboater to do well at Liverpool. Wingers in England keep it simple. They beat their man then cross the ball. Diouf wanted to beat his man and then let him get back into position so he could try to beat him again. It pissed the strikers off to see him dancing down the wing but never giving them a cross. Houllier tried to coach him to cross the ball, but being a team player wasn't in his nature. On one occasion Stevie shouted for him to track back on the left and Diouf simply told him to "f*** off." If someone hadn't stepped in, Stevie would have flattened him. Diouf didn't speak good English either so maybe that was part of his problem, but he knew how to swear and no matter what the occasion was it would normally end with him using the phrase 'f*** off'.

Steve Finnan

Steve was a very humble Irish international who didn't sound Irish. He was a good lad but I still wonder whether the fact that he got substituted at half-time in Istanbul is the reason why he disappeared from the football world after he retired. Maybe there is a mental scar about being substituted halfway through the most important game of his life when we were losing 3-0, and not being part of the famous comeback as he wanted to stay on in Istanbul? I'm not sure what happened to Steve and I haven't seen him for a while. It's a shame as Steve is a nice person and his contribution in getting us to Istanbul and Athens should not be forgotten.

Robbie Fowler

I used to ask youngsters who were training at Liverpool's Academy who their LFC idol was. Like a choir they would sing back in unison: 'Robbie Fowler'. It was always Robbie, never Michael Owen. I only got to play with him briefly before he was sold to Leeds in 2001 and then in a few games when Rafa brought him back in 2006, but I played against few players with a better left foot than Robbie. The supporters at Anfield adored him – they'd sing his name over and over when he was on the bench – and I have heard so many stories about him. Some of the tales about nights out he was on in Liverpool's pubs and clubs are legendary! Robbie was one of the most colourful characters you could meet. Myself and the lads could write a book of anecdotes just about him. He is big joker – I honestly think he could do stand-up comedy – and he has a quirky sense of humour. He came in for a few training sessions looking tired and Houllier asked where he had been last night. "Nowhere, boss," he replied, but Houllier didn't believe him. False rumours started to go around about his lifestyle and this pissed him off so one day he arrived at Melwood for training wearing a suit. Before Houllier got there he ruffled his hair up, loosened his tie around his neck, hung half of his shirt outside of his trousers and sat slumped in the canteen with a couple of rounds of toast and a coffee. Everyone thought he'd turned up straight after a night out and when Houllier walked in he flipped!

"Where the hell have you been?"

"Nowhere, boss. I was in bed at 10pm." And then, just to wind Houllier up a bit more, he added: "I overslept though boss so I just chucked on the first thing I saw."

"Look at the state of you..."

This gave Robbie exactly what he had been waiting for and he seized upon it. "What about how I look? Are you judging me on how I look rather than what I tell you?"

The penny dropped with Houllier. He realised Robbie had played him and was making a point. He just did it in a hilarious way. That wasn't the only Melwood incident that Robbie became legendary for. When the new Melwood was built Houllier allocated us all a car parking space but the one Robbie was given was very tight and difficult to manoeuvre in and out of. He got pissed off with this so he decided to park his car on a training pitch and, just to prove his point, did a few donuts, spinning the car around and around, churning up the grass. When somebody asked him what the hell he was doing he said that as soon as he got a normal parking space he'd start driving like a normal person again! There was also the fall-out he had with Phil Thompson shortly before he left. At the end of the training session Tommo was standing right behind one of the goals at Melwood so Robbie fired a shot towards the goal. With his typically precise left foot he hit the net, but the netting was so loose that it stretched and the ball almost took Tommo's head off. Tommo went ballistic and demanded an apology, to which Robbie replied: "What for? I hit the target!" It became a scandal in the newspapers and Robbie ended up missing the Charity Shield against Manchester United until it was all sorted out, but mischievous behaviour like that was all part of his character and added to the reasons why the fans loved him so much.

Luis Garcia

Over and over again we have asked Luis if the ball really did cross the line against Chelsea in the Champions League semi-final at Anfield in 2005. He always smiles when asked and gives the same answer: "One hundred per cent it was a goal!" To this day nobody has proved it either way for sure, but it was given and the fans still sing his name when Liverpool play Chelsea now because of that goal! Luis wasn't a player with great physical abilities, but he was technically very skilful. He found it tough to adapt to the physical side of the Premier League at first, but as the weeks passed he got better and better and had a habit of scoring crucial goals in the big games for us.

Steven Gerrard

Stevie could win a game on his own for us. We all know how important he was for Liverpool and I would go as far as to say he is the most complete player in the club's history. He's certainly up there with Kenny Dalglish as LFC's two biggest legends. It was an honour to play with him and the emotional approach he had towards football helped to make him such a charismatic character. He absolutely hated to lose and he'd show that both on the pitch and in the dressing room. If he had something to say he'd say it, no matter who it was he needed to say it to. Stevie also changed, matured perhaps, when he had a family. You think differently when you've got more women at home like Stevie has with his three daughters and it helped him to become calmer, which made him an even better player.

Didi Hamann

Didi and I were neighbours in Caldy so we used to travel in to training or for matches in the car together. I think he was underestimated as he was one of the best defensive midfielders in Europe and did a superb job for us. His reading of the game and ability to make interceptions made a huge impact on the team and I still think Houllier's decision to substitute him away to Bayer Leverkusen in the 2002 Champions League quarter-final cost us. We were losing 2-1 on the night but going through on away goals when Houllier took Didi off for Vladi. We ended up losing 4-2 and went out. That match showed how important Didi was, and it was no co-incidence either that we turned things around in Istanbul when he came on at half-time and neutralised Kaka's influence. The other thing about Didi was that he loved a bevvy and a bet, although doing the two things together didn't always turn out to be a good thing!

Stephane Henchoz

He was not the most technically skilled player, but Stephane was a proper rock-solid defender – a tough guy who got stuck into opponents and wasn't afraid of taking some hits back. I sat next to him in the dressing room and after some matches his legs were in such bad condition they looked like the grounds-man had run him down with a mower! That was Stephane for you though. He played with his heart and left nothing out there on the pitch. I loved playing behind him and Sami, with Carra at full-back. All three would put their bodies on the line to block the ball and if I was beaten, I always knew there was a chance one of them would still somehow clear the ball off the line.

Emile Heskey

Emile was my target! I'd look for him with long passes and he had the physical strength to deal with the ball while under pressure from opponents. Emile was a nice lad but I think he would have achieved more in his career if he'd had a Czech character.

He didn't argue with people or stand his ground enough. If he had, combined with his physical presence and talent, he could have done better.

Sami Hyypia

Sami was one of the best central defenders I ever played with. The captain of the team before Steven Gerrard took over, he was ultra-professional. He was also a true leader of the team and a guy who cared more about Liverpool FC the longer he was at the club. Sami wasn't a joker, but despite all the trophies he won he stayed very humble. He was a great friend of mine away from the pitch and a person I could trust and count on. He'd definitely be in the best XI players I ever played with.

Harry Kewell

In my opinion Harry was a fantastic winger, but the best period of his career was at Leeds. He was unlucky with injuries at Liverpool because when he was fit and playing he made a difference to the team on the left. It was a surprise when Rafa selected him to start in Istanbul just after he had returned from injury but I think he took the gamble because he felt Harry had quality and would be a bit fresher than some of the other lads. Obviously he didn't last on the pitch long, but fortunately it turned out well as it was Vladi who came on for him.

Chris Kirkland

Despite being rivals for a place in the team we got on very well. Chris was the big hope for English football when there was a lack of young goalkeepers coming through but he was fighting a losing battle against injuries. He couldn't understand how unlucky he could be to get consecutive injuries and this stopped his development, preventing him from fulfilling his ambition and potential to be England's number one goalkeeper.

Dirk Kuyt

It took me six years to learn how to correctly pronounce Dirk's surname! I don't have any problems now. He came to Feyenoord from Utrecht when I left Rotterdam to go to Liverpool, so we only met when he also came to Anfield in 2006. Dirk worked really hard every day and played with full commitment. He put his heart into playing for Liverpool, which made the fans love him, and has a very friendly personality. He's back at Feyenoord now and is a true legend at De Kuip.

Jari Litmanen

I met Jari for the first time in Holland – he was a star player for Ajax – and I still see him now for Liverpool Legends games. A true Finnish professional, he had fantastic skill and read the game brilliantly. Maybe you could criticise him for trying one dummy too many instead of playing a pass, but he was always looking for perfection. Jari was a good mate off the pitch and has a high attention to detail. He wanted to know as much as he could about everything that was going on and would ask a lot of questions.

Javier Mascherano

I didn't get to play with Javier a lot as he arrived at Liverpool close to the end of my career at the club but we could all see his quality in training straight away. Javier was made for Spanish football, even more so than the Premier League. He is a very

CHECKING IT IS REAL: With my winner's medal after a glorious night in Istanbul

BIG OCCASION: It didn't look likely that we would win after walking out to face the mighty AC Milan – especially when Hernan Crespo put the Italians 3-0 up just before half-time

THAT SAVE:
John Arne
Riise can't
believe
the double
save I made
from Andriy
Shevchenko
after we had
got the score
back to 3-3

BIG MOMENTS:
Milan keeper
Dida and
I share a
moment
before I
managed
to keep out
penalties
from Andrea
Pirlo and
Shevchenko

TURKISH DELIGHT: Jamie Carragher was the first to reach me after I saved Shevchenko's penalty...and then the celebrations really began

OL' BIG EARS: It was great to get my hands – or hand – on the biggest prize in European football

OLD FRIEND: After the Istanbul final I joined my former coach Bobo Kaczmarek at his testimonial game in Gdańsk. Right: The following season Pepe Reina was in goal for the FA Cup final

CONSOLING WORD: Pepe felt the pain of losing in the 2007 Champions League final but I was able to point to a victory two years earlier that I played a big part in

COVETED COLLECTION: A selfie that shows a large selection of some of the shirts I have collected throughout my career

NEXT CHAPTER: After leaving Liverpool I signed for another huge club – Real Madrid – in 2007 to provide back-up for Iker Casillas (left)

AMONG THE STARS: I got to work with such talented players as Kaka and Cristiano Ronaldo

THE SPECIAL ONE: Standing next to Jose Mourinho
Left: My gloves made it into Real's museum
Below: A guard of honour from my Poland team-mates at my final international game – against Liechtenstein in 2013

MINING HERITAGE: If football hadn't come along I could have been a miner

FULL STRETCH: It pays to be flexible when you are a goalkeeper – even on the dance floor!

REAL HONOUR: I had the great privilege of meeting Pope John Paul II in 2003

MANY INTERESTS: I'm now involved in motor sport and play more golf since I retired from football

CLASS ON THE GRASS: Here I am combining my motor racing skills with the pitch maintenance knowledge I picked up at Concordia Knurów, and (right) the medals I've managed to win

OLD FRIENDS: The Istanbul reunion night in May 2015 gave me the chance to catch up with many of the squad that combined to bring the European Cup back to Liverpool

NEAREST AND DEAREST: Family photos with the most important people in my life, my wife Mirella, son Alex and daughters Victoria and Natalia

tenacious player and has shown at Barcelona that he can play in central defence. I'm not surprised he has done so well in Spain.

Gary McAllister

Gary had a great personality and bags of experience. He used his nous on the pitch and it helped us a lot – it was like having the tactical brain of Jose Mourinho in central midfield for us! Gary could dictate our style of play and also the pace of a game. He knew how to slow a game down, but also how to raise the pace when it was needed. He was like a combination of a more attack-minded Didi Hamann and an older Steven Gerrard and I think Stevie learned a lot from him when he was younger. Gary's ability was obvious from the moment I arrived at Liverpool and when he left in 2002 we lost a lot of quality.

Neil Mellor

He didn't play many games for Liverpool, but he had a big influence on our triumph in 2005 because of the part he played against Olympiakos. We were 1-0 down at half-time and needed a miracle to win by the two clear goals required to progress to the knock-out stages. It was 1-1 when Neil came on and he made it 2-1. It was also his knock-down that Stevie fired into the Kop end net to send us through and that night Neil showed what a winning mentality he had. He was a good mate and it was a shame he had to retire early through injury.

David Moores

Mr Moores was the Liverpool chairman before the club was sold to new owners in 2007 and he was a real gentleman with a charming personality. His backing helped Liverpool get back to where the club belonged – being champions of Europe – and his behaviour was the complete opposite to how a lot of chairmen operate. I played in teams that had chairmen or owners who would storm into the dressing room after games and dish out rollickings like they thought they were the manager. Mr Moores had a different philosophy. He travelled with us to every game – even though he didn't have to – and would be in the dressing room before and after matches, but was never intrusive. I think he liked the matchday atmosphere. His attitude was 'Just imagine I'm not here. Don't think I'm putting pressure on you. No way. I just want you to know I support you.' When we won the Champions League, every player received a luxury watch. They were limited edition, I think 37 of them were produced, and we were supposed to receive the watch that corresponded to our squad number. I should have received the watch numbered one but the chairman spoke up: "I'm number one at the club..." This started a discussion with the boys. They felt it should be mine and there was talk of seeing if we could get another watch made with a number one inscribed on it so we both had one, but in the end the team as a whole decided I should get that watch and Mr Moores should receive one with a different number on it. This was explained to him and he accepted it, but I still wonder now if I should have let Mr Moores have the number one watch to avoid any awkwardness.

Fernando Morientes

'Moro' was a great striker with fabulous intuition, but he was cup-tied for the Champions League when he arrived at Liverpool in January 2005 so missed out on being a part of our success. Morientes was a positive person – he was open to meeting new people and experiencing new things – and although he spoke little English when Rafa signed him he was very well-liked in the dressing room. It didn't work out for Moro at Anfield but I liked him and regretted that he wasn't at the club for longer.

Danny Murphy

Danny was a solid midfielder who was big mates with Stevie and Carra, but he also integrated with the other lads and was helpful. He did well under Houllier but was one of the first victims of the clear-out Benitez had when he was appointed. Rafa decided that medical test results were proof that Danny couldn't handle the new fitness regime he had brought in. Danny disputed it, but Rafa said he'd find him a new club and immediately sold him to Charlton Athletic. I remember clearly the day Danny left. He walked into the dressing room, said his goodbyes and walked out, leaving us all a little shocked. It was a completely new and strange experience to all of us to see one of the first-team players leave so quickly.

Jose Ochotorena

'Ocho' arrived with Rafa as his goalkeeping coach and it took us time to get used to his training methods. We worked harder in the gym with Pako Ayestaran to improve our physical condition while Ocho focused more on analysing match situations, including providing us with a new level of detail about specific opponents.

We knew which players we had to expect to run in behind our high defensive line and also the finishing style of certain strikers. It was another element of goalkeeper coaching for me.

In Poland it was more physical and about agility, in Holland it was about technical skills and being good with the ball at your feet. In England it was about dominating your penalty area, especially when it comes to collecting crosses. This tactical approach helped me a lot when I moved to Real Madrid. Ocho is also a very nice person – we're still in touch now – and he knew how to deal with me when I was unhappy.

Towards the end of the 2005/06 season I was so annoyed with Benitez that I refused to even speak to him but he wanted me to play in a non-consequential game so Pepe Reina could be rested and also miss training to return to Spain to prepare for his wedding. I didn't feel like giving my all for Rafa so I told him I had a sore knee.

"So what now?" Rafa asked. "You want me to tell Pepe he can't go home to prepare for his wedding?"

"Do what you want," I replied coldly. "You're the boss. My knee is painful and I need treatment."

Rafa sent Ocho to talk to me: "Jerzy, I know you don't want to play and you're angry with Rafa, but you can't behave like this. You're a professional.

"You have a good reputation here. We have a good relationship and I will try to help you get the move that you want, but you should play. Take the rest of today and tomorrow off. Have a rest then come back and work hard like the professional you are."

He made me think about how other players react when they're frustrated. I've seen lots of aggression, including locker doors being kicked in, and I realised that I didn't want to be seen as that type of player. I listened to Ocho. He was a very good influence on me but even more importantly he recommended to me some very good wine and told me where the best place in Spain was to get paella, as he is from Valencia, where that dish came from.

Michael Owen

I had the pleasure of playing alongside some real football stars and Michael was one of them. I knew how good he was before I came to Liverpool, but I didn't know what type of person he was. I soon found out he was very humble. Michael didn't use his status as a star to manipulate situations. Everyone respected him for being an ordinary guy and keeping his feet on the ground, but because he was so popular he had to have two body-guards following him to ensure he didn't get mobbed! When we travelled abroad we used to tell him to turn left when he walked out of the airport so we could go right as nobody would notice us! Michael shared a lot of the same values as me and he was a good role model for kids. I met some famous players who couldn't handle the attention of fans and the press and it fried their brains, but Michael took things in his stride. People could learn a lot from him. He was also very superstitious. One day after training I was driving home with Didi to the Wirral and we spotted Michael, who was in good form at the time, in his car. He usually took the same route as us through the Wallasey Tunnel, but he drove off towards the Birkenhead Tunnel instead. It would take him longer to get home that way but Didi explained to me that just before he started his goalscoring run Michael had driven through the Birkenhead Tunnel so he was going to keep driving that way until he stopped scoring as it was lucky for him! It's fair to say he ended up driving home that way a lot!

Jermaine Pennant

Jermaine was a dynamic winger who could make a difference in one-on-one situations and was a funny lad to have around the place, but he was also from a younger generation of players who think they can do anything simply because they're famous footballers. It landed him in trouble with the police before he was at Liverpool – he had to play with a tag on at Birmingham.

John Arne Riise

'Ginge' had a ferocious left foot – of the players I trained against at Liverpool only Djibril Cisse could strike a ball as powerfully – and he was always in great physical condition. He was like a machine during pre-season training camps so we called him RoboCop! He would complete runs quicker than anyone else and then want to do it again so he could beat his own time, so we thought of ways to stop him from out-training us. In one session we got one of the young lads to set off far too quickly on a run, like a pacemaker, to try and tire Ginge out so Vladi, who was also a good runner, could pick him off at the end when he was fatigued. It didn't work. Ginge completed the run in less than six minutes and even though Vladi caught him he suddenly got a burst of energy into his legs and left Vladi for dead. He was pissed off that we didn't congratulate him for completing the run so quickly, but we were pissed off that he'd won again!

Momo Sissoko

Momo was meant to be Liverpool's Patrick Vieira; a tall, dominating central midfielder who commanded the middle of the pitch. He had the physical qualities to develop into that type of player – he was strong and won the ball back well – but he suffered from lapses of concentration. The bad eye injury he suffered playing against Benfica in the Champions League didn't help him either.

Djimi Traore

I remember Djimbo as a very good friend and a player who contributed much more to Liverpool than his famous own goal at Burnley in the FA Cup. He had some difficult days but he also made a crucial goal-line clearance against AC Milan in Istanbul that helped us to win the final, and that shouldn't be forgotten.

Sander Westerveld

I didn't think we'd get on because I was bought to replace Sander but my ability to speak Dutch helped and he behaved amazingly towards me. He never treated me like a rival, but as a friend, helping me to settle and explaining things such as the best route to Anfield and how to dress for away games. He helped me a lot and I remember him fondly for that. It also showed me how I should behave towards Pepe Reina when he arrived from Spain to replace me.

Abel Xavier

If I had to nominate the best-dressed team-mate I played with during my career then Abel Xavier would have no competition. He had clothes that somehow matched his hair and outfits that simply no-one else could have worn. Djibril Cisse was an eccentric dresser, but Xavier was stylish – although some days his outfits were so bright you could barely look at him!

Bolo Zenden

Bolo is a lovely fella who can speak Dutch, English, Spanish and French particularly well. He was small, but exceptionally strong and we could see why he used to do judo! He'd done really well at Middlesbrough and never been injured there but as soon as he started training with us he picked up a knee injury. That was a surprise for the whole team...

WORLD CUPS AND WORN GLOVES

I first thought about the Polish national team when playing for Concordia in the third division as they described me as a 'goal-keeper with a national team future' when trying to get a bigger transfer fee for me. Six months later – as a Sokół player in 1996 – I arrived in Tychy for another training session when one of the lads told me to see the coach as I had received a call-up from Antoni Piechniczek, who was the coach of the national team of Poland at the time. I was sure that it was a wind-up and ignored them. Then Bobo Kaczmarek came into the dressing room and said: "Gentlemen, we have a new international. We received a fax calling up Jurek to play against Russia."

I thanked the lads for helping me to achieve this milestone, but when I had to go to Bełchatów for the national team training camp – chairman Buller told his driver to take me there – the nerves kicked in. I wondered if the other players would accept me. Edward Socha, the Poland national team executive, was waiting for me at the hotel: "Here's the key to your room, we've booked you a single so no-one will interrupt you." I felt better, but then I panicked. If I'm alone who will tell me where to be and when? I was also given a Polish national team training kit, tracksuit and a pair of boots. I was so proud to get them. I must have tried the gear on five times before training and I've still got that tracksuit to this day.

Polish FA chairman, Marian Dziurowicz, gave us a motivational speech: "This is a very prestigious match for us. If you win I'll give you 500 million zloyts bonus," which was a huge amount of money at the time, but it didn't interest me at all. I knew that I had no chance of playing, because I was the third-choice goalkeeper, and was simply happy just to be with the squad. It then emerged that second-choice goalkeeper Andrzej Woźniak wasn't able to play so I immediately felt a great responsibility. I knew I would be the deputy for Maciej Szczęsny and would be on the bench for this prestigious friendly in Russia. My blood pressure raised immediately.

I went to the first training session and Maciej saw my gloves. He asked if they were the ones I wore for Sokół. I explained to him that I only had one pair as Sokół wasn't a rich club and I'd had to buy them myself, but hadn't been paid for three months so couldn't afford new ones. Szczęsny was shocked and called Socha over: "How can this kid be expected to train and play in these gloves?" Socha said he didn't have any gloves for me, but Maciej wasn't a guy who'd take no for an answer and I received a brand new pair of Puma gloves. Unfortunately they didn't fit me very well so I only wore them in training!

'Do you want a girl?'

We flew to Moscow and when the others realised it was my first ever flight they started to take the piss, saying Russian airlines crash a lot and to bring a spanner to screw my seat down properly. I sat next to Radek Michalski, who was a joker, and I asked him what the stewardess was handing out to the passengers.

"Cookies," he said.

"Oh great, I love cookies."

"Take two then, she won't mind."

I took two and as I started to open one Radek couldn't contain his laughter. They were disposable wet-wipes. "Don't worry," he laughed, "you'll need these in Moscow."

You don't see much of cities you travel to as a footballer but Moscow had big buildings and really wide streets. We stayed in the Rossiya Hotel, a Soviet-built enormous building that was probably the biggest hotel in Europe at that time. It was average at best – I'd stayed in better rooms when travelling away with Sokół – but as the new boy I wasn't going to complain. We ate after training and the food was awful. The waiters bizarrely sliced everything up, even the fruit, so our doctor went out to buy some more but the waiters sliced all of that up too! I went to see Red Square – and it reminded me of seeing the tanks driving through it on TV – but getting sleep was difficult. I had a single room and quite late on the phone rang. I assumed it would be a team official or the coach, but when I answered I got a shock.

"Good evening," said a mystery male voice. "Do you want a girl?" I was shocked! "No, I don't want a girl," I replied and hung up. At about 1.30am the phone rang again. "Hello, do you want a girl sending to the room?" "No, I really don't," I

267

said, "I want to sleep!" I wasn't very well the following day as I discovered salmon doesn't agree with me. I don't eat it now, but they served it for breakfast, lunch and dinner in Moscow!

Volleying a bread roll

My duty as deputy goalkeeper was to ensure Szczęsny was properly warmed up before the game and then obviously I was on the bench. We were losing 2-0 late in the second half when Szczęsny picked up a knock. I suddenly realised I might have to come on and that got my backside twitching! It stressed me out, I didn't feel ready, but Maciej was okay so my international debut would have to wait. After the game one journalist came to me to ask a few questions. I realised then that I was really part of the national team squad. The following day we were due to receive a packed lunch for our journey back to the airport but all we got was some stale bread rolls. I walked down the hotel stairs to see our striker Wojtek Kowalczyk shouting at TV commentator Andrzej Zydorowic, who had apparently been criticising our performance. "Why didn't you tell the full story? We've had nothing to eat and have been living in a shit-hole. Look at this roll with green ham on it." Kowalczyk then picked up his lunch and volleyed a bread roll across the street.

I took a step back and thought about things. Russia had been part of the communist Soviet Union until 1991 and I realised that we were still in the middle of the communist reality. Later I remembered that when teams came to Poland under the communist system, they complained about the standard of hotels as well. Because of that I knew I should have more tolerance.

After coming back to Warsaw the lads who complained, Kowalczyk, Tomek Iwan and Andrzej Juskowiak were all temporarily removed from the international team. I took the positives out of the trip. I didn't play, but it felt like my debut, and I had been able to work with one of the most famous Polish coaches, Antoni Piechniczek.

Hit by an orange!

Later that month I was called up to play for Poland Under-23s in friendlies against the Olympic teams of Argentina and Brazil in South America as part of their preparations for the Atlanta Olympic Games. What an amazing experience that was! Football in Argentina is like a religion. We had to have a huge police escort to stop the fans there mobbing us, even though they must have had no idea who we all were! We travelled to Tucuman in the north of the country and the military presence was so strong we thought some kind of revolution was on the cards. We weren't even allowed to train in the stadium; instead we had to use a square with two lamp posts at either end. It was ridiculous and hilarious in equal measure.

The stadium in San Miguel de Tucuman was a football ground with 15-metre fences all around the pitch. It was packed as Argentina had some of their best players in the team – Roberto Ayala, Roberto Sensini, Jose Chamot, Juan Sebastian Veron, Javier Zanetti, Diego Simeone and Claudio Lopez. Most of them were at big European clubs. We were in the dressing room talking about tactics when team executive Jerzy Koziński came in and said the match might be off as the Polish FA hadn't yet received their appearance fee. We finally got the go-ahead to play 10 minutes before kick-off and walked onto a pitch surrounded by policemen with rifles. I wasn't going to get in the way of their shots!

The Polish FA were desperate for me to wear Reusch gloves in the games as part of a sponsorship deal and gave me two pairs, promising me more if I wore them. They lied, which was a pity as they were good gloves. I ended up having to wear the pair I had used during the warm-up as in the first 15 minutes the other pair were very slippy so I changed them and ended up playing one of the games of my life. I was only supposed to play in the first half, but did so well that the coach, Edward Lorens, left me on. I was saving everything and the home fans were getting frustrated with me so one of them, who was sitting on a fence, chucked an orange that hit me on the head. A police officer immediately pulled him down after hitting him with his rifle butt, but it made me worry about what else they might throw at me. We ended up losing 2-0 – Abel Balbo and Simeone scored – and the next day I was awarded 8/10 in the local paper, a huge compliment as four of the Argentina team only got 6/10. We travelled to Buenos Aires afterwards and for the first time people recognised me. They were shouting 'portero, foto?' which means 'goalie, photo?' It was the first time I'd ever experienced any kind of popularity.

We flew to Rio de Janeiro next and I saw the famous monument of Jesus Christ. I thought to myself: 'Am I really here?' We had five days in Brazil but they were favourites to win Olympic gold and our coach feared we would get routed as they had Dida, Roberto Carlos, Aldair, Juninho, Rivaldo, Bebeto and Ronaldo in their team. I didn't play as well, and we lost 3-1 after taking the lead, but maybe that wasn't a bad result against that team!

'Put your cocks up!'
In February 1998 I made my full Poland debut away to Israel.

Many of the lads were scared to go there because of the Israeli-Palestinian conflict and seeing non-uniformed men carrying guns and having a helicopter hovering over our team hotel didn't exactly make us feel confident. I was told by the coach, Janusz Wójcik, that I would play in the second half, but now that I was playing week-in, week-out for Feyenoord I didn't feel nervous. I let one goal in and we lost 2-0, but I was surprised that the coach criticised my positioning for the goal. He didn't call me up again until August 1999 when we played Spain in Warsaw.

I didn't play much under Wójcik, but his team talk before that Spain game was one of the most memorable of my career. "The Spaniards are beautiful boys," he said. "They look great when they play on their guitars when the sun is shining, but not today. Not here in Warsaw. Nobody will f***ing pull the strings today except us. We start from the beginning and we press them from the first whistle. Put your f***ing cocks up! Off we go!"

I'm not sure if you would call that a rousing or an arousing speech! It motivated the lads and we went 1-0 up early on, but while I was sitting on the bench I noticed some strange behaviour. The Russian referee, Sergei Khusainov, and one of his linesmen were very favourable towards us so two goals correctly scored by Spain were adjudged as offside and disallowed. One of the Polish executives sat there praising the officials over and over again, saying what a great time he had with them the day before.

The following month Khusainov was accused of being drunk the night before he refereed a UEFA Cup game in Israel and was banned by UEFA for five months. It makes me wonder what he had been doing in Warsaw the night before we played

Spain! I came on in the 64th minute to make my home international debut and I recall making a good save from a lob by Raul, but we lost 2-1.

Under Beckham's skin

We still had a chance of qualifying for the play-offs to reach Euro 2000 if we got results in our final two games against England and Sweden. If we beat England we would finish above them in second and if we drew with them a point in our final game in Sweden, who had already won the group, would also be enough. The build-up was disrupted by arguments over how big our bonus should be if we qualified. Polish FA vice-chairman Zbigniew Boniek and Andrzej Pawelec, who was on the Polish FA committee, were meant to be on the same side, but ended up contradicting each other resulting in them agreeing to our demands of 120,000 dollars, making us all laugh. We then faced England in Warsaw and although I didn't play I learned a lesson in gamesmanship.

Wójcik started to talk to midfielder Tomek Iwan: "The pretty boy in their team, Beckham, has married a Spice Girl, Victoria. You need to use this. Don't be scared of the English; they are a team of cloggers. The only one who can play is Beckham. Tell him you've shagged Posh Spice. Tell him you've f***ed her loads of times. It will piss him off, distract him."

Iwan did as he was told. Every time Beckham was in earshot he told him he'd had Victoria. He told him he'd performed sexual miracles with her, over and over again. Beckham became more and more pissed off and by the end he'd lost his focus and was running after Tomek hoping for the opportunity to clatter into him with a challenge. David Batty also got wound up and was sent off for a reckless challenge on Radoslaw Michalski. We drew 0-0 and knew that a point in Stockholm would mean we would finish in second. Unfortunately we went into the game with the wrong mentality, thinking the Swedes would be happy to draw with us to put England out. They weren't happy with some of our tackling, though, and raised their game. We lost 2-0. That was the end of Wójcik. They decided to hire Jerzy Engel instead.

Number one

Engel called me up for a friendly against France in Paris in February 2000 and told me: "I am building a new team. You fit the profile of what I want from a keeper. You're my number one."

I was so happy that I drove from Rotterdam to Paris with Jan and Leo Beenhakker, my manager at Feyenoord, to get to the match! We lost 1-0 and I played well, but I was annoyed with conceding the winning goal to Zinedine Zidane in the 88th minute and the camera zoomed in on me saying "f***ing hell". That footage was even later used by politicians as an example of things that can happen when emotions are running high! I had to do a post-match press conference with Zidane and felt overawed sitting next to him. All but two questions were fired at him – he wasn't happy with the state of the Stade de France pitch – and I was relieved to get through my first international media engagement.

The battle of Yerevan

We led our 2002 World Cup qualification group from start to finish. We began with a 3-1 win against Ukraine in Kiev, beat Belarus at home, drew with Wales in Warsaw, won in Norway, beat Armenia at home and then got an important victory away to Wales in Cardiff. After that match we had to travel to Armenia, but we heard a rumour that the president of group rivals Ukraine had met with the Armenian president to motivate them by offering the players a win bonus to beat us. We knew we would face a battle in Yerevan, and so it proved.

The hotel we stayed in wasn't in a very attractive area and the only place where our mobile phones picked up reception was in a corner on the roof near the swimming pool that was about two metres squared. We had to queue up like we were waiting for a payphone to get into this corner and if two people got a signal no-one else could get one. It was very strange. The coach constantly repeated: "Don't get provoked! They are nowhere close to your football level so they will fight with dirty tricks," and it turned out to be our toughest game. They provoked us constantly and gave us all a good kicking. The referee was allowing this to happen when suddenly he decided he'd had enough in the second half. He booked five of their players and sent two of them off, also booking three of our players. Then someone kicked Jacek Bąk and he retaliated, sparking a mass brawl. Bąk and another Armenian were dismissed, meaning it was 10 versus eight, but we couldn't get a winning goal and it finished 1-1. Then the fun started!

Myself and midfielder Piotr Świerczewski were selected with two Armenians to do the random drugs test. One of the Armenians could piss immediately, but the rest of us were more dehydrated so they gave us each a beer. Piotr, who had been playing in France for eight years and was known as 'Świrek the nutter', started to speak in French with the Armenian player about what had gone on during the match. Their voices got louder and louder. I asked him what was going on and he was bubbling with rage. "Who the hell does this tough guy think he is? He's just said that if I say another word he'll call the boys in and have us buried alive!"

That really riled Świrek. He was ready to beat the living daylights out of this guy when the Swiss official conducting the drugs test intervened, telling me to split them up. Boniek happened to walk in at that point and helpfully told us they were fed up of waiting for us to piss so were leaving without us and would see us at the airport! I told him not to be so stupid. If he left us alone with the argument raging he might never see us alive again! Boniek wouldn't listen. He said a car was waiting for us outside and if we poured cold water over our legs that would make us pee. I followed his advice and within minutes I'd filled the sample bottle and was free to go, but Piotr asked me to stay. I figured I should wait and after he had finally peed he exchanged swear words with the Armenian and we left. Zdzislaw Krecina, secretary general of the Polish FA, was waiting for us in the car, but that was the scariest journey I'd ever been on. Every streetlight was switched off and I spent the 20 minutes it took to get to the airport thinking we would be ambushed and buried in a field in Yerevan. I've never been so glad to see an airport in my life!

The president called...

We had a crucial World Cup qualifier against Norway in Chorzow on September 1, 2001, the day of the 62nd anniversary of the German invasion of Poland that marked the beginning of World War II. If we won we would become the first Polish team to qualify for the World Cup since 1986. I had never experienced such an emotional build-up to an international game as the one coach Engel provided. Engel showed us a documentary about the start of WWII. He recalled that people remember that date as a start of the fight for life and honour. It seriously motivated us all to play well for our nation.

We travelled to the Śląski Stadium. It was buzzing. I heard one huge roar when I entered the pitch for the warm-up. It felt like the atmosphere was literally squeezing me. I'd never encountered such an emotionally charged noise before. I don't know if the Norwegians got scared, but they didn't turn up on the pitch. We won 3-0 and when news came through from Minsk that our closet rivals, Belarus, had lost we danced like madmen in front of the fans. After 16 years we were finally back in the World Cup and were the first European team to qualify.

I wished the international season had finished that night when I think back to what happened next. We had to go from meeting to meeting to speak to sponsors, appear on an evening TV show, visit more sponsors, attend banquets and then fly to Minsk for the next game. During the build-up to it Boniek told us that Aleksander Kwaśniewski, the President of Poland, had phoned him and said that it was important that we won in Belarus from a political perspective. Engel wasn't impressed and when Boniek left the room he said: "Don't lose your heads. If you get sent off you would be banned for the World Cup games and it makes no sense for me to take suspended players."

That was the moment when we realised what was at stake for us. The thought of missing a World Cup through suspension was unbearable so mentally we weren't preparing for a fight in Belarus. They could still finish second and make the play-offs so treated it like a cup final and won 4-1, Raman Vasilyuk scoring all four goals. It was my worst display for Poland. One of the goals I conceded was after a misunderstanding with Mariusz Kukiełka and I passed the ball straight to Vasilyuk for the fourth goal. Gerard Houllier had wanted me to miss this match to prepare for my Liverpool debut and I wished I had.

Dropping Tomek Iwan

We were drawn to play against joint-host nation South Korea, Portugal and the USA in Group D at the World Cup. All of our fixtures were scheduled to be held in Korea. We prepared for the tournament in Barsinghausen, near Hannover in Germany. It emerged that Tomek Iwan wasn't included in the squad and his absence was immediately the main topic during our conversations. Iwan wasn't playing regularly for Austria Vienna, but he was a key player in the team so we approached Engel about his decision. He said that it was due to injuries and his lack of games, but Tomek Hajto wasn't happy and snapped back that one of the lads he had selected instead couldn't even do keepy-ups. Engel was furious at having his selection questioned and told Hajto he'd gone too far.

In truth it ruined the atmosphere and team spirit before we'd even flown to South Korea. You wouldn't believe how the absence of one player could be so devastating, but it really was. Of course, the coach is responsible for the team and it is his right to make the decisions, but the atmosphere in a squad at a tournament is arguably more important than the training sessions. Engel said the Polish FA coaching committee above him had also been influential in the decision, but it created a division in the camp. That wasn't a good omen as we prepared for our journey.

A suitcase full of notes

We were told we would fly to South Korea in the president's plane and thought this was a great honour until we got on board. It looked like a piece of aviation history that should be in a museum, even if we were told it had new Boeing engines. TU 154 M LUX didn't have too much LUXury inside. There was water dripping, steam coming from behind a plastic casing and the take-off was nerve-wracking. By the time we reached the end of the runway only the front wheel was in the air. We thought the back wheels were going to catch the runway lights but somehow it took off just in time. The pilot later told us the plane was overloaded with food brought by our chef! Another problem was that the fuel tank wasn't big enough to get us to South Korea so we had to refuel in Novosibirsk, Russia. We were happy that we could get off and stretch our legs but the steps that would allow us to disembark were placed a few metres from the plane. Some ground crew guy started to negotiate: "$3,000 to get off the plane. No money, no chance." One of the lads shouted down that he was mental – that we'd rather jump off than pay him – but they won't refuel a plane with passengers on it.

We had no other option so offered him $2,000. Zdzisław Kręcina explained that the Polish FA would transfer the money, but the Russians demanded cash so Kręcina had to hand over a suitcase full of notes. Finally we got off the plane, only to discover the duty free shop in Novosibirsk Airport was three times dearer than anywhere else in the world. We finally got to Korea and, because we were on the president's plane, had to land at a military airport. The Koreans couldn't believe we were the Poland team and that our plane made it from Europe.

World Cup 2002

The Koreans welcomed us with hospitality that is typical of Polish people. They were warm and friendly, but we instantly realised the climate was a problem for us. It wasn't the temperature but the humidity we struggled to adapt to. Our shirts were permanently stuck to our bodies. We stayed in a resort near Daejeon. Nothing was too much trouble for the Koreans. We had a comfortable hotel and they gave us a Korean mobile phone for easier and cheaper contact with our families at home, but within a week or so we were bored out of our minds. There were no attractions in the local area so we got into a monotonous routine of training and eating. We also had problems with the centrally controlled air conditioning which had temperature swings from 16 to 34 degrees in a matter of moments. It left most of us with sore throats and other ailments. We later suspected the air conditioning problems weren't random because after losing our first game to the hosts the problems were miraculously solved. That can't have been a co-incidence.

Engel talked the Koreans up too much before the match: "They're a good side. They're well prepared physically. The atmosphere will be intimidating. It will be a hard game." It was the opposite of the things Houllier would say to us before a big away game – "It might be noisy but I never saw a supporter score a goal" – and it put us in the wrong frame of mind. The first 20 minutes were tight, then Hwang Sun-Hong put them ahead with a beautiful finish from a cross. After that the air, quite literally, went from our lungs. In the 53rd minute we lost possession and Yoo Sang-Chul struck a powerful shot from 20 yards. I got my fingers to it but the ball flew through them into the net. I was trying to push the ball away with an open hand but someone later blamed me for the goal saying I should have tried to punch it. That was a clueless thing to say as if I'd had my fist clenched I wouldn't have even touched the ball! We lost 2-0 and the media got stuck into us. Before the tournament Boniek had said we were "untouchable" and Engel said we had gone to Asia to win the World Cup. They were trying to be positive and talk us up, but Polish people don't like big-headed claims and now those waiting to put us in our place had their chance.

We were nervous going into the second match against Portugal. They had lost their opening game to the USA so it was 'do or die' for us both. We capitulated and lost 4-0, Pauleta scoring a hat-trick. It was a truly terrible experience that left us feeling broken. We'd hit rock bottom, were out of the World Cup with a game still to play, and the media had a field day. I was on the bench for the third game against the USA as Engel decided to give other players in the squad a game, but even though we won 3-1 it backfired on him. His critics blamed him for picking the wrong team in the first two games whereas if we'd lost again the players would have been held more culpable. Jerzy Engel was sacked when we returned home.

Zbigniew Boniek was quickly announced as his replacement and I was surprised as he was high up in the Polish FA as vice-chairman and hadn't managed a team since 1996. He was a brilliant footballer, notably for Juventus, and an outstanding ambassador for Polish football so it was surprising he wanted to be a coach again as every coach knows he will be a loser in the end. Instead of building on what Engel had done, Boniek went for a revolution and almost completely changed the squad and our style of play. It was catastrophic. We won our opening Euro

2004 qualifier in San Marino, but then lost at home to Latvia. In November we went to Denmark for a friendly and it was obvious that the team was broken and had no fighting spirit. Maybe his personality overshadowed us as nobody wanted to even discuss tactics with him. We lost 2-0 and Boniek resigned.

His replacement was Paweł Janas, who had previously coached the Polish Olympic Games squad and I liked him. He told me I was a key player for him, that goalkeeping coach Jacek Kazimierski has been told to let me introduce my Liverpool training regime to the national team, and that he wanted my opinion on all kinds of issues as he respected my views. He also reverted back to the style of football that Engel had introduced and we started to progress again, but we missed out on the play-offs for Euro 2004 to Latvia on goal difference. That 1-0 home defeat to the Latvians when Boniek was in charge had proved to be crucial.

Crazy wedding guests

Our opening two World Cup 2006 qualifiers were away to Northern Ireland and at home to England. We won 3-0 in Belfast – the scoreline suggested it was easy but the Northern Irish made us fight every step of the way – and then returned to Poland to prepare for England in the Aria hotel in Sosnowiec. There was a wedding party on and the guests went crazy when we walked in. The music went on loudly into the night, keeping us awake, and I heard guests drunkenly running down the corridor knocking on rooms in the early hours shouting: "Where is Dudek? We want a photo." When we went down for breakfast the next morning there were guests smoking and drinking, curing their hangovers with 'hair of the dog'.

The following day a political party were due to arrive at the hotel for a rally! We were meant to be preparing for a crucial game against England, the best team in the group, and this was what we had to contend with. We were eventually moved to another hotel and fought hard in Chorzów but lost 2-1. The preparations didn't help us.

By the time we played England again in October 2005 we had won seven qualifiers in a row and qualified for World Cup 2006. We were top of the group, two points ahead of England, and knew that even if we lost we would qualify automatically as one of the two best runners-up. If England didn't win, however, they might have to go into the play-offs and this meant their coach, Sven-Goran Eriksson, was under great pressure. The Poland-England rivalry is a big one back home. We have great memories of Jan Tomaszewski from Wembley in 1973, so there was a huge demand for tickets and, because we had a 100 per cent record away from home, there was plenty of belief we could beat them. Maybe we got over-confident. England controlled the game and won 2-1, my former Liverpool teammate Michael Owen getting the opening goal. They won the group and we realised we had to learn from it. We lost against ourselves that day.

Confident of a call-up

I knew in early 2006 I would remain at Liverpool for the rest of the season, even though I wasn't playing so a new fitness regime was devised for me. Because I wasn't physically exhausted with not playing I had to arrive at Melwood 90 minutes before everyone else and do a strenuous session. It was also important to retain my sharpness and concentration. I made myself available for every Poland game, including a friendly in Saudi Arabia that Rafa Benitez didn't want me to travel for, and I was completely focused on these games. I felt if I made any mistakes it would be used as a reason for me not to go to the World Cup in Germany with me not playing for Liverpool, but my form was good. I was on the bench when we beat West Ham in the FA Cup final on penalties in Cardiff and afterwards I went for a short holiday absolutely convinced that I would be in Janas' World Cup squad.

It has to be a joke

I texted Maciej Skorża, assistant manager to Janas, before the World Cup squad announcement to remind him of my contribution: "When you pick the squad don't forget the lads who worked hard in qualification. We have a great atmosphere and we don't want another experience like in South Korea." I was thinking of what happened with Tomek Iwan in 2002 and I had a feeling that Janas might wobble over his selection of some of the senior players, but surely wouldn't break the trust he had built up with the squad.

On the day of the announcement I was in Knurów, opening a brand new football pitch built with the help of my foundation, and I told everyone the squad announcement would be on the TV soon. I was driving back home when a series of text messages came flying through and lots of different people tried to ring me. I knew something must have happened. As soon as I walked in I switched the TV on and there it was on the screen: 'Breaking news: Dudek, Kłos, Rząsa and Frankowski left out of Poland World Cup squad'. I thought it was a joke! Janas then appeared for his press conference and I was expecting him to pull a piece of paper from his pocket and say "Sorry lads, got you there, this is the real squad," but he didn't.

I wasn't in his squad. At no point had he told me I wouldn't be going to Germany – I had to find out through the media – and it also caught his assistant Skorża by surprise as he'd spoken to me after I'd texted him to say he'd let me know where we'd be meeting for the first get-together!

I still can't find any rational reason as to why I wasn't called up. I hadn't been playing for Liverpool, but he had selected me for seven of the 10 qualifiers and I now had over 50 caps for my country. Janas didn't have very good interpersonal skills – he had a repressed personality – but I cannot forgive him for failing to tell me I wasn't in the squad, leaving me to find out by watching TV. If he'd phoned and said "Sorry Jurek, I only want to take goalkeepers who have been playing regularly," or whatever I'd have been gutted, but I would have accepted it and got over my omission a lot quicker. For Janas not to tell me the bad news man to man is something I will never forget.

Leo

It was another catastrophic World Cup for Poland. Defeats in the opening two games against Ecuador and host nation Germany meant we were eliminated before a 2-1 win against Costa Rica, which counted for nothing. Janas was rightly sacked.

I was disillusioned about the national team at this point but my spirits lifted when Polish FA chairman Michał Listkiewicz decided it was time to hire a foreign coach and appointed Leo Beenhakker.

I texted Beenhakker straight away to congratulate him and he phoned me back: "You are the most important player for me,

Jurek. You will be in the team for sure. I make the decisions now and nobody will tell me what to do."

It was good to hear, although Leo hadn't yet realised what a problem off-the-pitch interference is when it comes to the Poland national team. I told him about them in a conversation, but he thought it wouldn't be a problem. He underestimated the issue!

Leo took stick for calling me up for a friendly against Denmark. Jan de Zeeuw was also involved in the national team now and people said there was a Dutch clique and Leo should be looking to the future, not picking a 33-year-old who couldn't get a game at Liverpool. I desperately wanted to help Leo but before our first Euro 2008 qualifier, at home to Finland, I got so involved in off-the-pitch issues that I didn't focus properly on the match. With the score at 0-0 in the second half I cleared the ball straight to one of their players, who chested it to Jari Litmanen and he chipped it past me into the net. We then had Arkadiusz Głowacki sent off for conceding a penalty, which Jari converted, and went on to lose 3-1. I told the media I was responsible for the first goal, not the result, and afterwards Leo took us for dinner. He told us to be honest and open about the problems within the team. We stayed up talking to him until 5am!

Serbia were our next opponents and I sat with Leo and told him not to play me. I wasn't playing for Liverpool and if I made a mistake it would give the media another bullet to fire at him. He thought I was over-reacting: "Jurek, I have worked every-where in the world. I have even dealt with the mafia. I'll be fine, don't worry." My intentions were honest, but I think he perceived me as being a smart arse who was telling him what to do. I didn't play against Serbia and Leo didn't call me up for international duty again. Poland made it to Euro 2008 in Austria and Switzerland, our first ever European Championships, but finished bottom of the group. Leo had Poland in contention to qualify for the 2010 World Cup for South Africa, but a 1-0 defeat away to Slovenia proved to be costly. He was sacked inside the stadium in Maribor with two qualifiers still to play. He later admitted to me that the off-the-pitch problems I'd warned him of were a nightmare: "Jurek, you were right. It's the first time I've been in a football environment where not everyone wants success. In other countries the media, footballers and the FA work to the same goal. In Poland everyone has a different agenda."

An unexpected return

Stefan Majewski became caretaker-manager and surprisingly called me up for the final two qualifiers at home to Slovakia and away to the Czech Republic. I was chosen to play in the first game and that meant a return to the Śląski Stadium in Chorzow, a venue that holds great memories for me after we qualified for the 2002 World Cup by beating Norway there. Unfortunately the squad was disillusioned, the Poland supporters were boycotting the game in protest at how the Polish FA were running things and it snowed heavily. I'm not sure if they forgot to turn the undersoil heating on that morning but the pitch was almost unplayable.

Slovakia needed to win to qualify for their first ever World Cup and did so 1-0 after an early own goal from Seweryn Gancarczyk. I left the pitch feeling sad as I thought this would be my final cap for Poland. The new coach would have to build a squad for Euro 2012, which we were hosting with Ukraine, and

I knew I wouldn't be a part of it, so it upset me that my final appearance looked like being in an empty stadium on a dismal night. It wasn't how I wanted my international career to end.

At the beginning of 2013, two years after retiring from club football, I was part of a Polish FA delegation that was invited by the Spanish FA to Madrid. I had a chance to speak with Zbigniew Boniek, elected as the new chairman of the Polish FA a few months earlier.

"Jurek, what would you say if I could organise one final game for Poland for you?" he asked.

I was delighted and we started to talk about the details.

We had a friendly against Liechtenstein in Krakow in June and if I got to play it would be my 60th cap, but I would also make it into the 'Club of Remarkable National Team Players' for which you need at least 60 caps to qualify. I was 40 in 2013, but was still very active. My overall fitness was good, but I hadn't done any specific goalkeeper training for a long time so I trained on my own with Piast Gliwice, a club where my brother Dariusz was an assistant coach.

The match was in the cosy Cracovia Stadium and I started it as captain with the number 60 shirt on my back. All the memories came back to me and there were many familiar faces in the crowd. I was presented with a memento before kick-off and after 34 minutes I was substituted, receiving a guard of honour from my team-mates. The crowd were great too, singing my name a few times during the first half. I felt great relief when I left the pitch. I'd kept a clean sheet, not embarrassed myself and the lads went on to win 2-0. It was a great way to officially end my career. Finishing as a footballer is not easy, but all of us have to do it one day.

There were rumours in the media that I took the other players for a massive party afterwards ahead of the World Cup qualifier against Moldova, but it wasn't true. I simply attended a function arranged by one of my business partners, had a symbolic beer with the coach and I was presented with a cake. I wished the players luck in Kishinev and went home because I was in absolutely no mood to party.

We miss them so much

Life is brutal. It painfully teaches humility and I experienced it during my last game for Poland. Instead of being happy about making my final appearance, I was reeling from a family tragedy. A fortnight earlier my father-in-law, Edward Litwin, a retired miner, suffered a stroke while visiting our house.

He survived the stroke but fell into a coma and was cared for in a Kraków hospital. We visited him every day and hoped and prayed that he would wake up. I still had to prepare for my final game, but all my thoughts were with him. After a dozen or so days I said to the head doctor there: "I play in my last game for Poland tomorrow. He badly wanted to see it." The doctor said it was unlikely that he would wake up but that they would put the game on in his room on television. "He will be with you in the stadium subconsciously, Jerzy."

You have to behave like normal around a person in a coma so the day after the Liechtenstein match I went to the hospital to tell my father-in-law all about it. He passed away before I got there.

Comedians joke about in-laws and I know it can be difficult for some people with the parents of their partner, but my father-in-law was unique. He was a fantastic man with whom I got on extremely well. He was a true football fan who travelled to see me play in as many matches as he could. He may not have been able to see me play for one final time, but I felt he was there with me. He stayed until the final day of my career.

We really, really miss him and will do forever, but it wasn't the only tragedy we had to deal with. The following year we lost my father, too. We celebrate All Saints Day in Poland and go to cemeteries to put candles and flowers on the graves of our beloved ones who have passed away. That day we went with Dad to visit a cemetery. He didn't feel well, but he thought that it was nothing serious, so I started to joke: "Hey Dad, what's up? You've barely walked 500 metres and you're struggling to breathe? You need to get fit." We went our separate ways and I was visiting my mother-in-law when I decided to call my younger brother, Piotr, to see how my father was.

"Mum is giving him water," he said before he suddenly started to get upset. "Jurek, you'd better get over here quickly."

I ran from one block in Szczygłowice to another as quickly as I could. Dad had suffered a major heart attack. The ambulance arrived quickly and the paramedics tried to resuscitate him for 30 minutes, but they were unsuccessful.

My dad was 63 when he died. My father-in-law passed away when he was 62. Both of them were miners. Some people in Poland are envious that miners retire sooner than other professions do, but they don't realise that miners also pass away sooner. We miss them both every single day.

THE REAL
EXPERIENCE

I got on well with the Spanish lads at Liverpool. Luis Garcia, Xabi Alonso and Pepe Reina were not only players with quality, they were all bubbly, positive characters who always spoke well about the Spanish way of life. They taught me what type of wine to drink, introduced me to new foods like jamon and Pepe got me into eating paella. I liked the atmosphere among them.

We prepared for the 2007 Champions League final in La Manga and Ocho asked about my plans for the 2007/08 season.

"The only thing I know is that I will leave Liverpool. I've had a few offers, but nothing concrete."

"I've got something concrete for you from Spain. Interested?"

"Yes, Spain would be brilliant. But which club?"

"Don't say a word, it's a secret for now, but Real Madrid are seriously interested in signing you."

I laughed. "Come on Jose, I'm an experienced player. You're not getting me with that one."

"I'm being serious. They've done their homework, contacted me a couple of times and spoke to Pepe about you. I'll put you in touch with them if you want..."

When the initial surprise of what Ocho had said wore off I didn't think about it for long. Real wanted me to be back-up for Iker Casillas, but having spent two seasons on the bench I wanted to be number one somewhere so I was more interested in other offers. Recreativo de Huelva, a newly-promoted La Liga team, made an offer, but I didn't want to join them. The more interesting offer came from Real Betis. Mark Gonzalez, who had just agreed to move there from Liverpool, spoke to me about it: "Come to Betis, we need a goalkeeper. It's a superb club, very chilled out. The chairman wants you, the coach wants you... you'll get a new lease of life and I'll help you settle."

Betis had made me a good offer so I decided they were the best option and instructed Jan to set up contract talks. In the meantime I received a call from Predrag Mijatović, the sporting director of Real Madrid. He said he understood my decision but if I changed my mind to contact him before July 14, as there would be an offer on the table from them until that date. It left me feeling confused. I wanted to play regularly again and Real Betis were offering me that, but could I really turn down Real Madrid? The only place I could switch off from thinking about it all was on the golf course. I played a lot of golf that summer as, unlike my previous transfers, I had a number of options and needed to take time to weigh them up. For the first time in my career I had no club. I didn't know my future and it stressed me out a lot.

During the second week of July, Betis finally set up a meeting with myself and Jan so we flew to Sevilla. We were sitting in a hotel waiting for the Betis chairman, Jose Leóna, but after 30 minutes there was no sign of him. We phoned his personal assistant and she said: "Don't worry, he'll be there." But then she turned up at the hotel, told us to have a meal while we were waiting and presented us with a new version of the contract.

There was one important change. Only 40 per cent of my salary was being paid by Betis, the rest was to be paid by the chairman's company. I called Mark Gonzalez and he admitted his contract was the same. I didn't like it because if there were any issues regarding payment the Spanish FA would only guarantee I received the money Betis were due to pay me, not what the chairman's company would owe me.

Another hour passed, still he hadn't arrived, but we thought that perhaps the Spanish are a bit more relaxed about time so didn't panic and took our time over lunch. Then, about three hours after he was due to arrive, Jan received a text saying a Dutch TV station was reporting Real Betis had signed a contract with Portuguese international goalkeeper Ricardo. I was stunned. I came to the conclusion that Leóna had brought me to Betis to put pressure on Ricardo to sign a contract. He had me sitting there waiting as an alternative and I didn't like the game he was playing. I told Jan that even if Real Betis still wanted to sign me it was too risky. The deal was off.

Recreativo de Huelva were still interested but a week earlier a friend of mine, who had been to Huelva on holiday, told me he didn't think it would be a great place for me to move to. I realised he was right. I'd become used to playing in front of big crowds at De Kuip and Anfield and trying to win trophies so, with all due respect to Recreativo and the people of Andalusia, fighting a likely relegation battle in front of small crowds wouldn't fulfil my ambitions. I turned them down. Jan decided to call Leo Beenhakker, who had managed Real Madrid twice, for advice about their offer. His view was clear: "In every country you can find a famous football club, but there is only one club that is unique, second to none. Real Madrid. If they give you a contract you are happy with don't think twice about it. Go to Madrid."

Jan called Mijatović immediately and said we could be in Madrid tomorrow. It's fair to say Leóna's PA was surprised when we asked her for the number for Spanish airline Iberia so we could book the flight!

The Real deal

It took an hour to fly to Madrid. We met Mijatović at 11am and by 11.30am I had agreed a two-year contract. The only sticking point was that I wanted a one-year deal so I could see if we settled in Spain, but Jan advised me to take the two years on offer as it gave us extra security. So I did. I signed the papers at the legendary Santiago Bernabeu and Mijatović told me to report for pre-season training on July 24.

A lawyer claiming to represent Real Betis then turned up at our hotel threatening us with legal action because he said I'd agreed to sign for Real Betis, but I refused to listen to him and we went to see the house I would be renting. I wished I hadn't even been to Betis and had just signed for Real Madrid straight away at this point, but I was happy to have got there in the end. We had to keep the deal quiet when I went back to Poland for a week, but I'm not sure anyone would have believed me anyway!

I was curious as to why Real Madrid had targeted me and Mijatović was very honest about it. They wanted a goalkeeper who was prepared to be second choice to Casillas but had the quality to be able to successfully stand in for him when called upon. They also wanted someone who could motivate Iker in training by proving they could take his place in the team without making him feel too threatened, and a goalkeeper who was focused on the job rather than just being in Madrid to make money while winding down their career. They decided I fitted the bill perfectly.

My first job as a Real Madrid player was to attend the official 'player presentation', an important part of the club's culture. I had to attend the Santiago Bernabeu, speak at a press conference and then I was presented with my Real Madrid shirt and squad number for the season by the legendary Alfredo di Stefano. Then I had to walk out onto the pitch where the supporters would be waiting in the stands. Depending on the class of the player, presentations can be attended by thousands.

Obviously I was never going to compare to Cristiano Ronaldo, who got an incredible 80,000 fans turning out just to see him walk onto the pitch, but when I walked out of the tunnel I felt like I was at a galactic club. Members of the Polish community in Madrid filled almost one section of the stadium and I had to stand on a podium on the pitch. I really felt like a Real Madrid player that day.

First impressions
I lived in room 910 at the Sheraton Madrid Mirasierra hotel initially as Real had a deal with them that meant the entire ninth floor was exclusively booked for us. We slept there before

home games. Spanish life was something of a culture shock for me. I walked into a bookshop at 1.55pm to buy a Spanish phrasebook and the woman looked at me like I was an alien. She wanted to close up because between 2pm-4pm in Spain they escape the heat by having a siesta. The streets are dead for two hours. I was also used to eating my dinner at around 5pm in England but in Spain the restaurants are closed until late. I walked into one restaurant at 7pm and the waiter explained that the chef only started at nine! Staying awake later than my normal bedtime of 11pm also took some adjusting to. For me, a home body, this change of routine and lifestyle took a lot of getting used to.

I remember my first training session well. We sat in the dressing room and all of the lads came over to warmly welcome me. In other dressing rooms you feel fearful or get an insecurity complex, but not here. I felt like I'd been at Real Madrid for years and this was a dressing room full of stars. Outside of the club few people spoke English, but with most of the staff speaking English at Real it was a lot easier for me to communicate quickly. It also helped that I spoke Dutch. There was a Dutch colony at Real. First it was Ruud van Nistelrooy and Royston Drenthe, then Arjen Robben and Wesley Sneijder. Rafael van der Vaart joined us the following year. Thanks to them my acclimatisation was a little bit easier.

Playing golf was also helpful – I often played with Julio Baptista – and there were other new things to get used to such as having a bottle of wine on every table at pre-match lunches and being told we could drink as much as we wanted, before going for a three-hour nap!

I quickly realised how enormously popular Real Madrid is.

Wherever we travelled, we were welcomed by a massive crowd of fans. They waited to see us at airports, in hotels, on the streets. In Holland and England these scenes were only common for cup finals; at Real Madrid it was normal before every game. I felt like a member of a famous rock band hearing screams every time I left the tour bus. We even had bodyguards responsible for our security who gave me instructions of what to do if I thought a car was following me, and where to go for help if I was being hassled in a shopping centre!

Valdebebas

Real Madrid's Valdebebas training ground is known as 'Ciudad Real Madrid' for a good reason. 'Ciudad' means 'city' in Spanish and the Valdebebas is the size of a small town! There are a dozen or so pitches, comfortable dressing rooms, several other buildings containing all kinds of facilities and in the centre is the 6,000-capacity Alfredo di Stefano Stadium, home of the reserve team, Real Madrid Castilla.

Security is exceptionally tight, you get a better parking space if you arrive for training in an Audi due to a sponsorship deal, and the whole thing is set up to give first-team players privacy. No-one can interrupt the players there – it's not like at Melwood where photographers and fans can look over the wall to watch training sessions – and they even close the window blinds when journalists and guests are there after allowing them to watch the first 15 minutes of training from a balcony.

When Jose Mourinho became manager he had the complex redesigned to include 12 hotel-style double rooms. Benitez had done the same at Melwood and the idea was that after midweek matches we would sleep there to save us having to drive home, then have breakfast as a squad the following morning. Attention to detail was very much part of life at Real Madrid.

One of the other surreal things was that celebrities and VIP guests would be invited to watch training from a special balcony. One day I looked up to see Colombian football legend Carlos Valderrama; another day his compatriot, Rene Higuita, was there. Stars from other sports would turn up too. Andy Murray came to one of our training sessions and Rafa Nadal would also attend. Nadal is a massive Real Madrid fan who would rather have played for them than play tennis!

I was at training one day when I recognised a guy but couldn't think who he was. Then the penny dropped. It was Kurt Russell! I think he was there to promote a movie premiere and a couple of the Portuguese lads who weren't training that day, Cristiano and Pepe, were standing with him getting photos. I was bored in goal so, for a laugh, kicked a ball towards them, but I struck it a bit too hard. It was flying towards Kurt Russell's head when at the last second Pepe spotted it and made a brilliant catch, one Pepe Reina would have been proud of!

I was grateful to Pepe as taking a Hollywood star's head off before he went to a film premiere wouldn't have been my finest moment!

Diego Maradona also came to watch a training session when he was coaching the Argentina national team. He looked great, in far better condition than the media would have had you believe, and was a really nice guy.

He was very relaxed, down-to-earth and I was impressed with how he talked. Maradona has a huge football knowledge and did not come across as the arrogant character that he is often painted as.

You're in, you're in...

Real Madrid traditionally play for the 'Mayor's Cup' in different cities during pre-season and I learned that the bigger a trophy is in Spain, the less important it is considered.

We won one in La Coruna that was so big it took five of us to lift it! We played a semi-final against Real Betis that summer that was goalless with five minutes to go when suddenly Manuel Ruiz, a former goalkeeper who was coach Bernt Schuster's assistant manager, turned to me and said: "You're going on. This goes to penalties if we draw and you're an expert. You're going on for Iker."

I was surprised! I hadn't warmed up, my boots were untied and I had to find my gloves! After a quick warm-up I came on in the 90th minute praying that I didn't make a mistake and that I saved some penalties.

In the 94th minute Betis got a free-kick on the edge of our box that Juan Pablo Caffa fired into the top corner. Game over, and I hadn't even touched the ball! The lads were laughing at Ruiz in the dressing room, sarcastically calling him a genius for bringing me on. He told me again that he had seen what I did in Istanbul and thought I would be an ideal substitute, but it wasn't the perfect start for me.

A quiet cathedral

The Santiago Bernabeu is a football cathedral. Anfield is unbeatable in terms of the smaller stadiums, and I like the design of the San Siro in Milan and Old Trafford in Manchester, but the Bernabeu is one of the best looking stadiums in the world. It's also a massive tourist attraction – I read that a million people visited it last year – and in the huge club museum they list the names of every foreign footballer to have played for the club. Underneath the Polish flag is the name 'Dudek'. It gives me a huge sense of pride to have my name and photo there, especially when friends or family mention it to me after going on the tour, as while I may not have played too often for Real Madrid, it is fantastic to just be mentioned alongside some of the biggest stars to have played at the Santiago Bernabeu.

The atmosphere can be amazing, but not as intense or noisy as it can be in English grounds despite there being more people there. People come to watch Real Madrid like they're going to the theatre; it's almost like a cultural event.

I invited friends over from Warsaw, Poznań and Silesia and I remember the Lech Poznań supporters not being very impressed: "The stadium is bloody amazing, Jurek, but the supporters? One group of lads behind the goal sing and try to make an atmosphere, but the others sit around and do nothing. Are they here for a picnic?"

My experience is that in Poland the fans sing and make noise for 90 minutes irrespective of what is happening on the pitch, in England the fans react to events during the game and in Spain, where Real Madrid fans are very demanding and treat a draw like a defeat, they are a lot quieter and only become more vociferous when they are unhappy.

Mourinho tried to change this. He said publicly: "We have to motivate them to become the 12th man" and the club ran a promotional campaign with slogans like 'let Santiago Bernabeu be alive'.

It worked. The Bernabeu became noisier for a longer part of matches and I believe that when a player feels such support it gets an extra 10 per cent out of him.

Iker does his homework

Iker Casillas spoke less English than I spoke Spanish so we had some funny moments trying to communicate when we went to a pre-season training camp in Austria. Thankfully our goalkeeping coach, Pedro Jaro, a great professional and a good man, spoke fluent English so he helped us out. Iker knows Pepe Reina very well and had sounded him out about me. He'd also been in touch with Ocho, who was the goalkeeper coach for the Spanish national team. He'd asked every question about me and had notes! I was surprised by this, but it was a positive thing. It showed how professional he was.

Iker has great goalkeeping abilities but had problems dealing with crosses into the box and when the ball was at his feet. Both of these issues were evident when Real Madrid played Liverpool in the Champions League in 2009. I was stronger in these areas so Jaro introduced training exercises designed to help Iker improve. It helped him. Schuster had a reputation for resting his first-choice goalkeeper for the La Liga game before Champions League matches so I thought I would get some game time, but Iker was in such good form in 2007/08 he couldn't leave him out. He was the main reason why Real won the title in my first season in Madrid.

The man with the briefcase

We crashed out of the Champions League to Roma in the first knock-out round in March 2008, but had the La Liga title wrapped up with three games to spare when we scored two late goals to win 2-1 away to Osasuna. Our final away game was at Zaragoza, who were involved in a relegation battle, and this was when I discovered the Spanish culture of 'el hombre del maletin' – 'the man with the briefcase'. Spanish football club owners offer incentives for other teams to do well in crucial games against their rivals. I might surprise you saying this, but I don't mind that kind of motivation. If there is extra motivation to win rather than throw a match where is the problem?

Zaragoza needed to win to help their chances of staying up and obviously their relegation rivals wanted us to win, but with the title already wrapped up we had little to play for and Schuster had decided to give some of the lads who didn't play regularly a game, including myself. It would be my La Liga debut for Real. I don't want to say too much as I don't want Spanish prosecutors paying me a visit, but it was rumoured that we were incentivised by Zaragoza's relegation rivals to play well. I never saw el hombre del maletin – I played for pride and made a couple of crucial interventions – and we drew 2-2, much to the annoyance of the Zaragoza players. They were relegated the following weekend in dramatic circumstances.

We finished the campaign with a 5-2 win against Levante and celebrated in traditional Real Madrid style with the supporters around the fountain on Plaza de Cibeles. We met at Santiago Bernabeu and travelled to it on an open top bus down Paseo de la Castellana, the main street in Madrid. It was madness and reminded me of the scenes in Liverpool after we won the Champions League.

These are the moments you play football for – it's like a trip to the gates of paradise through thousands of people that admire you. You feel like a god to them. We had a celebratory dinner and then went to trendy Madrid nightspot Buddha del Mar, where we partied until dawn. It wasn't like at Liverpool though – the lads were too well behaved! I had only played five times that season, but I had another medal around my neck and if me being there had helped Iker to improve his form then perhaps I'd contributed more than the appearance statistics suggest.

It was a pleasure to work with you

I haven't got a bad word to say about Bernt Schuster. The German, who was a cool player during the 1980s, was a charming and intelligent man during face-to-face talks but could become a little introverted when he was with a group of people. It was a strange quality for a coach to have, but he was good to me.

I considered quitting Madrid after six months to try and get games in the hope I could make it into Poland's Euro 2008 squad, but Schuster called me in for a chat and told me he relied upon me as much as Iker and wanted me to stay. I listened to him and, with no alternative offers on the table anyway, decided to remain in Madrid. The team were playing poorly though. We were knocked out of the Copa del Rey by Real Union and after a 4-3 home defeat to Sevilla, Schuster was sacked. We all received a text message from him that read: "It was a pleasure to work with you. I wish you luck for the future. Unfortunately, we will not be working together any more. I wish the team the best possible results in the rest of the season."

Juande Ramos was Schuster's successor, having been sacked by Tottenham Hotspur himself. He was a good personality, like an older brother, and I got on well with him, but he liked to moan about how unprofessional players are in England and that they didn't like his training methods. It was like working with Houllier again! Results improved, but we were knocked out of the Champions League 5-0 on aggregate by Liverpool

– I was on the bench for both games and while being back at Anfield was special, it wasn't enjoyable to lose 4-0!

We had four games to play after an embarrassing 6-2 home defeat to Barcelona and I thought Ramos would give me some games, but he announced his strongest XI would continue to play. Iker was tired, having barely had a break after playing in Euro 2008 the previous summer – Guti told me: "Iker is so exhausted he couldn't catch a taxi in the street!" – so I was very, very disappointed. We lost all four games and Ramos was sacked. He didn't even text us to say adios.

Alcorcón

I decided to stay at Real in the summer of 2009 so signed a one-year deal with the plan of returning to Poland in 2010. Chilean coach Manuel Pellegrini, who had done very well at Villarreal, was hired as our new coach and he was brilliant with training sessions and tactics, but he didn't have a strong personality and found it hard to capture the imagination of the club's biggest stars. He didn't get to sign the players either – the sporting director did that – and ended up with a squad overloaded with central midfielders including my old team-mate from Liverpool, Xabi Alonso. We finished the season with 96 points, a club record at the time, but lost home and away to Barcelona, who beat us to the title by three points. We were knocked out of the Champions League by Lyon, but personally it was what happened in the Copa del Rey that defined my season.

We were drawn to play third division AD Alcorcón, a club from the suburbs of Madrid where many Real fans live. They played in a cosy 6,000-capacity stadium, were playing brilliantly in the league and this was like a World Cup final for them. We travelled there for the first leg and Pellegrini selected me to play, but made life harder for us by selecting three lads – Metzelder, Arbeloa and Guti – who needed games to build up their fitness. Even though 80 per cent of the stadium were supporting Real, we had a catastrophic night and lost 4-0. It was 3-0 at half-time and Guti was ranting in the dressing room. He screamed: "It's a scandal and shameful. It's impossible to play in this way. This is only a third division team..."

Pellegrini took exception to this: "You talk too much. Take a look in the mirror. Where have you been on the pitch?"

If you know Guti's temperament you'll know what happened next. He had a right go back at Pellegrini. It turned into a blistering row that ended when Pellegrini told him he was being substituted. We were a bit better after the break, but it was written the next day by someone that our 4-0 defeat was the biggest football sensation of the 21st century. He might have been right. Ironically, I was named as Man Of The Match for keeping the scoreline down to four, but a lot of people made fun of what happened. To a certain extent, it destroyed my reputation, something that really pissed me off.

Pellegrini is a polite, charming gentleman, but perhaps lacks the devilment you need at the top level. His replacement certainly had it!

One of the best phone calls I've ever had

I was one of the first people to know that Jose Mourinho would be the new coach of Real Madrid. I was meeting with Jorge Valdano, Real Madrid's chief executive, about whether I'd be getting a new contract and he told me: "We are getting a new coach, Mourinho. It depends on him if we extend your contract. I would do it now, but there is no guarantee he will want to work with you."

It seemed that Mourinho would have more influence on which players he could sign than his predecessors. He was appointed as Real Madrid coach after his Inter Milan side beat Bayern Munich in the Champions League final, a game I commentated on for Polish TV as, ironically, it was held in the Bernabeu, and 10 days later I was back in Poland when Valdano called me. "Jerzy, I'm with Jose. He wants to talk to you."

"I have heard good things about you. I need two goalkeepers. You should get on a plane back to Madrid now and sign for me for another season."

I was delighted; it was one of the best phone calls I had ever had. The chance to work for Mourinho could not be turned down. It proved to be the best experience of my time in Spain.

I quickly learned that Mourinho was a brilliant strategist. He not only told us how to play tactically, he told us how games would turn out. I remember his team-talk before an away game early in the season: "Gentlemen, this team are dangerous at home. If you start slowly, they will score. 1-0. A quarter of the game gone. It will make you nervous. Maybe you'll score. 1-1. But they can score again. 2-1. And if that happens you will be coming off." He pointed at one of the players as he said this.

"But, we start aggressive? We score. 1-0. They must attack. We have the best counter-attack in the world. We score again. 2-0. Then we protect the result." We started well and won.

He was clever at preparing for situations that other managers don't anticipate, such as a player getting sent off. We all knew how the tactics would change if we went down to 10 men no matter who was sent off. It was all planned in advance. He had us playing eight-a-side training sessions and then would call one player to the touchline for a chat, leaving it as eight versus seven for five minutes. The player he called over was carefully chosen, making us learn how to play without him. It was a lesson in how to take responsibility if things went wrong.

'My wife doesn't want to see me'

We had to adapt to a different way of doing things under Mourinho from the outset. It started on the summer tour of America when he arranged a meal to introduce his coaching staff to us and then took their credit cards off them. He shuffled them like a pack of cards and pulled one out. I forget whose card it was, but he had to pay the full bill for the entire squad. Believe me, it wasn't a small bill! Hopefully they eventually divided the bill between them. Honestly, it was too much for one person to pay.

Mourinho told us of his expectations: 100 per cent commitment, mutual respect, ambition, responsibility and maximum focus in training.

That essentially summed up his entire coaching philosophy and if someone didn't agree with a decision his door was always open to discuss the matter.

For instance, he insisted that we slept in a hotel the night before matches in Madrid, something the lads didn't understand, so Iker and Sergio Ramos went in to ask if we could spend the night before at home instead. He addressed us all with his decision: "You have a great captain and deputy. Iker and Sergio are on my back. They come to me 24/7, but my decision is final. I'll tell you why. One day a week my wife asks for a rest. One day a week she does not want to see me. So we stay in the hotel. Okay?"

I was fascinated with his personality. For want of a better phrase, Mourinho has balls! He's like a football general who is not afraid to lead his soldiers into war. Right from the start he tries to reach everyone in a squad by saying we are all part of the same army, whether in the starting XI or not. Achieving this at a club like Real Madrid where there are 20 internationals, most of whom were star players at previous clubs, is very challenging. That's why the Real Madrid coach has to be an authoritative figure. Mourinho was exactly what the club needed. He hadn't played at a high level, but it was evident that he had learned a lot from his father, who was a goalkeeper and coach, and from Bobby Robson at Porto and Barcelona.

There are no gym sessions in Mourinho's training philosophy. Everything is done on the pitch with a football. He believes a footballer can gain the necessary strength, speed and fitness on the pitch and warned us about what happened to Frank Lampard at Chelsea: "I told him not to do more in the gym. I told him the training sessions will strengthen his leg muscles enough. But he didn't listen. He did more. He did more running. And when he was running he injured his thigh. I told him 'Frank, I warned you. But you didn't listen'." That got the message across loud and clear. We had to buy into and trust his methods.

'You're cheating your team-mates'

Disciplining players is a crucial part of being a manager and we found out how Mourinho goes about it following a 0-0 draw away to Levante in September 2010. Pedro León, a right winger, arrived from Getafe that summer for €10 million and thought he was a superstar, but he didn't go straight into the team. This annoyed him and he was on the bench at Levante. We were drawing 0-0 and Mourinho asked him to warm up, but rather than do so properly he simply stood by the corner flag and did a few stretches. I was sitting on the bench near Mourinho and he spotted this. He was fuming: "Look at his lack of effort. And then he gets f***ing offended when I tell him he's not buckling down..."

He put León on for Angel di Maria for the final half-hour but when he twice had perfect opportunities to put crosses in he failed to deliver them and we drew 0-0. It was evident he was lacking concentration and commitment, something Mourinho bollocked him for in the dressing room: "You are unprofessional. You think you're cheating me? No. You're cheating your team-mates. I saw your f***ing warm-up. You couldn't care less about it, but I put you on. Two balls you had to deliver. Two balls for the strikers to put into an empty net. But you were not prepared. Do you care about playing for Real Madrid? Everyone has their five minutes here. You've had yours."

The following day we had training ahead of a Champions League tie away to Auxerre. León thought he would play, but Mourinho called us all into the middle of the pitch and singled him out: "I'm really sorry that you're not interested in playing for Real Madrid. Really sorry. Others would sacrifice everything to wear the shirt. But you're not interested." He turned to a young winger who was training with us by the name of Juan Carlos.

"How old are you?"

"Nineteen."

"Do you want to play for Real?"

"Yes."

"Would you sit on the bench and he happy?"

"Yes."

"When I ask you to warm up will you show full commitment?"

"I will."

"Good. You're on the bench on Tuesday night."

Then he turned back to Pedro León: "You will watch it at home on TV. I need people who will die for Real Madrid. Enjoy watching the Champions League on television."

We understood that there were no half-measures with Mourinho. He made an example of León in front of us all to make us aware that if we didn't put the effort in there would be no hiding place. Pedro León made just 14 appearances for Real Madrid and was sold the following summer.

The rat

As the title race intensified we drew 1-1 with Barcelona at the Bernabeu in April 2011. Mourinho entered the dressing room and said it wasn't a bad result because we'd played most of the second half with 10 men after Raul Albiol was sent off. But then he surprised us.

"I see your relations with the media are quite good. I know we have to get along with them but I didn't think you were getting along that well. I heard from them that you do not want meetings before the games, that we practise set-pieces the wrong way and our tactical training sessions are not good enough. I turn on my TV four hours before the game and what the f*** do I see? That a journo is giving away our line-up. How could we ever surprise them if one of you is a rat? Yes, yes. A rat! Somebody released the starting XI before the game. They knew everything about us. We trained all week. We wanted to surprise them."

He continued to shout about how Barcelona knew of his plan to play Pepe in midfield to man-mark Lionel Messi: "I'm always on the front line. I control what happens at this club. I lead you into battle like a general. But as we're about to attack, one of you stabs me in the back. You stab me in the back before such an important game?"

His eyes started to mist up. I'd never seen him in such an emotional state before. "Where is the rat? Who is it? Who could it be? Maybe you?" He pointed a finger at Esteban Granero, a midfielder who was from Madrid. He then pointed at three or four senior players. "Maybe it is somebody who has played here the longest? How can you destroy what we've been working for all week? You screwed me over. But you screwed yourselves and your families and friends too. I will get to the f***ing source."

With that he launched a plastic bottle against the dressing room wall, stormed out and slammed the door. We sat in silence in the dressing room like beaten dogs.

Mourinho was resentful towards us for a couple of days. Silvino, Mourinho's goalkeeping coach, told me that it had left a scar on Jose's soul and he even considered quitting Real Madrid. The media started to speculate that he'd lost the dressing room, that he'd fallen out with Cristiano Ronaldo and that he privately suspected Iker of being the rat because his girlfriend, now wife, was TV journalist Sara Carbonero and she must have inside stories from the dressing room. I never found out who leaked the team that day, but it was the start of problems between Mourinho and Casillas. After I'd left Real I returned to watch the first leg of the 2012 Copa del Rey semi-final as part of a Polish FA delegation and bumped into Mourinho in a hotel at lunchtime. I asked him how things were going and he said: "We have a problem with one girl, but we'll handle it." It was easy to work out he was referring to Casillas' missus, who was sharing all kinds of juicy anecdotes from the Real dressing room on TV, and he dealt with it by signing Diego López from Sevilla when Iker suffered a hand injury. When Iker returned to fitness, López remained in goal.

Learning from Iker

Iker Casillas is well aware of his own skills. He knows exactly what he can do best and what people love him for. It helped him to build his position as Real Madrid and Spain's number one keeper. One of his biggest assets is his extraordinary concentration. He has really strong legs and good reflexes which, despite his lack of height for a goalkeeper, help him to be fantastic on his line.

Pedro Jaro and other goalkeeping coaches saw some elements in Iker's game that he could improve on, but he calmly told them he would prefer to focus on what he could do best. At a certain time he was, in my opinion, the best goalkeeper in the world, but there was rivalry for that title with Juventus and Italy goalkeeper Gianluigi Buffon. Fabio Cannavaro was well aware of this and once said loudly in the dressing room: "Iker is a fantastic goalkeeper, a real genius, but Buffon is a goalkeeper from a different galaxy."

Maybe he was just saying so to wind Iker and the other Spanish lads up, but I think Fabio was convinced that Buffon was better than Casillas. When I spoke with him, he constantly reiterated the same stance. Buffon won a World Cup in 2006, but Iker won the World Cup in 2010 plus two European Championships in 2008 and 2012. He was a real leader who had so much to say on and off the pitch and could pull up the team in the toughest moments.

I learned a lot from him. First of all, a self-awareness that you should not push too many things as it can lead nowhere or, if you're not careful, to self-destruction. He also taught me to shun ambitious goals which you cannot achieve because if you push for perfection at all costs you can neglect the assets that got you to a certain level.

I thought that Iker was done at Real and I knew the reason for his poor form. He'd played too many games during the season and only had a two-week holiday after it. It wasn't long enough for him to recharge his batteries. After 15 years at the top level a loss of form had to come, but he still managed to maintain a decent level despite playing something like 80 games in a year and not having much of a break. He deserves credit for that.

The problems began when his girlfriend, now his wife, started to leak information from the Real Madrid dressing room. That's when his run-in with Mourinho started. When Carlo Ancelotti took over in 2013 he said he respected both goalkeepers and whoever trains best would play. I knew it wouldn't be Iker. He wasn't the type who trained hard before a game. He had great experience and was aware that he had to prepare for the game professionally, but he saved energy in training sessions ahead of matches. The reserve goalkeeper, on the other hand, can train twice as hard knowing that he won't need his energy on a matchday, nor does he have to prepare mentally in the same way. Ancelotti let Casillas know that it didn't matter to him that he was a club icon or how long he had been at Real so it was no surprise to me when it emerged that Iker was no longer first choice for the 2013/14 season.

'Papa Dudek'

Iker always laughed at me because I have three children: "You're almost a grandpa, Papa Dudek!"

I laughed at him and replied: "You'll see, it'll be your turn soon." He shook his head: "Not too fast mate, not too fast."

I reminded him of that conversation when Real Madrid arrived in Warsaw to play a friendly game against Fiorentina in 2014. I thought it would be great to visit the lads in the hotel and say hello. There was no pressure at all, as they were playing a friendly, so I had a chance to talk with them. I caught up with Pepe, Marcelo and Cristiano. It was nice, but I talked with Iker for an hour or so. He knew he wouldn't play, so he didn't have to concentrate before the game, and I asked him about the Mourinho conflict. He just shrugged his shoulders: "I really don't know what it was about. I read in the papers comments attributed to me, but those words never left my mouth. He didn't even ask if what the papers were saying was the truth. He treated me like he really suspected me of something and he didn't defend me during the press conferences. Mourinho said that Antonio Adan is better in goal than me. I really didn't know what was going on. It was strange."

I knew that Iker felt it a lot. I told him: "It's a perfect moment for you. Now you can figure out who your real friends are. Once you get through it, you'll find plenty of new friends." Iker started to show me the pictures on his phone: "Look, this is my mini me. He was two weeks at the time of taking this picture…" That was the thing I expected to happen to him when I said 'you'll see'. I know how it feels to have kids!

"Iker, we all have this moment. Football is not as important for you any more. You have different priorities. You don't sleep well and your routine has changed. I experienced it for a year after Alexander was born. I wasn't focused on football, even when I played, because I had more important stuff away from the pitch. When Alex snored I wondered if everything was fine. When he coughed I froze until he stopped."

Iker had learned from the same life experiences, so he didn't laugh at me or call me Papa Dudek. He said something completely different: "It's really amazing. I didn't ever think I'd experience such a thing."

Iker is now at FC Porto and when I look at his displays I can see his worst moments are behind him. I'm glad, because I consider him to be a good friend.

CR7

After much speculation, Cristiano Ronaldo signed for Real Madrid from Manchester United in the summer of 2009. You've probably read a lot about him, but he is one of the most professional players you could ever meet. If training was due to start at 11am he'd be there for 9.15am. He did extra work in the gym before and after our 90-minute training sessions. I watched him for almost two years and I can say that everything he achieved on the pitch is through his own hard work. He also symbolises the modern football superstar – not many others have their own brand like his CR7 – and very quickly became the number one name at Real.

Cristiano is ambitious. He wants to be the star. If he doesn't receive a pass when he thinks he should, he sulks. This some-times pissed the lads off, but we got used to it. His personality and character is similar to Raul's. Raul wasn't always happy when we won 3-0 and he didn't score. He preferred a modest 2-1 win with him on the scoresheet. He adored scoring the winning goal, being the hero, and Cristiano is the same. He wants to be the goalscorer at all costs and has an egotistical mentality about it. I think he sees team-mates as assistants who are working towards his greatness and this irritated Mourinho.

Mourinho worked with him a lot. He knew his compatriot cared more about his own success than that of the team, but wouldn't accept it. He explicitly warned him against provoking supporters and team-mates with his gestures and reactions on the pitch and told him he must become more of a team player. Mourinho was keen to avoid Ronaldo thinking that if Real Madrid won it was because of himself and if we didn't it was because of the rest of us, but that took a long time to happen.

Ahead of one game against Barcelona his instruction to the front three was not to press the Barca players in their own half but to draw them forward to try to hit them on the counter-attack. Ronaldo ignored him. Right from the kick-off he chased the ball from right-back, to centre-back to left-back in their half, was unable to win it and then turned around to the other lads and gestured 'why aren't you backing me up?' The crowd booed, thinking the others weren't putting any effort in!

Afterwards, Mourinho asked him in the dressing room why he had ignored him. Cristiano is the type of guy who is not afraid of exchanging words and he and Mourinho then had a frank, aggression-free discussion in front of the rest of us about their differing tactical views.

Several of the other lads had their say and I sat there thinking if they'd had the discussion six months earlier then maybe the team would have gelled quicker and we would have won La Liga, and perhaps the Champions League, rather than Barcelona.

I regularly stayed late after training so Cristiano could practise his famous free-kicks. Obviously he had to get good at them to score past me! He can make a ball move at a different trajectory than any other player and this is always put down to the way he connects with it, but there is another reason. Ronaldo has small feet. I have faced a couple of other players who can hit a ball like him, but with less power, and they had small feet too. Cristiano takes a UK size seven boot and I think having smaller feet allows him to control the power in his legs better than others. He effectively crushes a ball when he strikes it so it flies off like a balloon that is losing its air. Trying to stop a ball that moves in different directions at such pace is incredibly difficult. I came to realise that in training!

I also have to say that Cristiano is a perfect role model off the pitch for young players, but he is very image conscious. He got his hair cut every couple of days and would spend a long time in front of the mirror in the dressing room to ensure he looked his best before TV interviews and matches. He would join in the banter with the other lads in the dressing room, but he didn't take losing very well.

We lost to Lyon in the Champions League and I had invited the boxing champion, Dariusz Michalczewski, to the game as my guest. He came to watch us train the next day and was shocked when he saw Cristiano arrive and refuse to sign autographs for some kids: "I'm going to f***ing smash him," said

Darek. "F*** getting a picture with him and his autograph. How can he be like that with kids?" I calmed him down and spoke to Cristiano.

"I'm not here for f***ing autographs," he said angrily. "I'm here to win. We went out of the Champions League to f***ing Lyon last night. I'm pissed off, leave me alone." The kids were especially disappointed with him and it came across like he was being a prima donna, but Ronaldo is a perfectionist who takes defeats personally. Thankfully Darek didn't get to him... Ronaldo might never have won a Golden Boot after a knock-out blow from him!

El Clasico

El Clasico is different from any other game in world football and I was at Real Madrid during a period when Pep Guardiola's Barcelona were enjoying a golden age. The games between Real and Barca were real battles – international team-mates put friendships aside during those matches – and you would see sly tactics in operation such as Guardiola getting his players to surround the referee after almost every foul. Pressurising match officials is as big a part of Barcelona's identity as tiki-taka.

Mourinho knew that everyone thought Ronaldo was arrogant so he tried to turn more attention onto our biggest playing rival, Lionel Messi: "The truth is that the biggest football smart arse is Messi. He covers his mouth to protect himself from lip readers when he is provoking defenders. He irritates opponents, even if he doesn't show emotions on the pitch." He was right.

Messi said things to Pepe and Sergio Ramos that were offensive, in contrast to his golden boy image in the media. If I told you what he'd said you probably wouldn't believe it came from a player who is a role model for many people in the world. Mourinho used Messi to convince us that every great player must have an ego and a bit of menace about them, no matter what their image, to go with their will to win. Messi was part of a provocative Barcelona team that would do things out of sight of the referee in the hope that there was a reaction which he spotted. They also knew how to fall down at the right time in the penalty area. Small details like that made a difference to Barcelona winning big games and Mourinho wanted to open people's eyes to it.

Real played Barcelona five times during 2010/11, my last season in Madrid, including four games – La Liga, Copa del Rey final and Champions League semi-finals – within 18 days in April and May. Earlier that season we had lost 5-0 at Camp Nou. We had started the season well and Mourinho decided to go there with an attack-minded strategy but they were too aggressive, too fast and too dynamic for us. We were shocked to lose 5-0. Mourinho walked into the dressing room and slammed the door: "Be quiet and listen. Listen to them singing in the dressing room next door. They won 5-0 but what do they get for it? Three points. Nothing else. Remember this before we play them next time." Then he surprised us.

"Tomorrow, take a day off training, but you still have to work. Go into town. Take your wives and children out. Go to your favourite places. Let the people see you. Talk to them about losing 5-0. Nobody will say a bad word. They will support you. It will get it out of your system. Our opponent was better. Tell them. But we will be ready next time."

Other coaches would have been full of anger, rage and recrimination. Not Mourinho. It hurt his reputation to lose 5-0, but he refused to let it create internal divisions in the dressing room. The greatness of Mourinho was visible in that moment. He showed his great experience and how he could raise players' spirits in difficult moments through smart psychology. He then started to pin newspaper quotes on the wall in our training complex, like Phil Thompson did at Liverpool, before we played Barca with headlines like 'Xavi: Beating Real Is Like Having An Orgasm' and a photo of Gerard Pique holding five fingers up celebrating the 5-0 win. It worked to a certain extent as later that season, days after drawing 1-1 in the return league game in the Bernabeu, we beat them 1-0 in the Copa del Rey final. They went on to win La Liga and knocked us out of the Champions League, but that cup final defeat prevented Barcelona's greatest-ever side from winning the treble.

Mourinho's messenger

During a Champions League group game against Ajax in Amsterdam in November 2010 I was asked by Chendo, a former Real player who became an executive, to sit next to Mourinho on the bench during the second half.

We were 2-0 up, through to the next round and still had one game to play. Mourinho told me that if Xabi Alonso and Sergio Ramos, who had been booked, got themselves sent off they would miss the final meaningless group game against Auxerre and have no suspensions hanging over them going into the knock-out phase. He asked me to run down to Iker and pass on the instruction of what they needed to do.

I nodded and jogged down the touchline with a bottle of water to pass to Casillas. "Iker, the boss said tell Xabi and Sergio to get another booking so they miss the next game."

I jogged back to the bench and noticed that Iker was whispering in Sergio's ear. He then ran over to Xabi. In the 87th minute, with the score at 4-0, Xabi was given a second yellow card for time wasting. Sergio was also given a second booking for time wasting in stoppage time. We finished the game with nine men, but it hadn't gone unnoticed and UEFA started an investigation.

UEFA asked me for an explanation as to why I'd run down to the goal to see Casillas. I told them: "He wasn't feeling well so Mourinho had instructed me to see how he was feeling and if he should save a substitution to bring him off. Iker told me he was fine so I returned to the bench."

The UEFA disciplinary committee didn't believe me. I was fined €5,000, Iker was fined €10,000 and Xabi and Sergio both received €20,000 fines. Mourinho was fined €40,000 and given a two-match ban, although this was reduced on appeal, and the club received a €120,000 fine.

I started joking in the dressing room: "I won't pay it for sure! It was the masseur's fault that he didn't give a bottle of water to Iker. And it's your fault too doc, as you didn't check whether he felt well. I am not going to do your jobs for you!"

More importantly though, Xabi and Sergio were free to play in the knock-out stage and carried no yellow cards over. Mourinho's tactics had worked and, to be honest, I really admired him for that plan.

'I've lost some teeth'

I played in the Auxerre game at the Bernabeu. It was my first appearance of the season, but I only lasted for 44 minutes. Auxerre's Roy Contout was running towards me with Raul

Albiol alongside him and I ran out to clear the ball. Albiol realised I would get to it first and moved to the side but Contout was right behind him and, like a runaway train, clattered into me as I cleared the ball. He caught me in the face with his shoulder and I hit the ground.

The adrenaline was pumping and I jumped to my feet as my team-mates rushed over. Lassana Diarra got to me first and I think I said to him: "I've lost some teeth."

"It's okay, there's nothing," said Lassana, but I could feel two teeth on the right side of my jaw were moving and pointing at a crooked angle. The doctor arrived on the scene and started to check my head. He pressed his finger against the side of my face and when he touched an area just below my ear a bolt of pain ripped through me. I had to go off. I was gutted as I'd made two important saves earlier and it was good to be playing in the Champions League again when we were trying to win 'La Decima' – Real Madrid's 10th European Cup – but I was in agony and didn't even realise the supporters were giving me a standing ovation as I walked off. I was rushed to hospital where I was diagnosed with a fractured jaw and I had to have surgery the following day. It was two months before I was fit enough to go back on the bench.

I only played 12 times in four seasons at Real Madrid but I always gave 100 per cent in training. Football was never a job for me – it was a pleasure – and I was determined to be in the best possible shape if ever I was called upon. That's what I had been signed to do and I fulfilled that, but it was difficult. Training hard but knowing you won't play at the weekend is like teeing off on the golf course knowing there isn't a hole on the green. I stuck at it though and I think this is why I was respected in Madrid and why they twice extended my contract. When I arrived in Spain I was also one of the few players in the Real squad who had won a Champions League medal and that earns you respect in a dressing room. I was also mindful that many others dream of being in my position so it would have been wrong just to go through the motions.

Feeling like royalty

I decided to retire in 2011. I had turned 38 in March of that year and concluded there was no point looking for a new club. I wanted to see out my contract then move on to the next stage of my life. Real was an ideal club to finish my career – I completed my football education there – and I was given an opportunity to stay. Mourinho phoned me shortly before the end of the season: "Jerzy, I respect your decision, but you cannot retire like a nobody. You have to play one last game. Come to the Bernabeu so we can talk."

I went there straight away and told him perhaps I'd find a new challenge in Poland, but it was likely that I would be hanging up my gloves. Mourinho and one of the club's executives asked me to reconsider leaving and if I'd consider remaining at the club in a different role. A lot of ex-Real Madrid players end up working there in different positions. I had already been offered promotional work for Euro 2012 in Poland at that point so I politely declined their offer. "Okay," said Mourinho, "but you will play in the last match. You will be my captain. If it goes well I will take you off late on to wave goodbye to the supporters."

We played Almeria and although I didn't captain the team – Florentino Perez said it was tradition for the longest-serving player to wear the armband in the final game – it was a fantastic occasion for me. After Cristiano scored in the 77th minute to give us a 7-1 lead my number went up on the touchline and that was my club career over. I applauded all four sides of the Bernabeu as I came off and could not believe it when I saw my team-mates making a guard of honour for me. Ronaldo, Ramos, Pepe, Albiol, Arbeloa, Özil, Alonso, Benzema and Adebayor lined up and made me feel like royalty as I came off. It showed they appreciated my commitment over the previous four years.

It was definitely one of the most beautiful moments in my career. I didn't play a big part at Real Madrid, but it was worth the sacrifice of not playing regularly for a moment like that. Guti texted me when he saw it: "You bastard, they didn't say goodbye to me like that!" and the Spanish press ran articles questioning why I was given a guard of honour when some of the club's biggest legends, including Raul, hadn't been. The answer was simple. I was one of the few players who was leaving Real Madrid on good terms without any conflict.

Many players leave Real Madrid after falling out with the chairman or coach. Some are forced to leave when they think they should be staying. Instead of wanting to shake hands with everyone, they leave feeling angry, whereas I was going on my own terms and with the blessing of the club.

After the match I stayed in the dressing room for a long time. I think I was the last person to leave. There were plenty of thoughts in my head. Was it really my last game? I sat there and thought to myself that for a kid who started out playing on a patch of grass in Poland that was sandwiched between a block of flats and a workers' hotel, I hadn't done too badly...

MY MADRID
TEAM-MATES

Cristiano Ronaldo, Iker Casillas and Jose Mourinho weren't the only big names I encountered and played alongside during my time at the Santiago Bernabeu...

Xabi Alonso

A Spanish bookworm, Xabi is one of the most intelligent players I've ever shared a pitch with. He couldn't speak English when he arrived at Liverpool so did his talking with his feet, spraying passes around over 50 or 60 yards that only Steven Gerrard could match. He scored twice from inside his own half for Liverpool, one of them at home to Newcastle, and he would try that in training against me for both Liverpool and Real Madrid! Xabi is a very humble guy away from football and I'd love to see him follow a big name like Clarence Seedorf by winning the Champions League with a third club at Bayern Munich.

Alvaro Arbeloa

Alvaro also loves to read. He's always got a book in hand. We met in Liverpool. He had some problems there – mostly regarding failing to settle in England – and I wondered if Real Madrid was the right move for him. Alvaro is a very aggressive defender, but the demanding Real Madrid fans want to see technical skills too. I underestimated him. His commitment and defensive capabilities more than compensated for his weaknesses and he wasn't part of the Spain squads that won two European Championships and the World Cup by accident.

Julio Baptista

I saved a penalty from Julio in a League Cup game at Anfield when he was at Arsenal. I don't recall anything else he did that night! A common passion for golf meant that Julio and I became good friends at Real and we'd sit together on the team bus travelling to games. He still owes me a pack of golf balls!

Karim Benzema

When Benzema first arrived for a summer training camp he reminded me of the Brazilian Ronaldo. He was very relaxed, but his problems started when he didn't learn Spanish straight away. He was the type of guy who thought nothing about driving, and crashing, a Lamborghini. I think he shunted three cars in his first six months with Real! Despite that he seemed like a nice guy. His friend, Lassana Diarra, was a bad influence on him. If both of them weren't playing regularly they were like two loose cannons ready to blow in the dressing room. It didn't help the atmosphere. After Lassana left, Zinedine Zidane got into Karim's mind and helped him turn things around. He learnt the language and grew up.

Emilio Butragueno

El Buitre – 'The Vulture' – was a sporting director at Real when I was there and I found him to be a very intelligent man who attracted people to him through his positive character. He was a brilliant striker and his reputation means he is still very well thought of in the football world. He got things done for Real that others couldn't have achieved, purely because he was Emilio Butragueno.

Fabio Cannavaro

Fabio was a very chilled out guy who ate a ton of salad and pasta! I sat next to him during a training camp meal when I first signed for Real Madrid and there was a big bowl of salad on the table. He took a clean plate and put a portion of salad on it. He then left the plate and walked off with the salad bowl! "What are you doing?" I said. "That bowl is for all the lads." "No, no," he replied. "This is for me. It is not my fault we only get small portions." He then did exactly the same thing with a big bowl of pasta on the table! We teased him a lot about this but he taught me about nutrition. He also had a much-repeated response to anyone who dared criticise him: "I have nothing to prove to anyone. I'm a World Cup winner."

Ricardo Carvalho

Very professional, very serious – Carvalho reminded me of my

Polish team-mate Marek Koźmiński. A footballer has to learn to react to stress in a natural way, but I think Ricardo lacked that ability. He was also lacking the speed and manoeuvrability he had at Chelsea when he came to Real Madrid and that made it difficult for him.

Vicente del Bosque

I didn't work with del Bosque at Real Madrid but he made more of an impression on me than any other Spaniard during my career. I visited the Spanish national team's training facilities as part of a Polish FA delegation and he was a class act, answering every question we had and spending a lot of time with us. He came across as a mixture of Beenhakker and Mourinho and I could see why he was so successful at Real and has been with Spain. He was also very down to earth and said something about coaching that stuck with me: "When you sign a contract and everyone praises you, imagine how their faces will look when they want to sack you." Del Bosque has won everything there is to win as a player and manager, but he keeps his feet on the ground.

Alfredo di Stefano

It was a sad day when di Stefano died in 2014 as he was the best example in world football of how a club should respect a legendary former player. He promoted the Real Madrid brand all over the world and they named the stadium at the training ground after him. When he presented me with my Real Madrid shirt his handshake was that of a confident old man and when I saw archive black-and-white footage of him playing I realised what a great player he had been.

Mahamadou Diarra

One of the best defensive midfielders in the world, Mahama-dou is from Mali and is a practising Muslim who takes religion very seriously. He always had a prayer mat and compass with him so he knew which direction Mecca was. His faith impressed me and he asked the other Muslims at Real, Lassana Diarra and Karim Benzema, to follow his example, but they had a much more relaxed attitude to religion.

Angel di Maria

Only Cristiano Ronaldo and Arjen Robben were faster than him and he was able to win a game on his own, but di Maria wasn't very resilient to criticism that came his way. I saw him in Warsaw when Real visited for a friendly in 2014 and he was upset with the club for pressurising the Argentinian FA not to select him for the World Cup final against Germany in Brazil because of an injury he'd picked up in the quarter-final. He joined Manchester United a month later – and has since moved again to Paris Saint-Germain – and having seen how South American players struggled to adapt to the climate at Liverpool I sensed it wouldn't work out for him at Old Trafford.

Royston Drenthe

The most colourful personality at Real Madrid in the last 10 years, he was supposed to be a new Clarence Seedorf but the boots were too big for him to fill. He had a fantastic left foot but thought he was a star before he had achieved anything and lacked discipline, which was best summed up when he turned up for a training camp a day late. Such carelessness got him nowhere.

Fernando Gago

Another Argentine at Real Madrid, he and his compatriots Gabriel Heinze and Javier Saviola were always drinking yerba mate – a South American type of tea. He introduced me to it but I wasn't impressed. It just tasted like green tea.

Esteban Granero

He was one of the biggest talents at Real, a very technical player. He didn't get enough trust from the coaches and, just like other home-grown players, he didn't get enough time to show his skills. Granero was a perfect free-kick taker. When he took them against me in training I just stood and looked as the ball flew into the top corner of my net. When I published my autobiography in Poland in 2015, Granero was unfairly labelled as a 'rat' in Madrid's dressing room. The international media quoted just a part of the whole story from the book. I think everyone understands now after reading the whole chapter that Mourinho pointed at him purely as an example of a home-grown player from Madrid. Mourinho pointed at other people too, but poor Granero was singled out for something which, in my opinion, he had nothing to do with.

Guti

A great golfer, he showed me the best places to play in Madrid. He also had the potential to be one of the great footballers but lacked the motivation to go with it. He'd turn up 10 minutes late for training and blame the traffic, ask to be substituted because he had a headache or stomach pains and would even disappear for a couple of days. He had the talent to have achieved a lot more.

Gabriel Heinze

Heinze was like an Argentinian-German dog. When he caught an opponent, he didn't let him go, like a dog with a bone. He was very feisty in training and tackled as hard as he did in matches, but was a nice guy off the pitch. I lived in the same area – Ciudalcampo – as him, Saviola, Robben and Sneijder. Gabi told me a lot of stories about how tough life was in Argentina during the economic crisis. Because of different restrictions and blockades they invented a new way of delivering meat – in an ambulance that sped through the streets with the siren on and lights flashing!

Gonzalo Higuain

The most underrated player during my stay at Real. 'Pipa' – he was nicknamed after a sunflower seed – didn't receive a fair chance to show his talent. He would have scored a lot more goals for Real if they'd treated him as a number one striker and I was pleased to see him doing well at Napoli. Maybe Real decided to sell him to Napoli because he is better suited to teams with a more defensive style who play more on the counter-attack. Pipa needs more space to use his speed.

Klaas-Jan Huntelaar

Real thought Klaas-Jan was going to be the new Marco van Basten and he had great technical skills but, like Higuain, wasn't given the opportunity to be first choice centre-forward. He was the type of guy who would huff and puff in training because he wasn't playing and you can't be like that at a club like Real Madrid. They just move you on and after just six months they did that.

Kaka

Liverpool fans will always associate Kaka with Istanbul – he was brilliant in the first half – and when I was with him at Real he would practise penalties against me in training. Before he took the first one he always shouted "2005 final" and then hit the ball. I struggled to save any of them, he was that good. He joined Real from AC Milan for almost €70m but he arrived with an injury and that stopped him from having the immediate impact expected of him. I think that difficult start had a negative impact on him and then he got injured again. I used to chat to Kaka in the gym and I tried to motivate him by saying he had to believe in himself as when he was fully fit he would be a star. Not long after he scored a goal and ran to the bench to celebrate with me to say thanks for the encouragement.

Marcelo

When I was playing in Istanbul for Liverpool, Marcelo was still playing futsal in Brazil so it tells you of his progress that he signed for Real Madrid in 2007. I marvelled at how well he took to being at a gigantic club and I noticed that he continued to adopt some of his futsal techniques such as using the sole of his boot to control a ball. He was one of the jokers in the dressing room – he'd juggle a ball like a circus artist before games – and because I was older he called me 'grandpa'. He also went on some remarkable trips. We were given a weekend off so he jumped on a plane to Sao Paulo, had dinner with his family, stayed the night and then after a spot of lunch jumped on another plane back to Madrid so he didn't miss training. He was in the air for 22 hours and in Brazil for less than a day, but Marcelo is very close to his family so to him it was worth it.

Christoph Metzelder

We arrived at Real Madrid at the same time and became friends from the beginning, which helped us when we received a painful lesson about Spanish life. As new players we had to buy the lads dinner so we arranged it for 9pm and arrived at the restaurant at 8.45pm. Nobody turned up until 10pm! Being an hour late for dinner is nothing in Spain, but it was the opposite of the German punctuality that Christoph was used to!

Mesut Özil

Mesut could not stand it when he didn't play. It was his biggest problem at Madrid. He was phenomenal when he was at his best – I'd compare his balance and technique with Zinedine Zidane – but his form was inconsistent. Mourinho expected more from him and the intense focus he was put under had a negative impact on him too.

Pepe

If he ever writes a book then I have a title for it: *Fifty Shades of Pepe*. He has a split personality. On the pitch he is a warrior who shows no mercy, would die for the shirt and is so passionate that he loses all common sense, but off it he couldn't be a nicer, more helpful guy. For instance, when I introduced the idea of Szlachetna Paczka – which translates as 'The Noble Box Project' and is a philanthropic scheme to help Polish families living in poverty – to the lads it was Pepe who met with representatives from the foundation and made a donation. We were also connected by an Audi R8 from the club sponsors that I inherited from David Beckham and drove for three years before passing it on to Pepe.

Raul

We called him 'Rulo' and I believe he will go on to become Real Madrid's next great ambassador after di Stefano. He was very ambitious, a captain who tried to motivate us and he put extra work in with myself and Cristiano in the gym. As a striker he was very greedy. He cared more about scoring than the team winning – he'd be angry at a 3-0 win if he hadn't scored but happier if he scored and we had lost.

Arjen Robben

Almost my next door neighbour in Madrid, he told me a story about confronting burglars after he returned from the Netherlands to Spain following treatment for an injury. He opened the door and heard noises upstairs so grabbed a knife from the kitchen and went to see who was there. This startled the burglars, who escaped through a window and he started to chase after them but couldn't sprint because of his injury! He was injury prone at Madrid and there were rumours that he was suffering from stress, but it was a mistake to sell him to Bayern Munich. He is a world-class winger who plays with such egotistical self-belief that Raul said: "Give him two balls, one to take home and one for him to give us a pass!"

Robinho

Robinho was like a circus act. He could perform wonders with a ball, like a football freestyler, and had the same potential as Neymar but was given too much bad advice from those around him. When he fell out with Schuster he held his own press conference to give his side of things and that finished him at Real Madrid. He is one of the most unfulfilled talents there has been.

Javier Saviola

Javier was a nice lad but he was very naïve and easy to play pranks on. We were 2-0 up and Schuster had made three substitutions during one game, but Javier hadn't noticed and was still warming up so I signalled to him from the bench that he was going on. He ran to the bench, took his tracksuit top off and stood in front of Manuel Ruiz, Schuster's assistant.

"What do you want?"

"Who am I replacing and what are my tasks?"

"Replacing? Tasks?"

"Yeah, I'm going on..."

As Ruiz explained to Javier that he should know you can only make three substitutions he looked up to see the rest of us pissing ourselves laughing on the bench.

Sergio Ramos

An Andalusian from Sevilla, they boo him in his hometown because he signed for Real Madrid but he is an energetic person, the heart of the team and a huge fan of flamenco! He buzzes around so much that you'd think he has ADHD and this caused him problems at first because he wanted to do everything – like take a corner and still be the person who was trying to get on the end of it! His importance to Real and Spain can not be underestimated.

Wesley Sneijder

A perfect example of a player who believed he had made it too quickly at Real Madrid. He ran a lot, passed the ball well, scored goals and had a good first season, but he got complacent. You can't do that at Real Madrid! Nor can you party too much in the nightclubs either as people recognise you and partying takes its toll physically. When Wesley finally understood that he had chosen the wrong path it was too late.

Ruud van Nistelrooy

Ruud had the instinct of a natural goalscorer, a big heart and was one of the most liked players in the Real Madrid dressing room. We were rivals for a long time – Feyenoord v PSV, Liverpool v Manchester United – and he was the type of player who would still leave a foot in if I got to the ball first! In 2001/02 he scored in eight consecutive Premier League games and the ninth game was against Liverpool at Old Trafford. I said to him in Dutch before kick-off: "That's enough now, your record is good enough," and he joked back "we'll see, we'll see!" We did see – Ruud didn't score and we won 1-0! We became good friends in Madrid and he told me his retirement plan was to live in Spain for the rest of his life, but he returned to the Netherlands to work for PSV.

Zinedine Zidane

A legend. I tried to get Zidane's shirt after Feyenoord played Juventus in 1997, but he had promised it to somebody else. Zizou is a gentleman who never raises his voice but gets his points across when he needs to. He was Florentino Perez's 'advisor' when I was at Real but in reality he would pass his experience on to us, sometimes in the dressing room as if he was the coach. He progressed to be coach at Real and I think some of the passionate fighting spirit he showed as a player, most famously in the 2006 World Cup final when he headbutted Marco Materazzi, will be evident in his team.

DRIVEN BY ADRENALINE

There are two different things that can lead to your retirement from playing. Most commonly, you still feel mentally sharp but your body cries 'no more' and you just can't physically play at the level required. Or, you can still feel physically good, but your head is burnt out. For me it was the latter.

After so many years of leading a disciplined, routine-based life I felt relief when I retired. I missed the atmosphere in the dressing room, the team meetings and meals, the laughing, joking and unforgettable moments on the pitch, but I didn't miss the 90 minutes concentration you need as a goalkeeper on the pitch.

I came off from a game once and remarked: "F***ing hell, I feel knackered." Somebody replied: "But you only had one shot to save."

That was true, but as a goalkeeper you spend the rest of the time reading a game, predicting where danger could come from and anticipating when you could be called into action and what you have to do. I wouldn't even hear things shouted from the crowd or even my team-mates sometimes because I was so focused on what I needed to do and that takes it out of you mentally.

I've been asked a number of times about whether I had thought of going into coaching. The first person who asked me was Rafa Benitez while I was at Liverpool.

"Jerzy, what do you want to do after retirement?"

"I don't know. Maybe I'll become a coach?"

"A coach? Okay, but there are no top coaches that were goalkeepers. They are unsuccessful. This is normal."

"What about Dino Zoff?"

"He won some things in 1990. But then what? Who else?"

"Michel Preud'homme?"

"He has won nothing yet. The problem is you goalkeepers do not understand strategy like an outfield player. You look at everything from your position. Goalkeepers are too individually focused to be able to make a team successful."

I thought to myself that maybe Rafa is right, but then there are fewer goalkeepers in football than outfield players so statistically there will always be fewer goalies going into management. I disagree about his views on our outlook of the game, though. You see more when you can view the rest of the team in front of you so of course you can understand strategy. I took a lot of notes when I was a player about what each coach I was working under did so that, from a theoretical point of view, I would be well prepared to go into coaching if that's what I decided to do.

I made notes about training sessions and when I was at Real it became a real passion. I analysed everything, including conversations my coaches had with the players. It led me to conclude that coaching is very tough. Instead of focusing on yourself as a player there are a thousand things to consider, and problem after problem to deal with, to make a team successful. You've also got to plan for the future while dealing with the present and, at big clubs, live up to the expectations based on achievements in the past. It's a 24/7 job that you must do for 365 days a year and which requires an unbelievable amount of sacrifice and commitment.

I was fortunate enough to have some brilliant coaches during my career, but do I want to try and emulate them? After five years of retirement I can honestly say no. Not now.

My 'normal' kids

One of the main reasons I returned with my family to Poland after leaving Real Madrid was for my daughters, Victoria and Natalia. They were due to start primary school so we decided that returning to the country where myself and Mirella were born and bred made sense so we settled near to Kraków. This meant also uprooting Alexander, who was due to start middle school, but if we had left it any longer it would have been even more difficult to move them away from Madrid.

It isn't easy to be the kids of a footballer as you can be uprooted a lot. They make friendships and create their own little worlds only for them to be broken up, leaving them having to start again somewhere else. We thought it would be easier for them to grow their identities if we put down roots in a place that feels like home forever, like Szczygłowice does for Mirella and I. If you asked me where I was from, 'Szczygłowice' would be my answer.

My family had to make a lot of sacrifices for my career. They accepted it, but I am honest enough to say that they were forced to. I was quite happy living in Spain, but it was time to put Mirella and the kids first. Alexander was born in Rotterdam and the girls were born in Liverpool so it wasn't a 'return' to Poland for them as such, but I hope they will be more emotionally connected with Poland than their birthplaces by the time they have grown up. I'm also proud that they have remained grounded individuals despite their dad being a famous footballer.

Somebody told me once that my kids are normal and I took it as a great compliment. That is all down to Mirella. She has brought them up so they feel equal to other kids, not better than them because of my career. That is very important to us because we are humble people, although Mirella has had to play the bad cop role more than me! In fact, she reminds me of Phil Thompson – and I don't mean in how she looks!

Mirella keeps the house in order like Tommo kept the dressing room at Liverpool in order by saying things that you don't necessarily want to hear, but that need to be said. That made Houllier's life easier and Mirella has made my life with the kids easier in the same way. Of course, we have had arguments because a lot of decisions about the kids have to be made by her if I'm away, but we are so well matched that our relationship functions well.

Returning to Poland was even more important for her. We lived abroad for 15 years and it was easier for me to settle in Rotterdam, Liverpool and Madrid because I spent almost half the time with the lads so got to learn the language and about local cultures more quickly. Mirella had to do the same on her own and that is not easy, especially when you've got young children. Returning to Poland meant Mirella could breathe again. It allowed her to feel like I felt after Istanbul.

A chip off the old block

I realised how tough it was for Alexander to adapt to being uprooted when we moved from Rotterdam to Liverpool. I took him to his first day at nursery in Rotterdam and he was in floods of tears, shouting: "Daddy, don't leave me here," in Polish. I stayed for half-an-hour, but it tore me apart inside to see how upset he was. He settled well and was learning Dutch, but then we decided to move to Liverpool and that meant Alex had to start from the beginning again with a new school, new language, new culture and new friends. That was hard for him, but he finally adapted and was happy, only for us to then move to Madrid in 2007.

At least in Spain he was old enough to explain problems he had to us. For instance, he came home from school saying his teacher doesn't like him, never talks to him and he sits alone at a desk. I went in to see her and discovered she hardly spoke any English and with Alexander only just starting to learn Spanish they couldn't communicate well, leaving him feeling lonely. So it took time, but he got used to the Spanish way of life and had even started playing for Real Madrid's youth teams when we decided to relocate to Poland. It hit him the hardest – it took him six months to settle – and now he's back in Spain studying!

Alex didn't want to be a professional footballer like his dad, but a sports scientist. He then changed his mind and is now studying management in Spain. Because he speaks Spanish so well this gave him a head start with his studies and means I don't feel as bad for uprooting him.

Our daughters, Victoria and Natalia, were born in England and both arrived in this world in 2006. Victoria was born on January 23rd and Natalia on December 28th. I was so prolific hitting the target that maybe I should have been a striker instead of a goalie! I was made up to have a daughter as when I was at Concordia our goalkeeper coach, Jurek Ogierman, said to me: "Only the best players in the world have daughters. Pele, Lubański... and Ogierman!" When Victoria was born I thought 'I'm up there with Pele now!' Three months later, however, Mirella said to me: "I think I'm pregnant again... but this isn't good. A pregnancy after a pregnancy can be dangerous."

We panicked a bit so went to see the doctor the next day. He allayed our fears by saying everything was normal and Mirella had a good pregnancy. She was due to give birth around January 5th but we thought it was better that both girls were born in the same calendar year so Natalia arrived on December 28th by Caesarean section. I assisted with the birth, wearing a surgical gown. Rafa gave me the day off before the following game at Spurs, telling me to spend time with my wife and daughter.

The girls may have both been born in 2006 but they are very different – one of them is blonde, the other has brown hair. Victoria has my genes and is more well behaved, Natalia has her mum's genes and if she's not happy blows a fuse more easily! Victoria is the tallest in her class and already has a maternal instinct. She even wanted to be a nursery teacher and looks out for the smaller kids. Her teacher told us: "I could go for a coffee and know she would take care of the class – I have my own assistant!" They didn't see me play football but had to get used to me signing autographs, and to other kids teasing them.

"Kuba from school says that Casillas is better than you."

"Does he still support Barcelona?"

"He says he supports Real Madrid now."

"Tell him I said he's a typical Barcelona fan – they all support Real when Barca play badly!"

I played in a charity tournament and at the end we did a penalty shoot-out where anyone who donated 100 zlotys could take a penalty against me. Afterwards, Natalia wanted to go in goal and she was diving to make saves like me in my prime! Maybe she has inherited some of my goalie genes.

Reunited with Shevchenko

In April 2007, when Poland and Ukraine were bidding to be joint-host nations of Euro 2012, I was invited to Cardiff to take part in a presentation ahead of the decision by UEFA as to who the hosts would be. I saw Euro 2012 as a great opportunity for Poland to promote itself, to show Europe how the country has developed, and while the doubters – including Zbigniew Boniek, who said he wasn't interested – thought we had no chance of winning, I believed we could. Sports personalities from both Poland and Ukraine joined forces to back the bid and we all met up in Cardiff. It meant that I was reunited with Andriy Shevchenko.

The Ukrainian had signed for Chelsea in 2006 and, as fate would have it, made his debut against Liverpool in the Community Shield at the Millennium Stadium in Cardiff. He scored, past Pepe Reina, not myself, but we won 2-1. So it was ironic that I was meeting Shevchenko again in Cardiff and because of our shared history in Istanbul and for the national team – he scored against me in both qualifying games for the 2002 World Cup – it was important that we could put that behind us and present a united front.

Inevitably we were interviewed at the same time and while I was comfortable answering questions in English, Andriy wasn't confident enough to use what English he knew so spoke in his native language. Everything was translated, so the conversation was a little stop-start, but we explained how we were famous rivals on the pitch that were now united for the good of our countries. We told the audience how Poland and Ukraine were now ready to take on the responsibility of hosting a major tournament and it would be the best European Championships of the lot. If it was simply down to the passion of the presentations then we were certainties to win, but Italy and Hungary together with Croatia were also in the running.

The following day – having been introduced to Ukrainian heavyweight boxer Vitali Klitschko, who I exchanged pretend punches with – I was on the Liverpool team bus when Mirella contacted me to say: "Michel Platini just pulled a piece of paper from an envelope with 'Poland and Ukraine' written on it. We got Euro 2012! Everyone is jumping around like madmen." "Oh f***!" I replied.

A Polish-Ukrainian friendship wasn't easy – I'd liken it to having a couple of liver transplants until it works – but we had shown that we could work together for a common goal. Even so, Euro 2012 didn't turn out to be a good tournament for the Polish national team – yet again there was a group stage exit. And the following year I found myself in competition with Shevchenko again!

Vladimir Smicer invited me to join the Liverpool Legends football team and after attending the Amateur Golf World Cup in Durban I flew to Asia to meet up with the lads. Mirella didn't see me for a month! This was April 2013 and it was a sentimental trip for me as I hadn't seen lads like Robbie Fowler for years. We had a good catch-up and, despite having a team of 40-odd-year-olds with their bellies hanging out over their shorts, won an indoor tournament in Kuala Lumpur.

We played Manchester United and that got the adrenaline flowing. It was shown live on TV and it felt like we were fighting them for the title – there was even a spitting incident! – before beating a Premier League All-Stars team in the final. I enjoyed it so when Fabio Cannavaro called me to say he was organising a Global Legends Series game in Bangkok in December to raise money for charity I was up for it.

Luis Figo was in charge of the other team – I discovered from chatting to him that we both visited the same golf tutor in Madrid! – and I found myself sitting in the dressing room with players like Jari Litmanen, Paul Scholes, Dwight Yorke and Marco Materazzi. And in the other dressing room? Sheva. By now we had been friends for years, but I discovered during a training game to prepare for the match just how much what happened in Istanbul haunts him. It was meant to be a light-hearted warm-up match but old habits die hard and our competitive edges came to the surface. Andriy was desperate to score against me and had two great opportunities, but I produced two very good reflex saves. He got to his feet, looked at me and the expression on his face said a million words. It was like he saw me as a wall that was impossible to climb over!

As we walked off the pitch at the end he came over to me:

"What is it with you? You've got some kind of hex over me. It's like it's your destiny to stop me scoring."

I told him not to worry, our careers are over so he shouldn't care so much, but I could see Istanbul was still on his mind.

"What is going on? These saves are impossible. I shoot, I see the ball going into the net and then I see you coming from nowhere to save it. Again. How are you doing this to me?"

The following day, over eight years after Istanbul, Sheva finally scored against me again. When he did so I congratulated him and the entire stadium stood up and applauded our rivalry. I had the last laugh, though. Team Cannavaro beat Team Figo 8-5!

Back in the fast lane

I play a lot of golf now, and it makes me laugh that when I lived in Caldy for six years there was a links golf course at the end of my road and I didn't go there once! I got into golf accidentally. When I was moving out of my home in Caldy I found a rusty golf club in the garden. Me and Alexander messed around with it in the back garden – we were hitting tennis and table-tennis balls because I didn't have any golf balls – and I thought it was really cool.

At the end of that season adidas, who made Liverpool's kits, gave some of the lads a golf bag full of clubs so I asked the rep how I could get some.

"I didn't realise you played, Jerzy." The next day they delivered a full golf bag to my home in Caldy. After coming back to Poland I checked and discovered that the closest golf club to my home was 110 kilometres away, and it was an oasis of calm for me ahead of my move to Real Madrid. I started with my love affair with golf that summer although I'm not sure Mirella feels the same way!

> *"Jurek has always been going somewhere. I thought that after his retirement it would be different, but now he's away from home even more often. I have got used to it after 20 years, but sometimes it makes me mad when he goes to play golf for a week and I am left looking after our children."*
>
> **Mirella Dudek, wife**

Golf isn't the only reason I'm often away from home. I've got a new career now as a racing driver!

I became an ambassador for Castrol in 2011 and they became a sponsor of the VW Golf Cup, which is held in central European countries like Poland, Czech Republic, Germany, Hungary and Slovakia. There are drivers from all over the world – even South Africa and Argentina – competing and they asked if I would fancy competing as a celebrity guest driver in 2013 to get some publicity for the sport. I explained that I had never raced before in a professional car so to compete with professional drivers would be tough, but they convinced me I would be fine and I finished 14th out of 25. Everyone was surprised so I drove in a second race as a guest driver and when the season finished they proposed that I take part for the full season in 2014 as a proper driver. I did the same in 2015, but I had to learn a lot first. You're trying to attack the car in front of you while defending against the car behind you and you've also got to protect your tyres, but that's why motor sport engaged me. I wanted to gain knowledge about another sport but I can't say it is good fun because the fun ends when you close the door. You can have a laugh and a joke before a race, but when the door shuts you've got to focus on the race because it is a dangerous sport.

When I took Mirella and friends to watch me racing for the first time at the Lausitzring in Germany there was a support race on first – the ADAC GT Masters in which big cars like Lamborghinis are raced. I said to Mirella I needed to go and prepare so she should go to the stands to watch the support race to see what it is like. There were 30 cars on the grid and it was very noisy. The race started and there was a collision on the first corner with three cars crashing out. My phone beeped moments later and it was a message from the wife: 'Are you crazy? Do you really want to do this?' She didn't want me to race, but she was more relaxed after seeing me complete the race unscathed.

My daughters Victoria and Natalia like racing. They have impressed me with their perceptiveness. Not only have they learnt all the drivers' names, some of which I don't know myself, they ask questions like: "Dad, why did he race in an orange car in the first race but a yellow one in the second?"

They soon worked out it was because the driver had crashed the first one so needed a new car.

Racing is the biggest adrenaline rush I have ever experienced. The adrenaline keeps you going and wanting to come back to race even more. I remember my first race and everything was going too quickly for me to get my head around. We had the warm-up lap, the engineer wished me good luck and then I was left alone.

We have a button in the car that gives you more horsepower for an extra 10 seconds and during the start procedure you put your left foot on the brake and your right foot full on the throttle. It gives you 4,000 revs and when you release the brake the car goes.

Moments before the race started he said: "Left foot brake, right foot throttle, press the button and go."

I was thinking: 'What did he say? Left foot where?' The countdown clock was ticking down and I started to panic. I was thinking 'I can't do this, I need to go to the pits' but then I thought how embarrassing it would be if I drove off the grid into the pits in my first race. That's when the adrenaline kicked in. I focused on trying to remember the procedure and before I knew it I was racing. You can't compare the adrenaline of that to anything else.

Of course you get used to it. In football some players start to get nervous before kick-off, but others suffer from nerves during a game. It is better to be nervous before and let your adrenaline take over and when you are racing cars it is the same. I used my experience as a footballer to help me learn as a racing driver. When you are a goalkeeper you have to make split-second decisions, take responsibility for them and have good reflexes. It is the same in a car on the racing track. You have to make quick decisions and good decisions. Whether it's diving to the corner to save a shot or diving down the inside of a car on a corner, if you make the wrong decision it will cost you.

When you play football you cannot go car racing, go skiing or even drive go-karts because of the risk of injury. I have always enjoyed driving and was so crazy about it that when I was playing I even drove from Liverpool to Rybnik, where I lived, and from Madrid to Rybnik! It was over 2,000km, took me about 20 hours to Poland – I went via the Channel Tunnel

– and it was good fun. I used to look forward to the holidays so I could go driving, but when it was time to return to pre-season I sent my car back on a truck and flew to Liverpool. So when they asked if I'd like to do the Dubai 24 Hour Race I laughed and said: "Only 24 hours and we share the driving? I got to Poland from Liverpool in 20 hours on my own!"

I drove in the Dubai 24 Hour Race, the second biggest endurance event after Le Mans, after accepting an offer to compete in it without really thinking. There was only one place in the team left and another guy was being lined up so I said: "I'll do it." It took me 20 seconds to sign the contract.

When I got home I thought 'I've got a wife and three kids here, why am I going to Dubai to race for 24 hours?' I was full of doubts before it because I had never been involved in an endurance event and had watched the highlights of Le Mans on the TV. There were some bad accidents but I put the doubts behind me and went to Dubai. It was the best race I had ever done. You share the driving with four others and you're supposed to try and get some sleep, but in reality you're sat on a chair with your eyes closed hearing the noise of the cars fly past.

It was a fantastic experience. You have periods when you're chasing and spells when you're being chased by others. We led our A3 category for the first five hours but it took two-and-a-half hours to fix a gearbox problem so we dropped back to fifth. We thought we had no chance to catch up, but we chased and chased and eventually finished third, earning us a place on the podium. It was the best experience I have had yet as a driver and there were football fans who were there to support me.

When I looked around the track there were a lot of scarves

that I recognised! It gave me a great feeling. I now hope to race in England because there is a 24-hour race at Silverstone. To race in England in front of Liverpool fans would be a great experience for me.

Racing suits me because I am a competitive person and I'm already thinking to myself about what I can achieve as a racing driver. I won medals in football. I won a medal in golf in Poland when I was on a team of four and we were runners-up in a competition – much to the surprise of everyone – and I have won a medal in racing when we came third in the Dubai 24 Hour Race. But I also know that I cannot race cars forever.

A day will come when I have to move on to something else and I know that needs to be something that motivates me.

I could have ended up working as a miner in Poland. I played football for Feyenoord, Liverpool and Real Madrid. I represented Poland in a World Cup, will always be remembered for Istanbul 2005 and now I race cars.

But there remains one question in my mind, a question I cannot answer: What next for Jerzy Dudek?

I look forward to finding out...

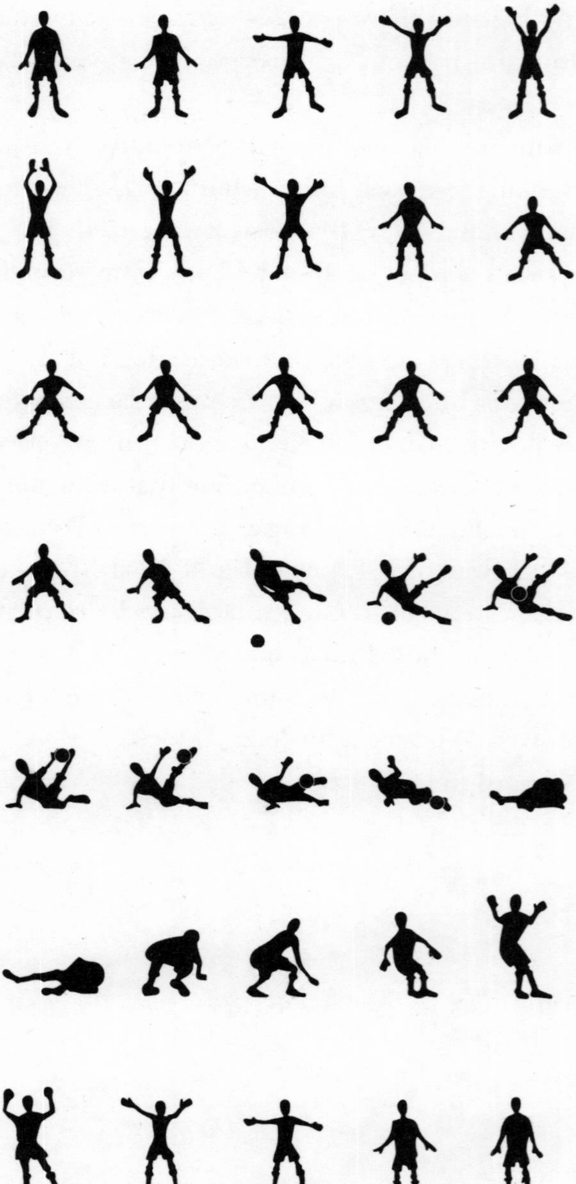